**Qualitology
(Unlocking the secrets of
qualitative research)**

Madrid 2008

Qualitology
(Unlocking the secrets of
qualitative research)

Edited by Pepe Martínez

ESIC
BUSINESS&MARKETINGSCHOOL

© ESIC EDITORIAL
Avda. de Valdenigrales, s/n. 28223 Pozuelo de Alarcón (Madrid)
Tel.: 91 452 41 00 - Fax: 91 352 85 34
www.esic.es

© Pepe Martínez

ISBN: 978-84-7356-578-3
Depósito legal: M. 48.570 - 2008
Portada: Gerardo Domínguez

Fotocomposición y Fotomecánica: ANORMI, S.L.
Doña Mencía, 39
28011 Madrid

Imprime: Gráficas Dehon
La Morera, 23-25
28850 Torrejón de Ardoz (Madrid)

Impreso en España

Index

Part I
THE GENETIC CODE OF QUALITATIVE RESEARCH

To Elena, David, Patricia,
my parents and siblings

Foreword

The world is changing faster and faster, and we cannot begin to imagine the changes that will take place over this century. Whatever happens, however, we do know that technology will play a major role in the rapid process of transformation.

In the world of marketing, the media ecosystem is growing ever more complex. What happens at point of sale is an increasingly important part of brand success, how products are distributed is undergoing major change, and developments in technology will directly impact manufacturers, service companies, markets and consumers.

As a result, new market research needs are emerging, and as researchers, we need to be able to offer our clients new approaches that better answer their questions. Many of those answers will come from qualitative research.

In this book we describe the qualitative techniques we have developed to answer the business and marketing questions of today's marketers, advertisers and sales personnel in both multinational and local companies. We discuss both how ethnography is being successfully applied to solve marketing problems, and developments in digital qualitative research.

This book centres on offering practical ideas and answers to many key modern marketing questions. It can be read from cover to cover, or a reader can go straight to the chapter of interest. We have included four international qualitative studies sponsored by Millward Brown, together with ten qualitative studies undertaken at a local level for major clients.

I hope you enjoy the book, and above all that you find it useful in helping to answer the types of question that often crop up in your day-to-day work.

PEPE MARTÍNEZ
Head of Client Service
Millward Brown Spain

Preface (or the proof that furry fish exist)

You only have to look at the index of *Qualitology* to realize that this is an excellent book about qualitative research. It is a valuable tool for professionals responsible for projects and studies, both national and international. An experienced reader will appreciate the uniqueness of this initiative. It is a bit like trying to catch a fish covered in soft spongy fur. Why is it so hard to find a good book about qualitative research? How has Pepe Martínez managed to compile such a book? It is useful to reflect on these two questions: if we get the answers right, we will be closer to the essence of qualitative studies, a fascinating side of social and marketing research.

First, no one who has worked in the field of marketing can doubt that qualitative research is more of an art than a science. With this idea in mind, we could do a wonderful study of, for example, the art works of Wassily Kandinsky. It sounds simple, but the very idea of writing a practical book on *How to Paint like Kandinsky,* or more generally a book on *How to Paint like the Great Painters*, sounds absurd. As with true artistic creation, qualitative research cannot be learned by just reading a book. It is something that has to be worked at over many years, using the researcher's innate talent and by watching the experts.

This book is full of practical information, and it is this practical approach that makes its content outstanding. The detailed case studies bring the practical information to life. And the book contains just the right amount of theory for us to understand how that theory is put into practice. The results of studies undertaken by some of the best qualitative researchers around enable researchers with less experience to learn from the experts, while those with more experience will be able to use *Qualitology* as an opportunity to reflect on their current working style and refine their professional skills.

Second, acquiring qualitative research skills is a little like learning a language: we can learn Swahili, Mandarin or Czech, but we cannot learn 'language in itself', because it does not exist. Although we can use the similarities between related languages to more quickly learn one language in a group if we already speak another, this doesn't help us if, for example we can speak fluent Hungarian and want to learn Portuguese, since these languages have different roots.

Qualitative research takes different forms in different countries and cultures. A Polish moderator in a focus group in Warsaw will have to work hard to guide his respondents who are likely to be talkative and energetic and want to talk about everything they can think of on the topic under discussion. His counterpart in Frankfurt will have to work equally hard, but in this instance to get German consumers to express their opinions or involve themselves in the task at all.

If every culture is different and the type of research we have to conduct is different in each country, is it possible to even imagine writing a book about qualitative research? Pepe Martínez knows qualitative research well. He has been conducting studies in the Spanish market for 25 years, and has conducted many international projects. For four years he was Millward Brown's Qualitative Research Director for Europe, which explains why his book is based on experience accumulated in so many different markets.

This publication provides a fascinating overview of the different approaches used in qualitative research, and it is proof of the success of Millward Brown's policy of expanding qualitative research into the main markets of the world.

Third, university professors who teach market research usually have little practical contact with qualitative studies. Researchers, on the other hand, spend most of their time moderating groups and conducting interviews, undertaking complex analyses and working in consultancy services, which leaves them little time to teach or to write about their knowledge and experience. The available books on qualitative research are usually written by theoreticians who are a long way away from being qualitative gurus. Most do not reflect the open, deep, expert, practical and useful approach that those qualitative researchers working for Millward Brown have to offer nor do they reflect the experience and the knowledge of the professional market researchers working for our clients.

Pepe Martínez is one of the few really outstanding individuals in the world of qualitative research who are able to combine theory with the practice of everyday research. This ability clearly separates him from authors of academic treatises. This may be the reason why this book is so vibrant and full of character, and why, as well as describing classical research methods, it also describes some of the most innovative and cutting-edge techniques.

I have known Pepe Martínez for a long time. We work together and I am proud to call him my friend. I know how much time he spends working, so I do not have the slightest idea how he found the time to write this excellent book.

Nor, to be honest, do I have the slightest idea of how to catch a furry fish.

KRZYSZTOF B. KRUSZEWSKI
Qualitative Research Director
Millward Brown Continental Europe,
the Middle East and North Africa

Acknowledgements

I would like to express my gratitude to those clients who have allowed us to publish genuine case studies of qualitative research work that Millward Brown has undertaken for them: Jesús Gallardo and Isabel de Julián of Coca-Cola, Spain, Alejandra Delgado and Luis Subias of Renault in Spain, José María del Pino, Cayetana Arce and Carmen Martín of Lilly in Spain, and Monika Cizkova of Vodafone in the Czech Republic.

I would also like to make special mention of the two people who taught me how to do qualitative research, José Luís Álvarez and Ignacio Martín Poyo. Their teaching and the confidence they showed in me have had a decisive influence on my work.

I would like everyone in Millward Brown to consider this book as theirs, because it has been written with the help of so many people in different countries and departments. I am sure that when they read it they will recognize their invaluable contribution.

Special mention should be made of the following people in the Client Service department of Millward Brown Spain: Enrique González, Adolfo Fernández, José Ramón Arteta, Cristina González, Mar Álvarez, Bárbara Guinovart, Felipe Barral, Rosana Rodríguez, Jorge Benito, Sara Durán and Stas Mencwel. Some have written a chapter of the book, while the others have made an active contribution. I would like to give special thanks to Rosana Valverde, the TGI team manager in Spain.

Mention should also be made of contributors from the Client Service departments of Millward Brown in other countries: Mimma Novelli and Monica Spinola in Italy, Guillaume Cadet in France, Henk Schulte and Pieter Willems in the Netherlands, Krzysztof B. Kruszewski in Poland, Lenka Robosova in the Czech Republic and Andrés López in Mexico.

I would like to thank my boss, Juan Ferrer-Vidal, Andrea Bielli, Krzysztof B. Kruszewski, Cath Booth, Erika Némethi, Cécile Conaré, Gordon Pincott and Jean McDougall (and her team) for their support, which made it possible for this book to be written.

Cath Booth, Kate Southwood, Jean McDougall, Krzysztof B. Kruszewski, Cécile Conaré, Andy Truslove and Juan Ferrer-Vidal helped me to find a title for the book.

A special thank you to Eileen Campbell, CEO Millward Brown, for her invaluable ideas, help and support.

I would like to express my gratitude to Vicente Rubira, who is in charge of publications in ESIC (Business & Marketing School), because he became interested in the idea of this book when it was only a contents page and a simple outline.

Without the help of Carmen Agudo, Dave Fricker and Susan Curran it would have been impossible to publish this book.

I would like to thank Marisa Rovidarcht and Dani González for all their work in preparing the manuscript and graphics. I would also like to thank Reyes Neira, who has provided invaluable help of administration and information storage — she has acted as my right hand.

Elena, David and Patricia, thank you for your patience and the time you have given me, as well as your support, hope and enthusiasm.

PEPE MARTÍNEZ

PART I

THE GENETIC CODE OF QUALITATIVE RESEARCH

1
Qualitative or quantitative?

PEPE MARTÍNEZ

The market is a highly complex reality

The aim of qualitative research is almost always to understand a relationship between two elements: the consumer and the market, in the sense of a category, brand, product, service, advertising campaign, pack or label, or psychosociological phenomenon. It is almost impossible to cover fully all the aspects of research because there are so many: external reality, different markets, the internal reality of consumers, psychological and social factors and so on. Consumer markets are universes influenced by many factors and with multiple meanings.

So we never have complete knowledge about a category or brand, and in qualitative research the process of interpreting information never comes to an end. It is always possible to reach a deeper level.

We need methodological pluralism

The methodological research toolbox includes qualitative research, 'ad hoc' quantitative research and standardized quantitative products. It is very effective, but also limited: each tool has blind spots. To get a true picture of the market, our vision must centre on a combination of approaches *(methodological pluralism)* and/or use information from different sources *(data and knowledge integration)*.

Triangulation is the technical term for combining different sources of information, techniques, methodologies, researchers, teams of experts, disciplines and theoretical frameworks in a single study. This enables us to understand the topic as fully as possible.

'Qual' or 'quant'? Both

Quantitative research

- It is used more commonly than qualitative in company market research departments.

- It typically uses structured or semi-structured questionnaires, which obtain information from the conscious or preconscious mind. The unconscious level is secondary. There is no free discourse by respondents; they answer what they are asked.

- Sampling is used: the data obtained refer to a defined segment of the population.

- The results are expressed numerically, allowing us to measure and quantify. This provides a sense of security – our guarantee we can believe the results.

- It tends to be descriptive. Different variables are measured, and we can use the results to seek explanations.

- It uses scientific procedures from mathematics (statistics and data analysis).

Qualitative research

- It is based on the richness of words and the potential of language. Its resources come from free discourse, an adaptation of the free association discovered by Freud* in the context of clinical psychology.

- Typically fewer people are consulted, so we can delve deeper.

- Techniques such as focus groups and in-depth interviews allow us to connect with the conscious, preconscious and importantly, the unconscious.

- It aims at understanding rather than description, which suits the complexity of the many factors that influence the consumer–brand relationship. Psychosocial reality is highly complex, and qualitative models get closer to it.

- It uses procedures from social sciences such as psychology, psychoanalysis, sociology, anthropology, psycholinguistics and semiotics.

COMPARES ASPECTS OF QUALITATIVE AND QUANTITATIVE RESEARCH, SO DIFFERENT AND YET SO COMPLEMENTARY

Quantitative	Qualitative
Origins: mathematics (statistics) and the natural sciences	Origins: human and social sciences
Paradigm: positivism	Paradigms: constructivism, phenomenology, hermeneutics
The power and security of numbers	The richness of language
Measurement, description and explanation	Comprehension
The hypothetic-deductive method	Induction and intuition
Extension and amount	Depth, intensity and density
The nomothetic approach (many cases)	The ideographic approach (few cases)
Description	Reflection
A non-holistic approach	A holistic approach
Macrosociology	Microsociology
Society and the market	Individuals and consumers
Structures	Processes
'Objective' reality (physical facts)	Social and cultural reality
Social facts	Social phenomena
Denotation	Connotation
Objective	Subjective
Static	Dynamic
Standardized and closed	Flexible and open
Sometimes termed the 'hard' approach	Sometimes termed the 'soft' approach
Works at the manifest level of consumers	Seeks the latent level of consumers
Concentrates on the conscious and pre-conscious	Seeks the unconscious
Main quality indicators: • validity (internal and external) • generalizability/representativity • reliability • objectivity	Main quality indicators • trustworthiness • credibility • transferability • confirmability

Summary and conclusions

- The market research objective is to find the relationship between consumers and a product category, brand, specific product, service, advertisement, pack or a label, and so on.

- We cannot determine the true state of the market using a single technique, since every tool has blind spots.

- Methodological pluralism attempts to integrate information from different sources and combine qualitative and quantitative techniques to gain a better understanding.

- The arts represent the qualitative, the richness of words, the chains of association in free discourse and the power of interpretation.

- The sciences represent the quantitative, the power of numbers to persuade, the security offered by the figures and robust statistical analysis.

2

The pillars of qualitative research

PEPE MARTÍNEZ

Introduction

Qualitative research works well as an independent approach, but as noted in chapter 1, the ideal is to combine qualitative and quantitative methodologies depending on the needs of a project.

Words as a tool for working

The linguistic and social aspects of human life are key to qualitative research. It essentially centres on the proper interpretation of consumer discourse, which includes language, non-verbal communication and behaviour.

As the main link between a person's internal world (their thoughts and feelings) and their external world (of action), language brings us into contact with thought (representations), feelings (the world of emotions), expectations (desires and motivations), memory (significant memories, experience and learning), habits and attitudes. All this takes place at both conscious and unconscious levels. Qualitative researchers analyse the language of individuals (free discourse), their non-verbal communication (gestures, expressions and body language) and their behaviour (actions).

The next figure summarizes the role of language.

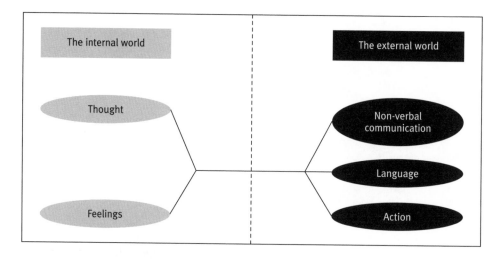

From language to free association

Slow progress has been made throughout history in understanding the key elements of human thought and feeling, but it was in the 19th century that psychology developed as a discipline, and contemporary thinkers focused on the structure and working of the human mind. Wilhelm Wundt* is considered as the father of experimental psychology, and Emil Kraepelin* and Gustav Aschaffenburg* developed the ideas of associationism. Within the Zurich School, Eugene Bleuler* and Carl Gustav Jung* stand out. Jung started to study free association in the early 20th century, before he met Sigmund Freud*, and used the word association test developed by Francis Galton*. He realized this made it possible to discover constellations of emotionally charged ideas centred on a theme (in his terms, a *complex*). This is exactly what qualitative researchers look for now: constellations of emotionally charged ideas which centre on, for example a brand, product, service, advertisement, pack or logo.

Free association, which in qualitative research we call free spontaneous discourse, is a very powerful tool, like a microscope that allows us to see into the psychological reality of the individual. It helps us discover people's 'true' thoughts, feelings, desires, attitudes and motives. In it we find a mix of the conscious, preconscious and unconscious, worlds the qualitative technician has to analyse, understand, weigh and interpret.

Free and spontaneous discourse

Freud* wrote:

> *'One more thing, before you start. In one respect your account has to differ from an ordinary conversation. While in the latter you try to keep to the subject while you talk, and reject all disturbing ideas and collateral thoughts, so that you do not wander, as they say, here you must act in a different way. You will observe during your account that different thoughts will come to mind that you would prefer to reject, with certain critical objections. You will have the temptation to say to yourself: this or that is irrelevant, or it is not important at all, or that it is ludicrous and therefore does not need to be mentioned. Never obey this criticism; say things in spite of it, and even exactly because you have noticed your reluctance to do so. Later on you will know and understand the reason for this rule – the only one, in fact, that you must obey. Say, then, everything that comes to mind. Behave, for example, like a traveller sitting in the train next to the window who describes for his neighbour on the corridor side how the landscape changes as he watches. Lastly, never forget that you have promised to be completely sincere, and never omit anything with the pretext that for any reason you find it unpleasant to express it.'*

Although it is many years since this was written, for a different field of application, Freud's advice applies perfectly to current qualitative approaches. The aim is to encourage consumers to tell us everything that occurs to them about the topic (for example, toothpaste, a cologne or a perfume). We look to find out about brands, products, purchasing habits, the reasons people buy or do not something, the variables that influence them when shopping and so on.

Consumers normally begin their free discourse with the most conscious aspects of the topic. The information from these first moments tends to be superficial and rational; it is often known or predictable. In this first stage, discourse is at a conscious and preconscious level. (Conscious material is nothing other than preconscious representations illuminated by the focus of attention.) But the free discourse tool, with its chains of associations, allows us to gradually gain access to a more unconscious level. Consumers do not realize this information is emerging. This is how the process of qualitative research develops: from the conscious and rational levels of the consumer's personality to the latent, unconscious level.

The general aim is to examine the nature of the relationship consumers have with (for instance) a certain brand. We aim to discover what it means for its consumers: for example, why they prefer one brand of mineral water to another.

In qualitative research we analyse how the brand connects with consumers: how it communicates through its advertising, pack and logo, and so on.

Children tend to express their desires in a way that is open, direct, natural, transparent and spontaneous. They are clear and direct about what they want and what they reject. But adult expressions have been moulded by the process of socialization. Their desires and dislikes, what they find pleasant or unpleasant, their motivations, barriers and symbols are protected by rationalizations. To access the motivational level, qualitative investigators have to break through this barrier. To do this, they rewind the process by which individuals are socialized. They progress from the outside to the inside; from what is manifest to what is latent, penetrating below the rational level to reach the level of the emotions.

There are two levels in free discourse:

- The manifest level corresponds to all the conscious and preconscious information people supply.
- The latent level is made up of the attitudes, motivations and barriers that explain their comments and behaviour.

In general, qualitative researchers operate at the latent level. Because of the richness of language and the power of free discourse, they need interpretation to gain an in-depth understanding of how consumers respond to a topic. Qualitative research uses the power of language, the strength of words. When consumers talk freely about a topic, this qualitative discourse represents the relationship established at a social level between them and the item.

The phases of qualitative research

The next figure shows the steps that must be followed in qualitative research:

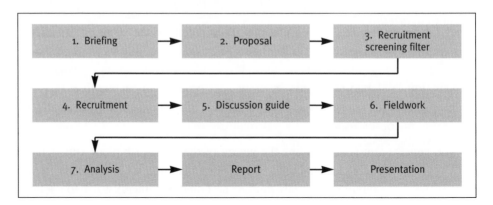

First, the client (for instance, a manufacturer or a service company) briefs the research company, outlining a problem it needs an answer to. This *research brief* typically includes information about the product, the market, the marketing problem, the objective, the target group and the research budget.

The second phase is the *research proposal*, which the research company prepares for the client. This includes the objectives, methodology, budget and timeline.

Once the client has given the go-ahead, the third stage begins: the preparation of the *recruitment questionnaire*, used to select individuals who meet the required sample characteristics. The next phase is the actual *recruitment* of respondents.

The fifth stage is the preparation of a *discussion guide* or moderation plan for the groups or interviews. This outlines the structure and order of the topics to be covered (*data gathering*). It is flexible because it is important to follow the order of the consumers' free discourse. It is important to move from general subjects to more specific and concrete ones, and from spontaneous to prompted conversation.

The next step is to conduct the *fieldwork*. This usually involves focus groups, in-depth interviews or variations of these. In this phase of the research it is highly important to listen to consumers.

The seventh phase is the *analysis and interpretation* of the information. First, each research professional involved in the study (usually psychologists or sociologists) prepares their hypotheses about the problem. The team then meet to compare points of view and reach specific conclusions and recommendations. This avoids the risk of subjectivity, and is the equivalent of a medical team studying a patient's case.

The penultimate step is the preparation of the *report,* which is often done in PowerPoint format. Finally, the findings are presented at a meeting with the client (a *debriefing*).

Qualitative techniques

In the next few chapters we look in depth at focus groups, in-depth interviews, projective and creative techniques.

The most widely used qualitative research technique is currently focus groups. Groups offer very rich information and make it possible to obtain results in a shorter time than using one-to-one interviews, although these have benefits particularly for in-depth research. Ethnographic interviews are a particularly popular type. Clients want to know what is happening in the places and at the times when people shop and consume products and services.

Free and spontaneous discourse in groups and interviews is the resource that qualitative technicians use most often. Projective techniques are the second most commonly used resource. Creative techniques are used less often. With free discourse we move within the rational and motivational levels of consumer personality. Projective techniques allow us to reach emotional and symbolic levels. Finally, with creative techniques we move into the imaginary level.

Each qualitative study is tailor-made

The qualitative researcher's job is exciting but difficult. There is no standardization: each study is specially tailored and every one is different. There are no magic formulae, no sure methods. Qualitative research demands that researchers be creative.

Qualitative research involves both action and reflection. It can be applied to many situations, problems and categories. It is used to study all of the elements of the marketing-mix for a brand, product or service. The main types of qualitative studies are:

- Category studies: basic studies (for example, on ice cream for home consumption) and studies on consumer needs within a category, to detect possible market niches that have yet to be identified.

- Conceptual studies: concept screening (testing multiple alternative product concepts and applying an initial screening filter to reject the ones that lack potential), concept tests (to determine the potential of a new product concept), and studies to develop a new product concept (this consists of several consecutive phases to identify opportunities and develop a new concept).

- Studies for the creation of names and brands, to develop a logo and to test names, brands and logos.

- Studies on brand image: brand equity, health and repositioning.

- Advertising studies: the development of an advertising concept, pre-tests (the creative concept, story board, animatic and finished advertisement), post-tests, usability of a web page. Advertising testing in smaller media (radio, print media and so on).

- Pack studies: tests on packs and labels, and creative studies on the creation of a new pack.

- Studies on promotions: tests on promotions and creative studies on the development of new promotional ideas.

- Prospective studies: creative research to detect market niches and opportunities for the development of new products, together with creative studies for the development of a brand (future scenarios).

Different views of the market and consumers

There are three levels of analysis in qualitative studies derived from psycho-sociology: macro-groups, micro-groups and individuals.

The macro-group concept is broad, abstract and distant – it provides an overview. This is the level of external reality, society, culture, the market, consumers in general, sociology: the macrosociological level.

When analysing the individual, we deal with a small, tangible, close reality. Here, we are in the terrain of psychology.

The micro-group falls between the macro-group and the individual. It combines microsociology, social psychology and the theory of groups.

In an 'up-down' model the macro-group is highly important. From this viewpoint there is a global framework of cultural and social structures which generates a cascade of attitudes. The micro-group also communicates social trends and fashions from higher levels to individuals. In contrast, in a 'down-up' model what is really important are individual preferences and interests. The activity of individual subjects gives structure to the social world, forming and constructing it. Social transformation occurs at the level of the micro-group and social reality is constructed upwards. From this point of view, each part plays its role in the formation of the whole.

The following figure exemplifies these two different ways of understanding the working of society and culture.

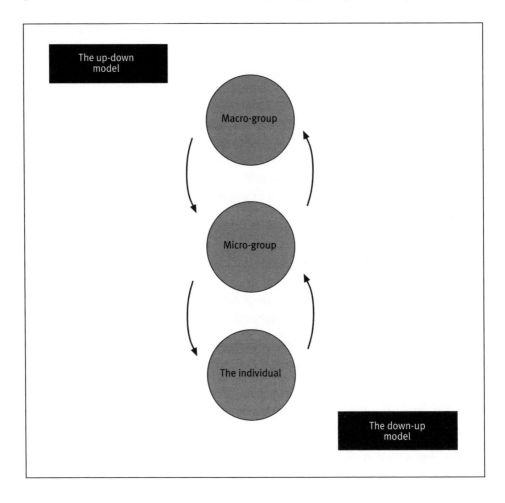

The *sociology* of the macro-group is best studied using quantitative research, which can handle large samples. At the level of the micro-group (*social psychology*), we use qualitative studies based on focus groups. We also use qualitative research – in the form of in-depth interviews – to study single individuals (*psychology*). The next figure shows these different options:

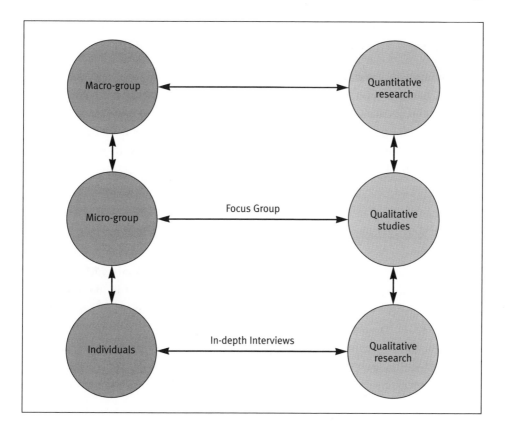

These three levels of analysis provide very different views of the market and consumers. *Structuralism* underscores the importance of the macro-group, society and social structures. In contrast, *methodological individualism* investigates particular subjects. At the intermediate point we have *symbolic interactionism* and *ethnomethodology*.

Structuralism

The forerunners of the structuralist approach are Auguste Comte* and Emile Durkheim*, but it really began with linguist Ferdinand de Saussure*, and spread from linguistic structuralism to other disciplines such as anthropology, psychoanalysis and semiotics. Other major figures are Claude Levi-Strauss*, Louis Althusser*, Michel Foucault*, Jacques Lacan*, Roland Barthes* and Jacques Derrida*.

The starting point of structuralism is social structures and facts. The aim of the market researcher is to find the latent deep structure that explains all social facts. The superficial structure is mere appearance, while the latent structure is the driving force for social and cultural life.

Structuralists believe that social structures generate the representations, feelings, attitudes and individual behaviour of consumers; in other words, that specific subjects are conditioned by the structure. This is an extreme viewpoint, one that proclaims the destruction of the individual consumer. The subject is a puppet moved by the strings of the system, and has no value in itself. It is not worth the effort to study it individually.

Symbolic interactionism

Symbolic interactionism derives from the work of sociologists Max Weber* and the Chicago School's George H. Mead*. Its starting point is the individual, whose social life is constructed on the basis of a constant exchange of symbols (with their corresponding meanings), although it also emphasizes social exchange. Market reality is made up of exchanges of symbols by consumers. Consumer behaviour depends chiefly on the meanings they attribute to, for example, products, services, brands, advertising campaigns, packs, logos and web pages.

This approach is eminently qualitative, based on the interaction of individuals and groups. It uses participating observation, interviewing and document content analysis to capture the meaning of the symbols in an interrelationship.

Ethnomethodology

The founder of this view of social reality and the individuals of which it is composed was Harold Garfinkel* in the 1960s. His starting point was the interactions between people, and he saw reality and social phenomena as born of the interrelationships between subjects. This means that the reality of the market and consumption phenomena are the result of interactions between consumers. Here we are at the level of the micro-group.

Ethnomethodology places almost all its emphasis on the practical meaning and rational dimension of human beings. Its normal methods are interviews, the ethnographic approach and researcher interaction with social groups. This approach is interpretive.

Methodological individualism

This is the opposite view to structuralism: that nothing exists apart from the individuals within a culture or society. There are no social structures as such, and social phenomena are the sum of individual subjects. Each individual is driven by their own interests and motivations, which is what researchers must study. The emphasis is on psychology. The most important antecedent is the behavioural psychology of John Watson*. This is a very mechanical view of society and culture.

The in-depth interview is the related qualitative research technique, because it allows us to examine individuals in depth, studying their thoughts, feelings, attitudes, motivations, barriers, remarks and behaviour.

Viva eclecticism!

These models and approaches offer interesting views of social reality. But at the same time, they are often extreme views that would lead to reductionism. In qualitative market research we tend to have an eclectic and inclusive philosophy, in which we take the best from each. This is not a simplistic type of eclecticism in which anything goes, but rather constructive positive eclecticism, in which we take the best model to explain each set of information.

Individuals, groups and social structures exist, and each one plays a role in the construction of society and culture. The market influences consumers. The products and brands launched by manufacturers condition the purchasing and consumption habits of individuals. The up-down model works. However, the tastes, interests and behaviour of consumers also influence the current market for goods and services, so the down-up model functions too. There is therefore an interplay between individual vectors and social phenomena. When a brand starts to be successful among a few people, then suddenly more and more people become interested in it, we move to a higher level: it is then that the brand becomes a social phenomenon and its success is exponential.

Paradigm shift

Important changes in market research occurred throughout the last century. These included a paradigm shift from a more positivist view of the market and consumers to a more constructivist approach. Quantitative research is closer to the positivist paradigm, that:

- There is an 'objective' external reality.

- Social facts exist.

- Data and information obtained are objective in nature.

- It is necessary to get as close as possible to scientific method.

- Researchers should distance themselves as far as they can from the object under study.

- It is necessary to seek a kind of final truth, which is hidden and must be found.

Qualitative research is closer to the constructivist paradigm, that:

- The most important thing is not external reality, but rather the internal reality of individuals. Consumers are motivated by their own perceptions and representations of the market.

- Social phenomena and processes are more important than facts.

- The information that is relevant and meaningful stems from the subjective world of consumers.

- A naturalist view is taken of the market and consumers.

- The researcher is within the same context as the object being studied; they are also part of the consumption market, and this must be acknowledged, since it cannot be changed.

- We live in a constant process in which social realities are constructed. Many different versions are possible, and there is no ultimate truth. Each consumer has their own truth, and their views of brands will derive from their personal experience of them.

Summary and conclusions

- Qualitative research uses words as its working tools. It centres on the proper interpretation of what consumers say, think, feel and do.

- Qualitative researchers seek constellations of emotionally charged ideas that centre on for example a brand, product, service, advertisement, pack, label or logo.

- The phases in qualitative research are briefing, proposal, recruitment screening questionnaire, recruitment, discussion guide, fieldwork, analysis, report and presentation (debrief).

- The work of a qualitative researcher is exciting but difficult. Each study is individually designed. This methodology has virtually unlimited applications.

- Up-down models of the market and consumers emphasize the importance of the macro-group (society, the market or culture), while down-up models concentrate on the individual (the subject, the consumer). The micro-group (social psychology) occupies an intermediate position.

- The market research philosophy is eclectic, inclusive and constructive. It uses models derived from, for example, psychology, psychoanalysis, sociology (symbolic interactionism, ethnomethodology, methodological individualism)...

- Major changes occurred throughout the last century in market research, including the paradigm shift from a more positivist view of the market and consumers (quantitative research), to a more constructivist approach (qualitative research).

3
Focus groups

PEPE MARTÍNEZ

Introduction

Focus groups are micro-groups which represent a macro-group or a segment of social reality. Respondents are able to interact and put forward different points of view. Well-moderated groups with a good sample provide us with a large amount of high-quality information.

In focus groups the whole dominates each part. The group prevails over the individual. The social level (sociology) stands out from the individual level (psychology). It is very important for the moderator to take group phenomena into account, as well as the need to balance the viewpoint of the group as a whole with that of each member.

The principal elements of a focus group

When organizing a focus group five factors must be taken into account.

First is the **moderator**: the person who controls the group, guiding respondents to undertake the task required. Moderators must know how to create a good working atmosphere in the group, in which the different respondents take part freely and spontaneously. Their mission is to listen to and understand the respondents.

Today, we usually work with seven or eight **respondents**. In the past we worked with 9, 10, 11 or even 12, but we have found that a group of seven to eight allows each respondent to interact with all others. For professionals such as doctors, we may reduce the number to five or six: they represent a smaller and more uniform universe, and each one will need more time to talk in depth about professional matters.

The third element is the **task**: for respondents to talk about the topic in a free and spontaneous way, in as much depth and with as much detail as possible.

It is important that the **space** used is suitable for undertaking the task effectively and comfortably. A circle of chairs around a low, small table helps to create an informal relaxed atmosphere and aids interaction.

The final variable is **time**, which determines the type of relationship that can be established between the respondents and moderator. Most groups last two hours but extended groups (typically from three to four hours) are used when the subject is very broad and deep, or it is necessary to use projective or creative techniques.

An average qualitative study comprises four to six groups, but small studies may involve two or three, and there are also larger studies (more than six groups).

The advantages of focus groups

This is the most popular technique in qualitative research, mostly because of the richness of its profile:

- A properly selected micro-group represents the discourse of a segment of the population (a social macro-group).
- Focus groups allow us to obtain a large amount of data, or a good number of ideas about a problem, in a short period of time.
- Different points of view are aired, and most importantly, respondents interact. The individual (psychological) dimension is combined with a social (sociological) one.
- The technique has great diagnostic power. If, for example, we show a group of consumers a television advertisement, they can evaluate it in depth.
- Focus groups need less time than in-depth interviews, so they fit better into clients' schedules.

The disadvantages of focus groups

The main disadvantage is the influence of the group structure and the group dynamic on the output. The moderator has to concentrate on the dynamic and ensure that it is correct and allows all relevant information to surface. Moderators must be highly attentive to issues such as leadership, and ensure that all the respondents take part. They must be committed to the group and ensure there is a depth of discourse.

It is not possible to go as deeply into the point of view of each respondent as it is in an in-depth interview. As a result, sociological factors predominate over psychological ones.

The key factors in good moderation

Each focus group is different. Regardless of how many groups they have moderated, a good moderator will feel uncertain at the start: they do not know what is going to happen, or what type of information will emerge.

In 2005 I asked my Millward Brown colleagues about the key factors in good moderation. I received feedback from 32 senior researchers, all with much experience in moderating, organizing and hosting focus groups, in 10 countries across three continents: Germany, Spain, France, the Netherlands, Italy, Poland, the United Kingdom, the United States, Mexico and China. I thank them all. Their input led to what I have called the Ten Commandments of Moderating, which are grouped into six areas in the next figure.

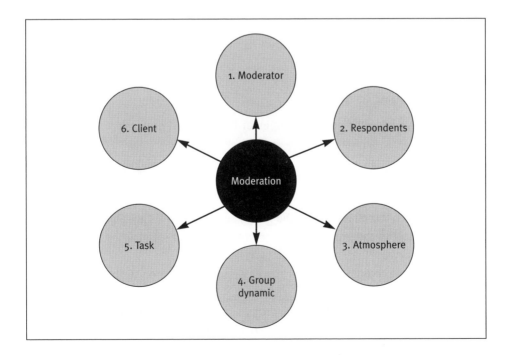

The moderador

1. Moderators must be in touch with themselves and their feelings.
2. They must be flexible and creative.
3. They must enjoy moderating.

The respondents

4. The moderator must connect with and listen to the respondents.
5. Target groups must be recruited carefully.

The atmosphere

6. Create a democratic atmosphere that encourages participation.

The group dynamic

7. Moderators must know how to 'read' the pace of the group.

The task

8. Concentrate on the task.
9. Always keep the core objectives of the research in mind.

The client

10. Listen to the client before the group session then forget about them while moderating the group.

Here are some comments about the key issues in relation to the moderator:

> *'It is important for the moderator to listen to themself and ask themself: How do I feel right now? What mood am I in?'*

'When you are going to moderate a group you have to feel curiosity, want to explore and find out.'

'Only use those techniques you feel comfortable with: for example, in the area of projective techniques.'

'Be flexible.'

'Know how to improvise, be creative.'

'Don't get stressed out, be relaxed and organize yourself.'

'Be happy and have a sense of humour.'

'Be yourself!'

'It's important that it is a rewarding experience for the moderator and the respondents.'

'Don't worry about joking and displaying your personality. Naturally, this is up to a certain point, and without being dominating – this makes the discussion more natural. Respondents then share their opinions and personal experiences in a more relaxed atmosphere. They prefer talking to a 'normal' person, rather than with an intellectual professional.'

Here are some of the things my colleagues said to me about the importance of the respondent in the group setting:

'You have to listen well, I mean respect the consumers and listen to each one of them, ensuring that they are comfortable and that they feel secure, recognized, important and unconditionally accepted.'

'Know how to place yourself in the respondents' shoes.'

'Be flexible and interact with the respondents. Don't boss them, don't constantly repeat the last things they said.'

'Include each respondent in the discussion. Talk to the quietest ones by name and encourage them to take part. Turn your back on the dominant ones or ask them to wait while you listen to the others first.'

'Treat the session as a unique meeting that will never be repeated in the same circumstances.'

'The group and their discourse has to be the core of the meeting.'

This is what they said about the atmosphere in groups:

'You have to create an atmosphere that is as democratic as possible.'

'Create a good group atmosphere (working together and taking part) which makes people enjoy the session (not getting bored).'

'Discourse should move around and nobody should monopolize it.'

'The aim is to create an atmosphere of spontaneity, sincerity, freedom, togetherness and involvement.'

And some comments about the group dynamic:

'Each group has its own dynamic and it's important to 'read' the pace of the group.'

'Focus only on the group and how it is going: analysis comes later.'

'Use and rotate different techniques (rational, emotional and projective), so the group moves ahead at a good speed.'

'Be alert at the different critical times a group goes through (tiredness, difficult tasks, creative phases), and do recovery exercises.'

'Encourage cohesion, integration, interaction, production and involvement and prevent silence, tiredness, insecurity and lack of commitment.'

A number of comments about the task help flesh out commandments 8 and 9:

'The study briefing can always be summed up in one or two key questions. Never forget these questions while you are moderating.'

'Always keep in mind the strategic objectives.'

'Ensure that you have understood the briefing properly, together with the research objectives.'

'Never lose sight of the task.'

'Always follow the main highway: only use side roads if it is absolutely necessary.'

'Prepare a diagram showing the main sections of the group.'

'Follow your instincts: if you feel there is an opportunity, go for it!'

'Always remove as many layers as may be necessary to find the true motivations.'

'Always go beyond the rational level! Ask them what a certain idea makes them feel.'

'Probe, investigate their replies as much as possible. Don't remain at a superficial level, the one that is easiest which explains the least; reach for the deepest reasons.'

'Pressure consumers gently and subtly: this will help you to evaluate the degree of commitment that they feel to their reply.'

'Ask open questions, avoid yes or no answers.'

'Progress from the large scale (what is general, the abstract level) to the small scale (what is concrete, specific areas): keep what is relevant in mind!'

'Start with what is spontaneous, then prompt.'

'You can stimulate discourse without even asking questions. For example, 'Let's talk about this brand.'

Lastly, these remarks give us a better feel for how to treat clients when they come to watch a focus group:

'Listen to your client attentively before the group, to understand clearly what they want to achieve.'

'Listen to your client attentively before the group and forget about them during the group.'

Different types of respondents

After many years of moderating groups we have identified nine types of respondent. These groupings take into consideration the respondent's approach to the subject being discussed, how they relate to the other respondents, how they relate to the moderator, and how they experience external reality.

The next figure shows these segments as discrete to better illustrate how people function in particular group settings. In reality, most people share the characteristics of several types or segments.

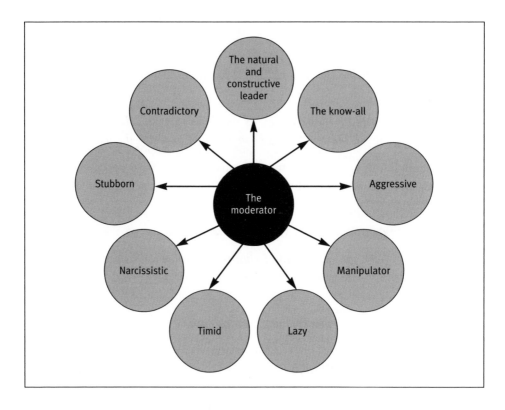

The natural and constructive leader

This type displays a positive attitude to the subject being discussed, the moderator, the others in the group and the reality external to the focus group. These respondents play an active role in the group. They use their energy in a constructive way, and know how to behave in the group. They participate actively and allow others to take part too. They collaborate, are committed and listen to other respondents. They have a good level of self-esteem, are self-assured and well-balanced.

They demonstrate the right level of involvement in the task set. Their contributions are effective and useful. They help to create a comfortable working atmosphere and good group dynamic. Sometimes these leaders express the opinion or feeling of the group as a whole. Because they are natural positive leaders and are not either dictatorial or monopolizers, they are accepted by the group.

Individuals like this present the moderator with an opportunity because they are good role models for other respondents. They are a resource that should be used, and they should be encouraged to participate.

The know-all

Know-alls are usually well informed and dominate the discussion. This is not always an advantage, and may become a major drawback. They are likely to play back what they have gleaned from the media on the topic. They play too much of a leading role in the group, always because of their 'wisdom' about the topic. However in focus groups knowledge is only relatively important. What are truly useful are individual opinions, attitudes, motivations, barriers and meanings, so this type does not usually help the moderator.

Know-alls sometimes impose their opinion on others. This hinders the creation of a democratic atmosphere. The moderator must control how know-alls participate. Dissuade them from providing information from the media; they need to express their own opinions, feelings and emotions.

A variant of the know-all is the charlatan, someone who plays a similar part but without being well informed about the subject.

Aggressive individuals

Aggressive people tend to destabilize the group dynamic. They make hurtful or destructive remarks. When they speak they create a tense atmosphere, but they do not tend to attack the moderator directly.

This type of person tends to question what the rest of the group accepts. It is a pathological form of behaviour which stems from childhood. They are angry and full of resentment or hatred, which they tend to direct at the other respondents.

The moderator must make it clear that personal attacks are not allowed. They must protect the other respondents from aggressive individuals, and try to get them to ignore them.

Manipulators

Manipulators seek power and authority. They want to control the situation. Because of this, they are most interested in the moderator, whom they see as holding authority.

Manipulators are usually intelligent, analytical and astute. They generally have good interpersonal skills, and usually have a 'card up their sleeve'. They might appear to help with the task, or to help the moderator in their role. They are quite skilful in their use of 'enveloping' strategies. They sometimes ask the moderator difficult questions, with the aim of embarrassing them. Sometimes they are more open, and launch swift and precisely aimed attacks against the moderator.

In all these situations the moderator must show the group their experience and positive authority. For example, they could turn things round and ask the manipulator to answer their own questions. In this way the moderator is able to show the other respondents they have seen through the manipulator's strategy.

Lazy respondents

Lazy respondents have a conformist attitude to what happens around them. They are passive and have a 'sleepy' personality. Lazy respondents are governed by the law of minimum effort. They only take part when the moderator asks them to. Curiously, they then tend to offer quite interesting points of view and opinions. Their view of life tends to be balanced, objective and realistic.

Whenever possible, the moderator should stimulate these respondents to take part because they often make a good contribution.

Timid respondents

Timid respondents tend not to take part because they are very insecure. They feel inferior and have low self-esteem. They usually have serious doubts about the validity of their ideas, and fear rejection by the other respondents. As a result their attitude during groups is passive. They adopt an attitude of listening to the others. When they say anything it is usually along the lines of 'I agree.'

The moderator should encourage such individuals to take part, praising what they say so they feel supported.

Narcissism

Narcissistic individuals feel superior to the other respondents. They are usually exhibitionists who try to show off their physique, image, lifestyle and so on. They often try to seduce the group. They are recognizable because they try to centre the group discourse on themselves. When they speak they use the subject to exhibit one of their own qualities.

These individuals do not usually fully join the group. They may be quite delicate and fragile when others do not respond to their exhibitionist attitude in the way they had hoped. The moderator should get them to concentrate on the subject, and talk about their opinions, point of view and feelings.

Pigheaded respondents

On rare occasions, we find these strict and rigid individuals in groups. They have fixed ideas and do not usually listen to other people or take their opinions into account. Their point of view is strongly rooted in values that may be religious, political or cultural. They tend to work more with stereotypes than with real situations. They display neither flexibility nor room for manoeuvre in how they see things. They often try to impose their opinion on the other members of the group. They usually have a dictatorial attitude.

The moderator must reduce the importance of such individuals. Other respondents must be allowed to speak, and the pigheadeds encouraged to defend how they see things. The moderator should make it clear that it is not necessary for everyone to think the same way.

The contradictory personality

This type of respondent has a dual personality. Their attitude can change frequently during the group. Sometimes they see something as white, at other times black. Their personality is unstable, and this gives rise to a lot of confusion within the group dynamic. Most of the time they do not agree with anyone or anything. Nevertheless, they are intelligent and may make valuable contributions.

The moderator should try not to conflict with their negative side, but encourage the participation of their positive side, and praise them whenever this happens.

Leadership of the group

The moderator has to ensure that everyone in the group takes part, and expresses their points of view. So they must watch closely the group structure and its dynamics, and in particular the phenomenon of leadership.

In general, leadership goes against the notion of balanced participation by all of the respondents in the group. However, we must distinguish between positive and negative leadership. A natural, positive and constructive leader is useful to the group dynamic. This type of leader works for the group. They listen to the moderator, themselves and the other respondents. They usually have the ability to play back correctly the way the group thinks or feels. Such leaders are accepted naturally by the other respondents. The moderator should actively support this type of leadership.

It is helpful to look at respondents' facial expressions and body language, which should show whether they feel the leader is representing them properly or poorly. Sometimes situations become complicated, particularly when respondents feel comfortable hiding behind a leader who does not represent their own ideas and feelings.

The moderator must deactivate all artificial, negative or destructive types of leadership. Know-alls, aggressives, manipulators and the pigheaded try to achieve such leadership. If they take control, the dynamic of the group will be seriously damaged. The quality of the resulting information will be affected, and the conclusions drawn will not be representative of the target group.

Silence

Some group members keep silent, are passive or hardly participate at all. Silence in a group has to be managed very carefully. It requires diagnosis.

Four types of respondent use silence. An aggressive person will keep silent while waiting to 'pounce' on other respondents. The manipulator will remain silent until the right opportunity presents itself for them to question the moderator. Timid respondents will be silent because they feel insecure, while lazy ones will be silent simply because they're lazy.

It is almost better for aggressive and manipulative respondents to remain silent. They must be kept properly under control, otherwise the dynamic of the group is at risk. Timid and lazy respondents should be encouraged to take part.

The introduction of the moderator and respondents

The main aim of the moderator's introduction is to clarify the roles of the respondents and the moderator. All the respondents should talk freely about the subject. The moderator must listen while carefully controlling the structure and dynamic of the group, monitoring what the different respondents say and ensuring the task is completed successfully.

Respondents may be invited to introduce themselves in several different ways. The choice will depend on the aim of the focus group, how long it will last, whether or not projective and creative techniques will be used, and the degree of respondent involvement required.

Five different types of introduction

- **Standard:** respondents tell the group their name, job, hobbies and so on. This is the most common form of introduction.

- **Involving.** This is on the lines of, *'Let's talk about your names. Who gave you them? Why were you given these names? Do you like your names? Would you like to have another name?'* Another alternative is, *'What is the best thing that happened to you over the past year?'*

- Based on **desires.** *'Imagine you suddenly have a free week and can do whatever you want. What would you each like to do?'*

- **Projective.** *'We are going to introduce ourselves one by one, as if we were a natural element.'*

- **Creative.** *'Let's imagine we have an eye in our fingertip. How would this change our life? In what way would it be different?'* This introduction is very useful for extended focus groups in which creative exercises such as brainstorming will be used.

Good grouping

Personally I like to gather information in an enjoyable, fun, pleasurable and comfortable way. If respondents are committed and involved, the group provides better-quality information. Sometimes a negative atmosphere emerges in a focus group: there is silence, insecurity, unpleasantness, tension, anxiety and distress. Respondents feel uncomfortable and the information derived is of lower quality.

Summary and conclusions

- The main elements in a focus group are the moderator, the respondents, the atmosphere, the group dynamic, the task and the client.

- This popular technique provides a good range and depth of information from a reliable sample of a population in a relatively short time. The chief drawback is the relationship between the content obtained, and the structure and dynamic of the group. The moderator must ensure that all respondents participate, they are committed, and all the relevant information emerges.

- Each individual's viewpoint is revealed to less depth than in an in-depth interview. Sociology predominates over psychology.

- Good moderators obey the Ten Commandments of Moderating.

- Respondents can be categorized as the natural and constructive leader, the know-all, the aggressor, the manipulator, the lazy, the timid, the narcissistic, the pigheaded and the contradictory.

4
In-depth interviews

PEPE MARTÍNEZ

Introduction

In-depth interviews provide rich information because we are able to look in depth at the personal point of view of an individual who represents a segment of social reality (a macro-group). This makes it possible for us to investigate the relationship between thought, emotion, language (verbal discourse) and action (consumer behaviour). This technique works well when we want to study the relationship between a respondent's:

- cognitive level: what they think
- emotional level: what they feel
- linguistic level: what they say
- level of behaviour: what they do.

In-depth interviews make it possible to study in detail the interrelationship between psychological and sociological phenomena: how individuals collaborate in the construction of social reality, and how it in turn influences them.

It is harder to conduct an in-depth interview than a focus group. In a group, more techniques are available for the moderator. In a depth interview, if the interviewee lacks resources, the moderator has to help them, without influencing their free and spontaneous discourse.

In-depth interviews have roots in individual therapy, either psychoanalytical (derived from Freud*) or humanist (founded by Carl Rogers*), and in anthropology and sociology. They are a development of the fieldwork anthropologists carried out in the early years of the last century, and use the life-story approach of sociologists.

Socrates*, the famous Greek philosopher, was the first 'interviewer' we know of. He stands out because his method of philosophizing was based on 'not knowing', the *mayeutic* way of thinking. Socrates was skilled at enabling people in a very natural way to gradually discover what they already knew. A strong similarity exists between the Socratic mayeutic technique and the attitude of qualitative researchers conducting an in-depth interview.

Plato*, a disciple of Socrates, later used his master's words to describe the mayeutic technique: 'and the reproach which has been levelled at me so often, that I question others but never say what I myself think of any subject, ignorant as I am, is a thoroughly justified reproach'. The humble tone of Socratic wisdom comes through strongly in these words. Again, the philosophy is relevant in our context: on no account should the interviewer make remarks, comments or suggestions about the topic which could influence the information obtained.

While an interpersonal relationship has to be maintained between the interviewer and the interviewee, all remarks the interviewer makes must be neutral. The really important thing in an in-depth interview is the consumer's point of view: their psychological reality.

The interviewee should take the initiative, become so involved in the topic that they tell us everything that spontaneously comes to mind. This generates different chains of associations. A useful analogy is a journey to a distant country in the company of someone who knows it. The interviewer must focus on listening; following the Freudian model of 'floating attention'. They must concentrate fully on the interviewee's discourse and fully respect the interviewee's viewpoint while avoiding value judgements.

Principal elements

The 'setting' of an interview has six elements, shown in the next figure.

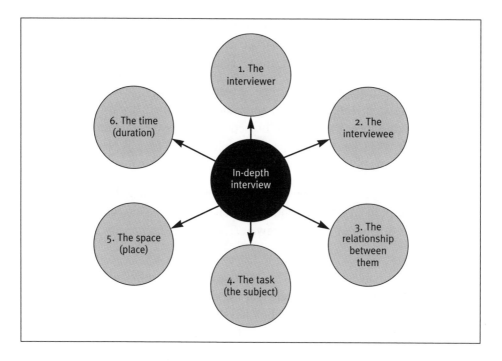

The interviewer must ensure the interview respects the rules of the game. They must create an atmosphere of spontaneity and openness, accepting unconditionally both the interviewee and their points of view. The interviewer's mission is to listen, understand and help the interviewee with the task.

The interviewee's task is to describe their point of view. They must therefore be involved and committed, able to go into the subject as deeply as possible. They must be encouraged to express their attitudes, motivations, barriers and feelings. We cannot simply ask an interviewee's opinion – the answer would be too basic, superficial and rational.

Because in in-depth interviews there is only one respondent, the relationship established with the interviewer is more important and intense than in a focus group. In the ideal scenario, the interviewee leads while the interviewer walks alongside, asking them to describe everything they see. Every interview is unique and unrepeatable. Each presents a different interviewee with whom the interviewer has to create a new relationship. The interview must take into account the real-time and classic nature of the relationship. Care must be taken to avoid falling into the 'question and answer' trap, like a game of tennis in which all energies are directed at returning the ball.

Interviews by judges, policemen, detectives or journalists can be pressurized and create tension, but in-depth market research interviews take place in an atmosphere of enjoyment, comfort, trust, security, sharing and informality.

The fourth element is the task: the subject or topic under discussion. This should be approached in a free and spontaneous manner. It must cover all the topics required to meet the research objectives. Any points that do not come up spontaneously must be prompted by the interviewer in a second part of the interview.

The space where the interview takes place must be suitable for two people to carry out the task in an effective and comfortable way. The interviewer must take care not to sit in front of the interviewee. The ideal is two chairs at an angle of 90 degrees.

The final variable is time. The interview length influences the type of relationship that can be established and the depth that can be reached. It also affects the types of exercises and techniques that can be used. In-depth interviews generally last between 45 minutes and one hour, although some are shorter or longer. Ethnographic interviews tend to be longer than average.

A medium-sized in-depth study usually comprises around 20 to 30 interviews, although there are sometimes more or less.

Advantages

In-depth interviews allow us to delve deep into the interviewee's psychological reality. Focus groups are better at detecting social phenomena – in the group situation, individual viewpoints are less important. Interviews show clearly the connection between consumption and lifestyle. They help us understand how purchasing and consumption habits fit into a person's everyday life.

In-depth interviews also enable us to make a realistic diagnosis of brands whose image is weak or damaged. When a brand declines, respondents in a focus group usually play back the brand stereotype: that is, its weak points. They might not admit they use it or see good points in it. Interviews can help identify which aspects of the brand could be kept and strengthened.

In the same way, in-depth interviews help us arrive at a realistic diagnosis of brands with an idealized image. Focus groups tend to underline and emphasize their strong points, without mentioning their weak points. With in-depth interviews we can explore in more detail the possible drawbacks of a leading or long-established brand.

The in-depth interview technique should be used for intimate subjects such as contraceptive methods, condoms and intimate hygiene products. It also offers advantages when studying subjects which give rise to social conflict such as gender differences, the lack of safety on the streets or immigration. In a group discussion, participants might say what they think others want to hear rather than express their true views.

Finally, in-depth interviews are particularly useful when we suspect there are problems with how an ad campaign is understood. In a group situation, we find that if one person understands the ad, this helps others understand it. In a one-to-one depth interview, we can look at the whole process of interpretation.

Disadvantages

In-depth interviews do not allow the simultaneous interaction of different points of view. Because the technique is based on the individual, it cannot reproduce social phenomena. The approach is more psychological and less sociological.

Another drawback is that this technique requires more time than conventional groups. Each interview lasts approximately one hour, and a minimum number of interviews must be conducted to show a range of points of view. The interviews also have to be analysed one by one. It takes three to four times longer to conduct and analyse 30 in-depth interviews than the equivalent, four focus groups.

What makes a good in-depth interview

First, think back to a time in your life when you were in the company of another person and felt especially good. Now think of a couple who get along well. Communication between them is good, at both a verbal and non-verbal level. They look into each other's eyes, their bodies are relaxed; they connect. There is harmony, understanding, synergy, collaboration, reciprocity and attraction. This is an useful model for a good in-depth interview.

A good interview is enjoyable, and the relationship is rewarding. Neither person gets tired because each is playing their role in a satisfying way. There is a desire to help, synchronization, and a certain chemistry between the interviewee and interviewer.

The interviewer and interviewee are relaxed, alert and concentrate on the subject of the interview. They are living in the present. They have taken a break from their everyday lives. The atmosphere generated in the interview space is different from that of any other experience. In good interviews a 'magic' atmosphere envelops the relationship.

The interviewer has to feel curious about the inner world of the interviewee. They must accept this world unconditionally. This creates a feeling of trust and security in the interviewee, which leads them to share their vision of the subject. Humour can also be very useful.

Body language

The interviewer must be aware of the role played by body language and other forms of non-verbal communication. It is important that there is direct eye contact. The look must reflect the interviewer's acceptance of the interviewee. At the same time, the respondent's eyes will give information about how they feel, as well as the type of relationship they wish to establish.

The interviewer needs to convey a sense of availability, accessibility, acceptance, receptivity, openness, listening and relaxation. Finally, the interviewers should take advantage of those parts of their body and personality with which they feel most comfortable, most secure and enjoy using most: for example, eyes, tone of voice, face or hands. They should try to avoid communicating in ways with which they feel less comfortable.

Tricks that help

The first trick involves using gestures and expressions to reinforce forms of behaviour or styles of remark we would like to see repeated. This positive reinforcement usually has an immediate effect. It can also be useful to offer feedback to interviewees when their behaviour or remarks move away from the research objective.

Repetition, or as it is sometimes known the mirror technique, is another useful trick. The interviewer repeats a word or expression the respondent has just used, to encourage them to continue to explore a subject in greater depth. It is particularly useful when the interviewer senses they have reached an area of meaning in which it is possible to delve deeper.

For example, imagine an interviewee has used the word 'smooth' to describe the shampoo she uses. This adjective has several different meanings (it is polysemic). She might for instance mean the shampoo is soft to the touch, does not harm the hair, leaves the hair soft, or is made from natural ingredients. When the term 'smooth' is repeated, the interviewee will offer more information about the subject, and this will aid understanding.

Used to excess, repetition can make the interview feel artificial. Use it only in situations where there is an opportunity to explore a subject in greater depth or clarify meaning.

Great care must be taken not to interpret what the interviewee says during the interview. Remember the interviewee is not aware of the latent level of discourse. If the interviewer attempts to interpret responses, they might disconnect from the interviewing process and appear distant. Analysis and interpretation should be left till after fieldwork has been completed.

Interviewers should be tactful and remember that verbal communication is just one method. They should control their tone, making sure they do not generate noise or interference in the relationship.

Adopting an innocent attitude can also sometimes be a great help, provided it is neither exaggerated nor artificial. The interviewee must find the interviewer's attitude credible. However, credible naïvety can encourage the person being interviewed to explain their point of view in greater detail.

The questions should always be as open as possible so the answers given by interviewees are not limited in any way. An example is, *'What do you think of this pack?'* This question gives rise to projective discourse in which the individual reveals their inner world. A closed question is, *'Do you like this pack?'* The interviewee can only answer *'Yes', 'No'* or *'I don't know.'* Closed questions can also make people feel defensive.

Projective questions can be a good way to ensure the interview is as successful as possible. Lastly, in some instances it is possible to develop a cooperative relationship with the interviewee. For example, the interviewer might say to the bartender of a discotheque, *'Just between us, why isn't this brand of rum served more often?'* This encourages the bartender to reveal the real reasons; the interview becomes more open and honest.

Summary and conclusions

- The richness of an in-depth interview lies in the fact that it is possible to delve deeply into the interviewee's point of view. It is ideal for studying the connections between what people think, feel, say and do.

- The main elements are the interviewer, the interviewee, the relationship created between them (the dynamic), the task (the subject), the space (the room) and time (duration of the interview).

- Studies that use interviews instead of focus groups take longer, and do not allow for interaction between different points of view.

- The interviewer must be aware of the role of body language and non-verbal communication.

- Tricks that can help interviewers include reinforcement, repetition, a naïve attitude and cooperation.

5
Ethnographic research

PEPE MARTÍNEZ with SARA DURÁN

Introduction

The term 'ethnography' is applied to a set of social research methods that evolved from the anthropological tradition. Anthropology aims to reconstruct the profile of a culture from the viewpoint of its members, identifying the causes, mechanisms and social rules that underlie actions, facts and forms of behaviour, of which the actors may not themselves be aware. It studies primitive societies, and was a forerunner of modern sociology, which applies the same techniques to contemporary society. In turn, qualitative researchers in market research have adopted and adapted this set of techniques.

Ethnographic research is based on fieldwork, and detects and studies behaviour that has a cultural meaning in a society. In modern market research (both qualitative and quantitative) the term 'fieldwork' is used in a broad way to refer to the stage of a research project in which information is collected.

Ethnography has made several major contributions to human knowledge, including:

- seeing and understanding life from the point of view of the members of a different culture
- avoiding ethnocentrism, the belief that one's own culture is better than others
- acceptance of cultural relativism, in which social values are not fixed and unchanging, but rather vary in different societies and historical stages.

There are two different approaches in ethnography:

- **The emic approach,** in which the researcher adopts the viewpoint of the world offered by those they are studying. When we listen to consumers while doing fieldwork we adopt the emic viewpoint and try to see the market features as consumers see them.

- **The etic approach**, by which the researcher establishes connections between the phenomena found and the theoretical models available for their interpretation. In qualitative research, we use the etic approach in the analysis phase.

Ethnography functions from the bottom up: it starts by describing facts and how phenomena are experienced, then moves upwards to construct a theory that explains the information gathered. The next figure shows this in graphic format.

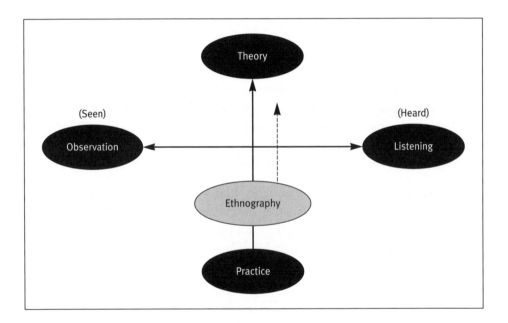

In market research, the ethnographic approach:

- is more than a methodology: it is a way of thinking, characterized above all by its openness, flexibility and relativism
- studies a small number of cases in depth and in detail, in a qualitative manner
- is an empirical and inductive method
- is humanist, affirming the value of the individual and their view of the world
- works with a universe of unstructured information
- uses an interpretative framework for analysis.

Interacting with the subject of a study

There are four basic types of interaction between a researcher and their subject of study, which are shown in the next figure.

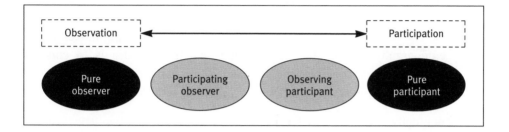

Pure observers do not interact with their research subjects (in this context, usually consumers).

Participating observers concentrate mainly on observation while also interacting with their subjects in a complementary way.

Observing participants centre on interaction. The main aim here is to form a relationship, although they also take advantage of the situation to observe.

Lastly, in the case of the **pure participant** there is no observation; the researcher puts all their effort into the relationship with consumers.

The most frequently employed stance in market research is the participating observer.

The fall and rise of the ethnographic approach

Qualitative market research started in the middle of the 20th century, in the United States and the most advanced European countries. Drawing on the traditions of both psychology and sociology, its practitioners developed a research style based on 'laboratory work': typically focus groups and in-depth interviews conducted in specially equipped rooms in their offices.

Laboratory research is a highly effective way of working. Respondents engaged in free and spontaneous discussion are a good predictor of what happens in real life, and it is very convenient for both moderators and clients. Over recent decades the majority of qualitative fieldwork has been laboratory-based, but there are some drawbacks:

- Verbal communication predominates. What respondents generally do is speak.

- The information that emerges has to pass through the filters of memory, thought and language.

- It may not be possible to explore certain aspects of how consumers experience or relate to a product or brand.

At the end of the 20th century there was a strong and growing movement to bring ethnography into qualitative market research. The idea is to conduct research in the natural shopping and/or consumption habitat, to open the door to experiencing how consumers interact with a product and use all five senses.

Ethnography opens the way for research to be conducted in two new settings:

- at the point of sale: these techniques fall under the banner of 'shopper research' and are becoming increasingly important

- at point of consumption, in or outside the home; this explores the consumption moment, the consumption ritual and the profile of the consumer.

The ethnographic variants on focus groups and in-depth interviews are ethnographic groups and ethnographic interviews. The next figure shows how the laboratory approaches and ethnographic techniques are related.

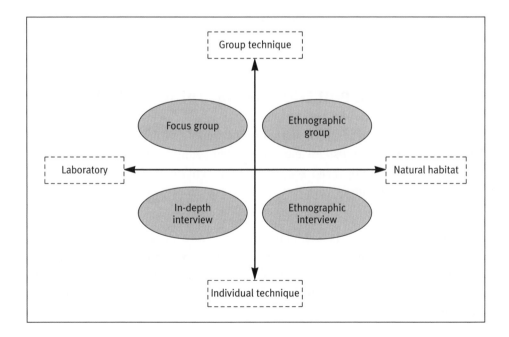

The range of ethnographic approaches

Ethnography offers us different alternatives within qualitative research, depending on the aim of the study, in both purchase and consumption settings:

- at the point of sale (shop visits), with both shoppers and sales staff

- in the home

- in the workplace

- in motion in the street (for example, studying the impact of outdoor advertising)

- in bars, restaurants and similar venues

- in hospitals, with doctors and nurses

- in schools and universities, with students and teachers.

These activities last from half an hour to a whole day, and can involve individuals, couples (heterosexual, homosexual or friends), nuclear families or groups (for example friends or workmates). A wide variety of techniques and methodologies run from pure ethnography to a purely laboratory approach, as shown in the next table.

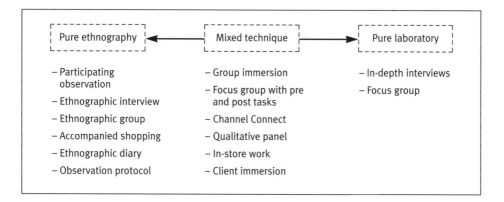

ChannelConnect and the Accompanied Shopping technique are discussed in detail in chapters 15 and 16.

With **pure observation**, there is no interaction with the individuals being studied. The tool is not very structured. **Participating observation** is also not a highly structured technique. The main difference is that the researcher responds to the subjects' behaviour, commenting, questioning and establishing a relationship with them.

Ethnographic interviews are more structured. The researcher prepares a list of points or an interview guide beforehand, and uses it as the basis for data gathering; observation is secondary. Observation protocols, however, may be used in any of the three methods, to ensure that specific types of information are recorded when it is felt it would be useful.

The following table compares these three approaches:

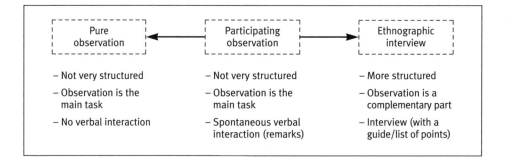

Pure observation	Participating observation	Ethnographic interview
– Not very structured	– Not very structured	– More structured
– Observation is the main task	– Observation is the main task	– Observation is a complementary part
– No verbal interaction	– Spontaneous verbal interaction (remarks)	– Interview (with a guide/list of points)

Participating observation is the principal ethnographic technique.

- It is a qualitative tool.

- A small number of subjects are observed.

- Subjects are selected according to the demands of the study, by (for example) their psychological, social, cultural, sociodemographic or socioeconomic profile.

- Observation always takes place in the natural habitat for purchase or consumption, with a focus on the individual's regular activities.

- The researcher records the behaviour and the experiences of the subjects.

- The researcher may invite respondents to talk about their behaviour, facts and experiences.

- The days of the week and times of day for study must be defined very clearly.

Millward Brown has used this technique in, for example, studies of:

- television programmes and advertising during prime time

- household rubbish recycling

- clothes-washing habits.

Ethnographic interviews also take place in the natural habitat where products are consumed or services are used. In-depth interviews are used to gain understanding of all the factors that influence the moment of purchase, consumption or use. Millward Brown has used this technique in, for example, studies of:

- doctors in hospitals, clinics, out-patient clinics and surgeries

- sales personnel in stores, to explore the dynamics of shopper–salesperson dialogue

- strong and weak points of refrigerators, interviewing the whole family in their kitchen.

The interviews can be recorded using a still or video camera. This rich visual material is used in analysis, and in the report and presentation.

The **ethnographic group** technique takes place in two phases. The first phase consists of participating observation: taking field notes in situ, recording the group's remarks verbatim, taking photographs or filming them on video. The group might consist of either strangers or previous acquaintances.

The second phase consists of a focus group, normally held either immediately after the initial experiential phase in situ (in the natural consumption environment), or the following day in the laboratory. The first phase experience engenders trust and support, and the moderator normally connects quickly and effectively with the respondents.

On occasions the client takes part in both phases of the research as either a passive or participating observer.

Millward Brown has held ethnographic groups, for example, on the consumption of alcoholic and soft drinks in bars and discotheques, and in amusement parks, theme parks and casinos.

Ethnographic diaries are usually combined with focus groups or in-depth interviews. The respondents keep a diary at home before coming to the laboratory. By maintaining it for several days while they are in direct contact with the product under study or a competitive brand, they provide a fresh point of view, and valuable and rich insights. A diary kept before a focus group also ensures that we receive both individual and group feedback.

An example of the guidance for an ethnographic diary on face care

We are researching how women today care for their face. Please spend 10 or 15 minutes each day keeping this diary for four days, two weekdays and a weekend (Saturday and Sunday). Please remember to bring the diary with you to the meeting arranged to discuss this subject as a group.

One each day please give details of:

- *all the things you do during the daytime, their duration and everything you believe to be relevant about them*

- *the times you spend on face care: the products you use, the routine you follow, the tricks you have, the place and time of day, the amount of time you use each product for and so on: every detail is important to us, so please try to include as much explanation as possible.*

Include photographs of the face care products you have at home, showing where you keep them, the time of day you use them, and what they mean in terms of your facial beauty routine. You can also include other images that you associate with facial beauty. Please also add a label, box or pack of a face care product that is very important to you.

So we can get to know you better, please tell us:

- *your first name and surname*

- *your age*

- *your occupation*

- *your partner's occupation*

- *how many members live in your household (including the ages of children)*

- *a brief description of yourself*

- *about your main interests or hobbies.*

We have a few further questions for you:

In a normal week, what physical exercise do you do? (type of sport, on which days, duration and with whom, etc.)

In general, how do you care for the skin on your face?

What personal 'tricks' do you have for facial beauty?

When you are considering a product for facial care, what concerns you? What do you look at? Please explain why.

What do you prefer, and try to avoid, when you apply facial care products?

In general, what personal 'tricks' do you use to keep in shape, to feel well, to stay healthy?

What magazines do you usually read? Which is your favourite, and why? Please include in your diary an article from a magazine that caught your attention.

Thank you very much for your help. We shall meet in the group.

As digital cameras are increasingly common, consumers are often able to send in photographs by email or bring them on a CD. This visual material enriches the information obtained, the analysis, the reports and the final presentations. Those without cameras are given disposable ones to use.

Millward Brown has used ethnographic diaries to research, for example, refrigerated food products, soft drinks and beers, deodorants, face creams, colognes and perfumes, mobile telephones; and in studies for pharmaceutical companies.

Observation protocols

It is becoming increasingly necessary to design an observation grid to structure the observation. This might seem simple, even trivial, but it is important that it is based on an understanding of how much time is needed to record the data, how it will be used and who will use it.

Observation grids make it possible to:

• take maximum advantage of observation time

- set guidelines for observation so there is consistency between researchers in a study

- summarize the observation records so that information can be optimized for subsequent analysis.

The grid might include (for example) diagrams, pre-coded categories or open fields, depending on the objectives of the study and the context of the research.

Observers must always avoid preconceived ideas, and be open to all the phenomena that arise. They should note non-verbal communications: facial expressions, gestures, looks, postures, mood states and so on.

The choice of a system of observation again depends on the objective and characteristics of a study: The options are:

- **Category systems**, often used to test a hypothesis in depth. For example, a researcher observing a couple might be asked to note how often they make eye contact: always, almost always, sometimes, almost never, never.

- **Descriptive systems** are used when there is no prior information about the topic: these field diaries are used to identify aspects before choosing some for study.

- **Narrative systems** are used when there is a clearly delimited objective for observation. These often combine, first, a note of everything the researcher thinks might be of interest, and second, a series of more specific observations.

- **Technological systems** involve audio and/or video recording, used in any of the above ways. Previous authorization may be necessary, depending on the type and location of the research.

There are two basic levels of observation:

- On the first level we record what is happening, what we are seeing, perceiving and intuiting, and so on. An attempt is made to differentiate between the objective and subjective.

- The second level refers to the interaction between the environment and the individual. We record both the location and what is happening in it, and the individual within it: what they do (for instance look, touch, eat), what they say, and their non-verbal communication.

Case study: the use of an observation grid

This example concerns the development of a concept for a new fast food restaurant. The study used ethnographic interviews among other techniques.

First came a series of participating observation sessions in existing restaurants of this type, during which a field diary was kept. A grid was then prepared using the data acquired and hypotheses that had arisen.

Researchers were asked to note, as objectively as possible:

- Interview number.

- Date.

- Interviewee characteristics (age, sex, etc.).

- Time of start and finish.

- Location and description of the site.

- Number of products purchased.

- Description of products purchased.

- Remarks about the selection of the restaurant and meal.

- The presence of any gifts, 'gadgets' or promotions linked to the meal selected.

- Description of the atmosphere between the people under observation.

- Whether any food was shared.

- Description of the tone of voice.

- Roles and leadership of the members of the group.

- Whether more food was ordered, details of it, and how the other members of the group reacted.

- Mood when leaving the establishment.

- Whether the tray was taken to the container before leaving, and by whom.

There was also a section for recording other comments and more subjective aspects of the observation: feelings, hypotheses, a 'mini-analysis' of the variables observed.

Mixed ethnographic and laboratory techniques

Group immersion

We use this term for extended group sessions lasting a minimum of four hours (depending on the country and context). They consist of three phases:

- The group start in the laboratory.

- In the second phase, they share an experience in a natural habitat: for example a supermarket, an outlet of a new franchise or a petrol station.

- In the final phase, the group get back together in the laboratory to discuss the visit.

This technique gives rise to richer insight than a conventional focus group.

One Millward Brown study concerned a new concept for a chain of shops selling newspapers, magazines and books. In the first phase, the group discussed the advantages and disadvantages of current outlets. In the second phase, respondents visited a shop that used the new concept. In the last phase, they provided feedback on this experience.

The respondents may also be asked to make a visit individually before coming to a meeting. We did this when testing a new concept of mobile telephone shop.

Focus groups with pre and post tasks

In this mixed technique, before attending a focus group meeting, respondents are asked to keep an ethnographic diary to an agreed set of instructions. This increases their sensitivity to the subject and enables them to prepare visual material for discussion (photographs, labels, packs, articles from newspapers or magazines, web pages and so on). Done properly, the task is highly involving.

A conventional focus group is then held, and finally all or some of the group may be requested to complete a post-task. This may involve taking a photograph related to something discussed in the group, or trying (or asking their family to try) a product. One or two weeks later they are interviewed by telephone: an individual phase that takes place in the consumer's natural habitat.

Qualitative panels

These involve a panel of consumers and/or experts who participate in a multi-stage study involving a variety of techniques, lasting from six months to a year, depending on the client's needs. A panel for a mass-market product like a detergent usually consists of approximately 70 to 80 consumers. A panel of experts (for example, to develop new mobile telephone services) is typically much smaller: about 15 or 20. The advantages are:

- The continuity of the panellists.
- The opportunity to examine in depth and over time consumers' motivations, barriers, attitudes, lifestyle, experiences, values and changes.
- Respondents are more committed, involved and available, leading them to adopt the role of information providers.
- The methodology is highly flexible, and often each new phase is not defined until the previous phase has finished, making this a very dynamic process.
- The marketing and research teams work together with consumers in a way that is united, progressive and interactive.
- It is especially useful when the objective is to innovate in a market.

Techniques used with qualitative panels include:

- workshops with the marketing and research teams and consumers
- focus groups
- creative sessions
- ethnographic diaries
- ethnographic interviews
- ethnographic groups
- group immersion.

In-store research

The aim here is to get as close as possible to the place where final purchase decisions are made – the point of sale. Core to this type of research is the accompanied shopper technique discussed in detail in chapter 16, which is used to:

- determine shopper types
- understand the role of planning and impulse in the purchase decision process
- determine the purchase decision process for the category in question.

Other in-store research objectives involve:

- improving the location and organization of products and variants in displays
- adding the purchaser dimension to negotiations between manufacturers and retailers
- becoming true experts in a category.

A category in this sense is not a catalogue of things (products, varieties, brands) but a concept that refers to consumer needs. We can distinguish:

- a category, defined by a generic need
- a subcategory, defined by a specific need
- variants, as defined by individual preferences.

The next figure shows how information in this type of research is structured.

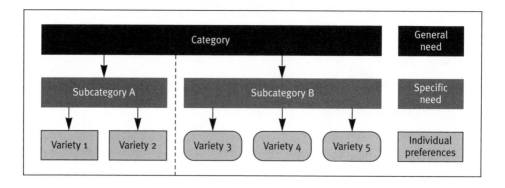

In-store research often combines conventional focus groups with accompanied shopping, using different respondents for each phase. In the focus groups, intended to help understand and suitably define the category, shelves in the room display relevant products, brands and varieties, which respondents can organize according to the criteria they use when purchasing. This information provides a framework for the accompanied shopping, which may be complemented by a quantitative study at the point of sale.

Client immersion

Though not a research technique as such, the Millward Brown client immersion process can be a very useful way of bringing client marketing and sales teams (and others) closer to the consumer by steeping them in the shopper experience and consumption environment. The programme has been designed to provide actionable input related to any specific point of sale or purchasing process issue.

First, the marketers are trained by Millward Brown qualitative researchers to conduct face-to-face interviews and accompanied shopping interviews. The in-house and client teams jointly develop a discussion guide.

The immersion journey then starts with each marketer conducting an in-depth interview at a shopper's home. The objective is to get a good understanding of the consumer's lifestyle, values, attitudes and behaviours, and consumption environment. It also enables the client to see where the product is stored and gain precious insight into consumption occasions and product usage.

Next is an accompanied shopping phase, again with the client as the observer. Straight after the product has been selected, an interview is conducted in front of the shelf to probe for relevant insights: for example decision criteria, and the role of packaging and promotions.

A Millward Brown researcher then moderates a workshop with the client teams, which is translated into key learning and actionable results that can help the client build future strategies.

Summary and conclusions

- Ethnography is a very powerful approach for researchers, marketing professionals, sales teams and distribution channels. Derived from anthropology and sociology, it involves getting to know consumers in their natural habitat.

- Ethnographic techniques seek facts, experiences, phenomena and behaviour, not only opinions. They therefore attempt to go beyond mere verbal discourse, to reach the dimension of experience.

- The two working environments of ethnographic market research are the point of sale and the consumption setting.

- Awareness of the stance of the researcher (which ranges from pure observation to pure participation) is crucial to good ethnographic research, as is the development of an appropriate research protocol.

- Ethnographic market research techniques include participating observation, ethnographic interviews, ethnographic groups, accompanied shopping and ethnographic diaries.

- Ethnographic techniques can also be combined with conventional laboratory research. Tools include group immersion, focus groups combined with pre-and post-group tasks, qualitative panels and in-store techniques.

- Client immersion is a Millward Brown approach designed to draw on these techniques to bring marketers closer to the consumer experience.

6

Projective and creative techniques

PEPE MARTÍNEZ

Introduction

Projective and creative techniques are used in qualitative research to elicit more information that comes from free and spontaneous consumer discourse.

The mechanism of projection

The concept of projection originated in psychopathology. It is the psychological mechanism by which we attribute opinions, attitudes, motivations, resistance or forms of behaviour to other people, when they are actually a reflection of what we ourselves think and feel. Understanding this allows us to identify aspects of a subject's personality from their free discourse. For example, if somebody in a focus group says that *'people drive terribly badly'*, they are probably not a good driver.

Because we are naturally narcissistic, we tend to project negative or unpleasant aspects of our personality onto others. At the same time, we tend to appropriate their positive and pleasant characteristics by means of a psychological mechanism that works in the opposite direction, *identification* or *introjection*.

Market researchers used these concepts to develop *projective techniques*. Within each individual we can distinguish two concepts — the 'real I' and the 'ideal I'. As its name indicates, the 'real I' refers to the person as they are, with their strong points and weak points. The 'ideal I' is the idealized image: what they would like to be like, their aspirations and expectations. The dynamic between these two 'Is' leads to projection and introjection, as shown in the following figure.

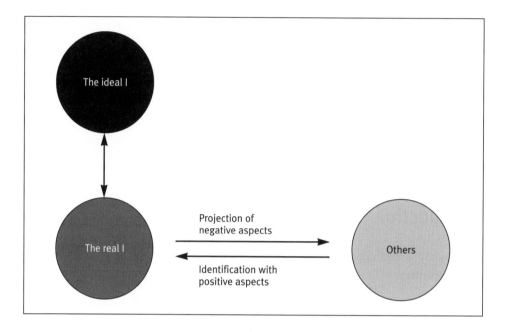

The application of projective techniques

Projective techniques are used to complement the free and spontaneous discourse we find most often in focus groups. They are very useful when:

- The aim is to discover opinions, attitudes, motivations and resistance. In such cases, consumers are asked how they think other people will react to a situation or some stimulus material.

- An in-depth diagnosis of the image of a company or brand has to be made, on its own or compared with its competitors.

- The main objective is to discover consumers' emotional and symbolic relationship with a brand.

- The need is to explore in depth what consumers think of a product, advertising campaign and so on, and their relationship with it.

It is much more effective to use projective techniques in focus groups than with individuals.

When consumers are talking freely and spontaneously in focus groups and in-depth interviews their discourse takes place at three levels:

- The rational level. This is the objective world, the conscious dimension; the most external and stereotyped part of social discourse.

- The motivational or emotional level, which alludes to deeper aspects of personality. This is the subjective world of consumers. It is the aim of the researcher to reach this motivational discourse.

- The symbolic level, at which people make unconscious connections between ideas and symbols.

The next figure shows these three levels.

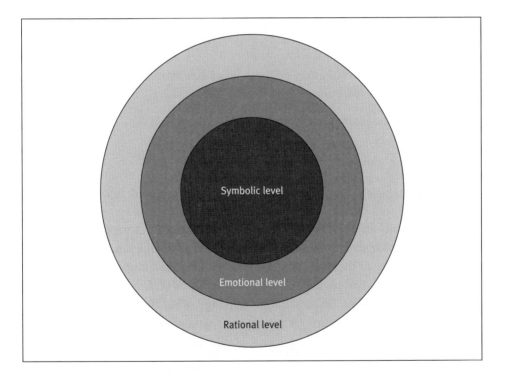

Researchers use projective techniques to try to tap the unconscious mind at the symbolic level, and draw on it to identify more fully and more clearly a person's perception of the topic, and their relationship with it at a motivational level.

In general terms, we can identify three types of projective technique, in which:

- the projective mechanism is completely integrated into the free discourse, in which it emerges spontaneously

- predetermined personification-type projective questions are used

- collage is used.

In the first type, the moderator asks questions like *'How will people out on the street react when they see this ad on television?'* or *'How will consumers of this product react when they notice the changes made, and how will non-consumers react?'* Again, respondents are likely to project their own views onto the answers they give.

In the second type of technique, the moderator asks, for example, *'What if a BMW turned into:*

- *A person? What would they be like? What kind of relationship do you think you might have with them?'*

- *A home? What sort of home would it be? What would the atmosphere inside it be like?'*

- An animal: *what animal would it be?'*

- A plant: *which plant do you imagine? Why did you think of this plant?'*

Other options for this class of question include a landscape, an object, a colour, a piece of music, a planet, a famous person, a feeling, an image; you can probably add more to the list. Each one can be elaborated in different ways. For example, *'Let's imagine someone who is driving a BMW. Is it a man or woman? How old are they? What do they do for a living? What do they do in their free time? What's their personality? What are their values? Where do they go?'*

This type of projective questioning can be used in many different ways and on many different occasions. Its use is limited only by the imagination of the moderator or the resources or skills of the group.

The third type of projective exercise involves respondents using different materials to create a collage which represents their thoughts and feelings on a particular topic. In this group technique:

- Respondents are given magazines, glue, scissors and coloured felt-tipped pens.

- Large sheets of paper (from a flip-chart) are placed on the walls of the room.

- Most importantly, the moderator gives the group an instruction, such as *'Let's express the personality of the Nike brand here'* or *'Let's show the profile of those who use the Puma brand on this sheet of paper.'*

The respondents then cut out images they think fit the task, and stick them on the paper, and write or draw whatever comes to mind. Once the collage is completed, the whole group talks about it. Collage techniques allow us to analyse the images and content used to create the collage, as well as further probe the group conversation.

These projective techniques enable us to transcend the purely verbal level of free discourse. They move us into the world of images and sensations, and broaden the ways we can talk about a brand, examine it and get to know its true essence. For them to work the group must be well structured, members must feel secure and the atmosphere must be trusting. At the same time, a sense of fun and enjoyment has to be created. Otherwise people will feel uncomfortable with the exercises.

Creativity

Many people, adults especially, feel uncomfortable and insecure when asked to show creativity or reveal their emotions. They might fear making a fool of themselves and appearing childish; not having any good ideas, or not knowing what to say; or saying things that are very unreal and coming across as a little crazy. However creativity can be very useful in qualitative research. Our working framework is based on the belief that everybody has creative potential, although many lack practice and technique. To be creative, people must develop a different attitude to their surroundings.

Applications of creative techniques

Creativity has many uses in market research. The researcher might be looking for, for example:

- new concepts for products or services
- new names for brands and sub-brands
- communication concepts for a product, service or brand

- possible follow-ups for an advertising campaign

- slogans and claims

- future developments in a category, product, service or brand

- new forms of distribution

- problem solving within an organization, company or department

- ways of training a marketing team for ongoing creative activity.

Creative focus groups are usually held with one of three types of participant:

- Professionals: for example representatives of the marketing team, the sales force, the R&D department, the advertising agency, the media agency and the promotions agency, together with the market research company.

- A group of experts in the industry. On other occasions groups are formed of, for example, psychologists, sociologists, writers, actors or artists. With the right training, people in creative jobs can offer original and useful ideas.

- A group of proactive and creative consumers, identified as such because they have passed a screening filter for creativity, or have been identified from previous groups as particularly creative. They should be excited by new products and services.

Creative techniques

The moderator must create an atmosphere that encourages the production of ideas. The ideal is an attractive, spacious, comfortable and naturally lit room. So they feel totally comfortable, members of the group should be free to move around. If the room has a carpeted floor, the group can sit on it if they wish. Creative exercises take some time to complete: allow two, three or four hours, a day or even a weekend.

The moderator should start by explaining the principles of a creative group to the respondents, who should:

- be very open, to the subject and to the ideas of others

- listen to and accept unconditionally the ideas of other respondents

- concentrate on the task at hand

- be involved and committed

- be natural and spontaneous in expressing their ideas

- be confident enough to express all their ideas without self-censorship or self-criticism.

All the ideas the group generates should be worked on and supported, not aborted. The moderator can encourage this by saying, for example, *'How can we take this idea further?'* or *'Following on from this, it occurs to me that ...'.* Creative activity should be enjoyed – motivation increases the richness and quality of ideas. When done well, it is very rewarding for both the moderator and the respondents.

Once the moderator has explained the principles, those taking part should introduce themselves. This can be done projectively, by asking the respondents to find an analogy to their personality in, for example, an element in nature. The moderator can begin, by saying, for instance, *'I'm a river that flows down the mountains. I'm narrow and very long, I like to refresh everything I find on my way: stones, grass, trees. I enjoy turning to the right and to the left, and I get bored when I move in a straight line.'* This technique helps respondents move away from reality and rational discourse and enter the world of imagination.

It is helpful to the group dynamic to continue with a few warm-up exercises. For example:

- Ask the participants to explore a fanciful topic, such as *'How would life change if we could fly?'*

- Word association: one respondent says a word, the next has to say the first word they associate with it, and so on round the circle.

- A chain story. One member of the group starts to tell the story and the next has to continue it.

- Physical exercises can also be included.

Once all the respondents are relaxed and interacting well, the core of the session can begin. This consists of three complementary and consecutive stages:

- The aim of the first phase is to fully immerse respondents in the problem that has to be resolved creatively.

- Next, the realistic approach is abandoned, and respondents are taken into the world of the imagination where everything is possible and there are no limits. The objective is to find new ideas to help resolve the problem. Useful techniques include brainstorming – ideas about the topic generated by free association – and future scenarios. For example, *'Let's imagine the home of the future, the materials it will be made of and the cleaning products that will be used in it.'*

- The final phase is to review the material generated, and select the ideas with the greatest potential for further exploration. (This task can continue after the focus group session.)

Finally, of course, the moderator will thank the participants and wind up the session in the usual way.

Summary and conclusions

- Projective and creative techniques are qualitative tools that can be used to elicit information beyond that generated by straightforward free and spontaneous consumer discourse. Both use symbolism and association to try to tap the unconscious mind and latent creative abilities.

- Both types of technique work best in group settings rather than one-to-one interviews.

- The main types of projective techniques are integrated discourse techniques, projective questions using analogies, and collage. Among the core creative techniques are brainstorming and future scenarios.

7
Digital qualitative research

FELIPE BARRAL with PIETER WILLEMS

An overview of current online research

The number of *quantitative* research studies that make use of the Internet is increasing. The rate of growth in individual countries is influenced by Internet penetration levels, and in some countries by the attitude of both clients and researchers. Because it is impossible to see or listen to respondents to online questionnaires, doubts are still raised about the degree to which samples are representative, but techniques for checking on people's identities are being developed. There is likely to be considerable short and longer-term growth in online research at the expense of telephone and face-to-face methods.

Qualitative studies, however, centre on the relationship between the researcher and the respondents. Non-verbal information, including facial expressions, gestures and body language, plays a highly important role, and this is lost in online studies. However, these issues should not preclude us from exploiting the opportunities that this new tool brings.

Digital qualitative research

Several types of digital qualitative research are now available:

- classical tools that have been adapted to the Internet, with digital focus groups and digital in-depth interviews
- digital ethnography
- accompanied browsing
- digital panels.

Digital focus groups

The main advantages over traditional group discussions are:

- They are convenient because respondents take part from home or work (in the case of professionals).

- Because they are in a sense anonymous, respondents feel able to contribute more freely.

- Respondents are less influenced by other group members, and the individual personality of each one stands out more.

- At the end of the group, the conversation is immediately available for analysis because it is already in text format.

- Clients are able to follow the group from their own office.

See Brüggen and Willems (in press) for a fuller review of the advantages and disadvantages.

Qualitative online research is particularly useful with groups who do not feel comfortable in the laboratory, such as teenagers, who can suffer from shyness and a closed or rebellious attitude. They are very familiar with digital chat using tools such as Messenger, so their self-confidence and comfort levels tend to be high, and this enables them to be more natural and open.

Online focus groups work well (though with variation between countries) for those aged between 13 and 40. They can be used for any subject, and are especially useful for sensitive subjects such as hygiene, health and sexual issues.

Most traditional qualitative research fieldwork takes place in large cities, but working online makes it is possible to organize focus groups with respondents from different (including more remote and rural) areas. In our experience they work best when there is a maximum of eight respondents and they last no longer than an hour and a half.

Digital in-depth interviews

These are particularly useful for interviewing professionals, for example a doctor or someone in charge of contracting for corporate telecommunications services. The researchers do not have to leave their offices to contact the interviewees, who might be located at a sizeable geographic distance.

Digital ethnography

Ethnographic approaches can be also adapted for the Internet. All ethnographic work requires us to ensure that the information collected is valid; that what has been observed reflects real life and was not caused by the laboratory situation. In digital ethnographic studies, we can experience consumer-generated content as an observer and chronicler of what is really happening – spontaneously and in the respondent's natural habitat.

We must look at the object studied not as an isolated idea, or as something self-contained, but rather as something that only makes sense when it is analysed as part of a cultural fabric. Because the content is spontaneously generated by consumers the range of potential topics is vast. For example, observation of chat rooms or discussion forums gives access not just to general chit-chat, but to respondents providing others with information: perhaps personal movie reviews or feedback on new professional products.

It is important to consider and respect the nature of what is observed: in its real context, the time of day, the time taken and so on.

In today's environment of permanent connectivity the possibilities of 'seeing without being seen' have widened: we can analyse blogs, discussion forums, chat rooms, information on social networks and so on without the usual interference of the researcher. Thanks to the widespread availability of webcams, mobile phones with cameras and digital cameras, we are able to access, observe and communicate in many more ways than previously.

More directive techniques are also possible. Using a digital ethnographic diary, the modern version of a traditional anthropological field diary, we can observe an individual and their everyday relationship with the product. Because technology makes it possible for researchers to look at respondents' diaries each day, and enables respondents to, for example, send photos and other material to enhance them, we can observe not only what is happening, but how changes take place over time. This provides an immediacy and richness of detail not previously possible.

The forums include:

- **Blogs**, in which the writer or blogger creates their own page, expressing their free and spontaneous views in much the same way as in an in-depth interview. Blogs may offer a lot of information about lifestyles and values, and can provide specific information about experiences and preferences with products, services, categories and brands. Some blogs centred on specific interests become widely consulted by Internet users: for example The Sartorialist, a site created by a traveller interested in fashion, is now an important site for those interested in trends.

- **Chat rooms** are sites designed so that users can communicate with each other, publish opinions and assess brands, products and services. These themed pages are segmented according to product and category, and are becoming a source of information and reference for consumers. In terms of collective interaction, they resemble focus groups, but because their content is generated spontaneously, they provide us with a new stream of research information. Attempts by brands to monitor and harness these spaces are signs of the importance consumers give to other people's opinions.

- **Online communities**, such as Facebook, My Space, Fotolog and Tuenti, are sites where users create their own spaces, like a window open to the world where they can display their personality. Members join communities of interest related to their specific lifestyle and leisure activities. Some pages get huge numbers of hits, more than many brand-owner sites, and are highly influential as recommenders of products.

Digital technology not only increases the tools available for research, it has also created new ways for consumers to learn about brands. The Internet has empowered individuals to make recommendations to others, beyond the control of the brand and its manager. Digital ethnography may make it possible for marketers to unlock and enter this new world.

Word of mouth (WOM) is an area of increasing interest to marketers. They sometimes exploit it through viral marketing. Consumers are starting to trust remarks made by their peers more than they do brand advertising campaigns. As researchers, we have to determine where, when and how WOM occurs.

Accompanied browsing

Websites have become an important touch point for most industries. Understanding how consumers perceive their content and navigate from the first link to purchase is key for marketing teams to optimize a cross-media communication strategy.

Both branding and usability aspects are considered: how the website contributes to brand image and perception, and how consumers navigate and conduct tasks on the site. Can they find products easily? Do they understand how to check out purchases? Does the textual style fit with the expertise of the target audience?

Various methods assess the marketing and usability strength of websites. Some, such as eye-tracking, require advanced technology. It indicates accurately how users focus on elements on the screen, and allows for relatively unobtrusive measurement of web browsing, but there are availability constraints, and it is tricky and expensive to set up and track each respondent.

Most website evaluation uses accompanied browsing. This is flexible and provides actionable recommendations. Respondents browse a website while in an observation room, in the company of a moderator, and often indirectly observed by clients. There is usually no introduction or warm-up interview, but a preparation task trains the respondent in what is required. The aim is to create a situation as similar as possible to normal browsing.

Respondents are given tasks such as *'Get a subscription to a monthly newsletter on furniture design,' 'Find the cheapest 3G phone, buy it together with a data subscription and pay using a credit card'* or *'Look for websites where you can compare rates for mobile subscriptions, and find out which brand provides the best rate for your usage pattern.'* The moderator does not comment or prompt the respondent, who is often asked to think aloud while browsing. Observers can watch their gestures and behaviour, and view mouse movements via a split-screen in the observers room. The researchers typically present the outcomes of the study in a workshop session, converting results swiftly into design and communication recommendations.

Accompanied browsing can also be conducted online. A portal is set up for this purpose, and the respondent logs in to the session from home. The moderator communicates verbally with the respondent via the phone. The software allows both moderator and respondent to navigate on the respondent's computer. The respondent's online behaviour, mouse gestures and page changes can be viewed by the moderator, and are recorded together with any oral feedback. The advantages are comparable to other online qualitative methods. Respondents can participate from home or from work, it is easy to include respondents from different regions or countries in the study, and the sessions can be scheduled flexibly. In particular with business-to-business websites, this is often the only feasible way to conduct a website evaluation since business users do not have time to travel to the research laboratory.

Digital panels

Researchers can create a social network, or 'online community', where the interactions on the site are monitored. This is the next step up from small-scale ethnographic observation. A group of respondents use the digital platform to communicate with each other in the same way as on other social networking sites. Their log-in times and tasks are controlled by the researcher, who adapts them to suit the aims of the study. In our experience, online communities are best for strategic studies where the aim is to study specific target groups in greater depth.

In 2007 Millward Brown Spain created a virtual community of young 'techies' (new technology enthusiasts), to study their values and lifestyle, including their use of technology and telecommunications, and leisure activities. In a digital extension of a focus group, respondents followed our instructions and created a virtual working space. We expected them to behave in an artificial way, but they interacted just as they would have done face to face: relationships developed, interpersonal conflict arose, and so on.

Recently, a client asked us to construct an online community to keep in contact with a group of 50 consumers (distributed over a whole country) of a personal care product over a three-month period.

We have also used the online community approach to create IdeaBlog. Developed by Millward Brown, this typically involves a sample of between 100 to 150 recruited consumers who come together in a specially created community website (to which only they and the researchers have access). An IdeaBlog may last from one week to several months. Participants take part in the discussion forum when and how they wish. The activity is moderated by the researcher, who encourages contributions from all the members and maintains the energy and direction of the conversation. As well as verbal input, respondents can upload videos and include photographs and images. This methodology, which is based on the idea of social networking, is new, involving and fun.

!DEABLOG

IdeaBlog can be used, for example, for looking for product ideas, discussing them, testing new product concepts, advertising alternatives, developing brand strategies and mapping brands. The tool uses a qualitative approach, but also allows us to quantify measures of particular interest. For example, we can ask respondents directly whether they like a particular concept.

Summary and conclusions

- Digital (online) qualitative research is a major area of growth. Respondents can provide free, anonymous, spontaneous and natural feedback.

- Techniques include digital focus groups, in-depth interviews, ethnography, accompanied browsing and digital panels.

- The most important limitation is the lack of access to respondents' non-verbal communication.

- Advantages include convenience for the respondent, the independence of respondents from each other's views, the ability to use respondents in remote and rural areas, and the fact that input is immediately available in a text format. Feedback can be provided over a long period, not only verbally but also using images, videos and so on.

- Among Millward Brown's developments in this field is IdeaBlog, a 'quali-quant' methodology using a sample of about 100–150 consumers who form an online community for from a week to several months.

8
Analysis & interpretation

PEPE MARTÍNEZ

Background

'The word is half his that speaks and half his who hears.'

*MONTAIGNE**

Data interpretation and the production of recommendations are a particularly appealing part of qualitative research. Most practitioners are passionate about the challenge of understanding, analysing, explaining and interpreting the workings of consumers' minds (the psychological viewpoint) and social consumption phenomena (the sociological viewpoint). However, it can be difficult and complex, with processes that are very different from those for quantitative studies.

The large number of respondents in a typical quantitative study makes it possible to carry out statistical analyses and test the significance of the findings, a rigorous methodological approach which offers clients a sense of security. Qualitative studies have smaller sample sizes and depend more on the researcher to reach conclusions. Quantitative research tends to be associated with objectivity and the hard sciences; qualitative research with subjectivity and the arts. There are few books or articles on qualitative analysis, often seen as a 'black box' process.

In practice, however, qualitative research consists of a mix of method and art. Because the researcher is immersed in and is a part of the reality under investigation, it is necessary to search for objectivity; to adapt a scientific paradigm to the object under study. By following rules and procedures, we can eliminate subjective distortions and get as close as possible to objective knowledge. This process guarantees to clients that the results obtained are valid. However, there is still a role for intuition, imagination, creativity and inspiration, which tend to develop the most powerful insights.

It is not easy to look at the qualitative discourse obtained in fieldwork and reach conclusions and recommendations that are solid, well-argued and clearly explained. It is like entering a large maze with many different pathways and dead ends. Applying method to the analysis and interpretation, and the experience of the researcher, are key factors in making sense of so much diversity.

Most of the information we obtain is verbal. However, what consumers express in non-verbal ways is also important. Ethnographic research provides a lot of non-verbal information, because it allows us to observe consumers in their natural habitat.

A qualitative research practitioner might be compared to a palaeontologist, an anthropologist or a detective. Palaeontologists study what is excavated – fossils, bones, the tools used by our ancestors. Their task is to understand this material, and use it to reconstruct the roots and first steps of humanity. Anthropologists do the same thing when they study ancient cultures. Detectives study the scenes of crimes, the clues left by criminals, then construct a line of investigation on the basis of this information. All these professionals, like qualitative researchers, use empirical data as the basis for the construction of a robust model which can provide explanations, predictions and recommendations.

Qualitative researchers cannot completely free themselves from their own point of view, cultural outlook or attitude to the topic. However, with training and experience they can control their subjectivity and adopt a position of neutrality. They must try to combat the phenomenon of selective attention: focusing on information that confirms their own point of view. And they must connect with consumers and empathize completely with their internal world, before finally carrying out an impartial analysis. Qualitative researchers must be aware of how consumers differ from themselves.

Care also has to be taken with the influence that theories have on the observation process. Theories, models or paradigms should not condition how researchers observe or listen to consumers, but instead be used to explain the findings in a subsequent phase of the research. It is prudent to adopt an open attitude from the outset, with unconditional listening to, and observation of, all of the material that emerges.

Qualitative analysis cannot and must not be influenced by the client. We have to get as close as possible to the reality of the market.

We mentioned on chapter 5 anthropology's concepts of the emic and etic ways of studying a culture. From an emic stance the researcher tries to see the world from the same point of view as the respondent, using the same rules and mental representations. The etic approach is more concerned with finding the connection between the phenomena observed and the theoretical models of the researcher's discipline. Qualitative researchers must combine these two ways of working.

It is important to keep in mind epistemology (the study of scientific knowledge), gnoseology (the theory of human knowledge) and hermeneutics (the discipline that studies comprehension and interpretation).

Mythical thought

The way of understanding the world in the very first human cultures was grounded in magic, myth and religion. Diviners or shamans specialized in the art of interpretation. The natural elements were personified, and the world was understood from an animistic point of view. Fantasy, imagination and emotion predominated; it was some time before the rational side of human thought came into play. Myths about gods and heroes were born within this context of magic and religion, and played a role in explaining both natural phenomena and human actions. We are all familiar with those Egyptian, Greek and Roman myths that have passed down to the present day.

Hermes, for instance, in Greek myth was one of the twelve gods of Olympus, immortal like all the gods. With winged sandals and wings on his hat, he was the herald of the gods, the messenger of Olympus in general and his father Zeus in particular, taking messages from the gods to humans and vice versa. He gave his name to the Greek word *herminia,* which means 'interpretation'; to Hermeios, the priest of the oracle at Delphi, and the modern term 'hermeneutic', which refers to the science and art of interpretation.

Market researchers play much the same role that Hermes once did: they are the messengers between manufacturers or suppliers and consumers. On the one hand they test concepts and products on behalf of marketing teams; on the other, they explore consumer desires and values.

Stages prior to analysis

These were discussed on chapter 2 the client briefing (not necessarily objective), the research proposal, planning the project and carrying out the fieldwork.

The researcher, like the client, starts to think from the initial stage about possible solutions, explanations and hypotheses: in other words, their subjectivity emerges. Care must be taken that this does not distort the analysis in even the subtlest of ways.

Analysis and interpretation are affected by three main elements in the planning phase: definion of the core aims of the study, the methodology and techniques in the study design, and the sample composition. These shape the kind, quality and relevance of information obtained, which in turn will affect the analysis. For example, focus groups are not a good way of checking comprehension of an advertisement, because the participants influence each other. Participant characteristics must be considered carefully, defined precisely, and carried through into the sample selection. This includes not only demographics but consumption characteristics: whether consumers are regular users or infrequent purchasers, users of the client's or a competitor's brand, and so on. Sample size is important too. A small sample (for example, two focus groups or ten in-depth interviews) makes it harder to analyse the findings properly. An over-large sample – *saturation* is the technical term – is neither cost-effective nor again, easy to analyse.

During the fieldwork, little by little the researcher will generate working hypotheses.

Levels or phases of analysis

Although 'analysis' and 'interpretation' tend to be used interchangeably, there is a distinction. While the entire process of analysis is a continuum, it contains three steps or successive levels: analysis of content, structural analysis and interpretation. The processes moves from the superficial, manifest, explicit and external, to what is deepest, most latent, implicit and internal. (See the next figure).

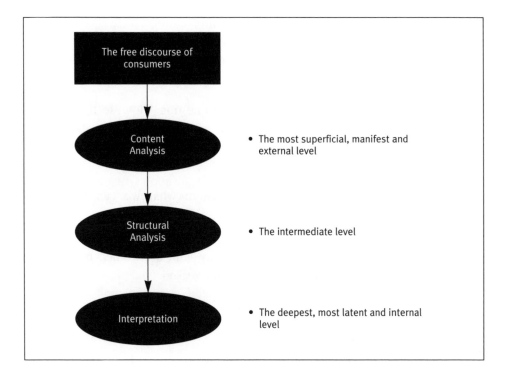

The first phase: content analysis

All data obtained is recorded, these days in a digital format. This discourse is then transcribed and turned into meaningful text, which becomes the raw material for content analysis. It needs be deciphered to uncover the hidden keys we are looking for: typically, information on customer attitudes, motivations and intentions.

In this phase the information is reduced and condensed. In quantitative research, the equivalent is putting numerical data into tabular form, but in qualitative research the starting point is discourse (by which is meant, both language and non-verbal types of communication). The whole power, richness and magic of free discourse is based on words and language. We turn this consumer discourse into a text which becomes our working material. It is empirical, observable, analysable, outside the researcher, and in a sense, objective.

At this point we are still at the most external and superficial analytical stage, where we are permanently connected to the consumer viewpoint. That helps make the first analysis rigorous and objective.

Content analysis is based on three dimensions:

- The **verbal** dimension answers the question 'What do consumers say?' In other words, it informs us about content.

- The **para-verbal** dimension answers the question 'How do they say it?' Consumers express desires, fears, doubts and so on; their remarks are not neutral, but have their own tone, style and intent. It is therefore necessary to read between the lines.

- Finally there is the **non-verbal** dimension: what we can learn from expression, body language and so on.

Sometimes these dimensions are in harmony with each other, but at other times not, and when this happens we must find a reason.

Most content analysis is based on the verbal dimension. Within this, we must distinguish between:

- significance: the content, on the semantic level

- the signifier: the container, on the syntactic and morphological levels.

All the most important elements in consumer discourse must be analysed one by one. The analysis of *significance* is crucial. Qualifying adjectives play a very important role here, because they allow us to enter the inner worlds of respondents.

To find the meaning or significance we are looking for, we use semantic and thematic analysis to identify concepts, categories, dimensions and cores of meaning. We are also able to record how often a category or subject is mentioned. The key categories are identified. The more exhaustive and exclusive the categories at this stage, the better. Distinction prevents confusion, as St Thomas Aquinas* said.

As we progress in thematic analysis and categorization, we are able to identify the primary and secondary concepts and phenomena. Little by little the initial perception of complexity is reduced. This makes the analysis task more manageable.

The para-verbal dimension can be approached by attributing a sign to each response we identify, typically:

- positive (+)

- negative (−)

- ambivalent (+/−)

- neutral (0).

The qualifying adjectives used, the verbs, their tense, the modal adverbs and other parts of speech reflect the nuances of the speaker, and offer highly useful information about the nature and intensity of attitudes. We can also analyse tone of voice (for example, irony or cynicism), as well as doubts, hesitations, silences, 'slips', errors of pronunciation, contradictions, an attitude of self-control, loss of control or the emergence of an internal conflict, and any other information that becomes apparent. All this helps us to understand the way in which consumers say what they say, and to reveal the pattern that determines specific opinions, thoughts, feelings, comments and forms of behaviour. And it gives us invaluable clues on how consumers react in 'real life'.

Non-verbal communication is handled much like para-verbal communication, by categorizing it as positive, negative, ambivalent or neutral, and adapting the categorization as necessary to deal with nuances: not just laughter but the type of laughter, the degree of surprise shown at something, and so on.

When respondents draw on their own experience their input tends to be more consistent and meaningful than when they make generic or impersonal remarks.

The second phase: structural analysis

Once we have distilled the text using content analysis, we move on to analyse the way in which the information is structured. We look for a fixed underlying structure, a set of generating principles which can order and explain the manifest superficial discourse.

During content analysis we moved closer to each element of the text, but in structural analysis we distance ourselves more from the material in order to see the structure as a whole. The text gradually emerges with a structured reality, in which the different elements occupy certain places. There is meaning in each one of the elements identified, the way they are combined and the dynamic between them. All this allows us to construct an interpretive model.

The third phase: interpretation

In the interpretation phase we need to distinguish between the manifest level – what is actually said – and the latent level – the deeper meaning conveyed, the unconscious elements that influence the person's opinions, attitudes and behaviour. Our mission as qualitative researchers is to reach the latent meaning. Interpretation is the key that allows us to open the door of comprehension and explanation.

Manifest discourse is not static text, but rather a dynamic reality. It is full of psychological mechanisms such as intellectualization or rationalization, idealization, identification, projection and negation. We must understand and identify these to interpret the material correctly. They offer us the clues necessary to shift from the manifest to the latent level.

A frequency–absence analysis can also be carried out. Significant absences are an interesting clue and may lead us to barriers or conflicts that prevent the emergence of relevant themes. We look for explanations for them.

Demographic and consumer characteristics such as gender, age, class, type of consumption, region and city must be kept in mind. The discourse must be related directly to the cultural context in which it emerged. We must therefore establish relationships with the psychosocial reality of the respondents (such as predominant cultural values and social trends). It is very fruitful and rewarding to link text with its social and historical context.

Gadamer* states that there is always a circular relationship between a text and its context, a part and the whole. He sees the hermeneutic task (that is, interpretation) as to progressively broaden the hidden meaning in concentric circles.

As well as relating the respondents to their own context, we need to relate them to the context of the topic (for example, a product or brand). Aspects to consider include its market category (for example, detergent, deodorant, cologne for men, cars, life insurance), its competitive position (such as leader, follower, niche brand), and its lifecycle stage. All of this helps us to reach a more complete and deeper interpretation of the material.

The following figure summarizes these contextual issues.

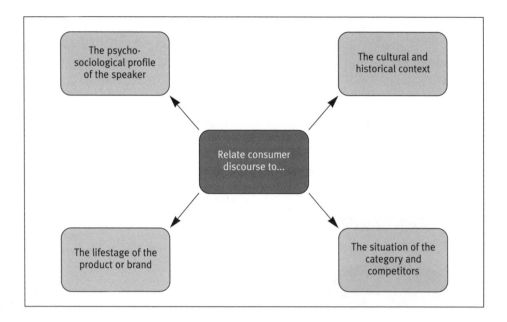

The process of interpretation is not easy. There is a risk of taking multiple readings that are erroneous or incomplete. We have no rules for deduction that are general in nature, valid for all cases and applicable in an automatic or mathematical way. Each study is unique, and each analysis is different.

It is not always possible for us to say whether the presence of a phenomenon in manifest discourse necessarily means that a certain attitude exists at the latent level. Our aim is to find the power of exact interpretation and to acknowledge the risk of subjective interpretation. However, if a rigorous process is used in conjunction with intuition, it should be possible to attain knowledge that is clear, solid and valid. It should always be remembered, though, that the findings are only valid for a specific topic, in a specific context and at a specific time. Each study takes us into a different world, one that has to be discovered, organized and understood.

As in other disciplines, experience is a major advantage. At the same time, over-confidence must be avoided. Qualitative researchers must always adopt an open and neutral attitude; they must practise mental flexibility and use creativity.

We often follow a rational, logical and deductive process to discover the causes of consumer behaviour, but on other occasions it is necessary to use intuition and creativity. Imagination is fundamental, even within scientific research, especially when generating hypotheses. Qualitative research is half-way between the rigour of content analysis and the intuition of interpretation, between science and art. It has to handle two different types of reality, the objective (the market, products, brands and so on) and the subjective (the internal worlds of human beings). It has to combine cognitive elements with emotional aspects.

The next figure illustrates the main differences between content analysis and interpretation:

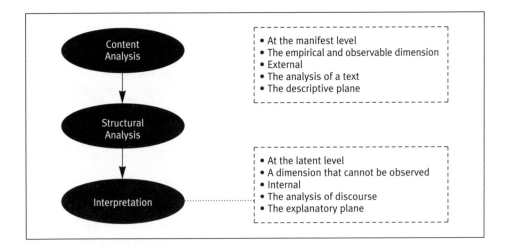

In this final phase of interpretation we contemplate the linguistic discourse of consumers from a great height. This allows us to adopt an aerial view, one that is global and complete, and in which the major conclusions and recommendations of the study are now apparent, together with the arguments that offer the necessary consistency and validity. Our final objective is to reach the latent level, which is neither observable nor empirical. This is why it is important to search the consumer discourse for proof and valid arguments to form a solid basis for our interpretation.

It should always be kept in mind that interpretation demands great care by qualitative researchers. It is important to be rigorous in the process.

The history of interpretation

Throughout the history of philosophical and scientific thought the human mind has tried to use every way it can to understand and interpret the world. At one extreme, trends have underlined the importance of sensations, perceptions, the senses and the physical world, and facts and experience. Knowledge comes down to the real (external and objective) world. This is the territory of nominalism (the individual case) and empiricism (experience). Positivism too is based on facts, and the scientific method is restricted to data.

At the other extreme are schools of thought that underline the role of reason, the mind and ideas. From this point of view knowledge ascends to the abstract world of concepts (the psychological, internal and subjective). This is where we find the idealism of Plato*, the realist view of the problem of universalism and the idealism of Hegel*.

Between these extremes we find the intermediate and balanced viewpoints of Aristotle* (based on observation and mental categorization), the moderate realism of Boethius* and St Thomas Aquinas*, the optimism of the Enlightenment, the work of Kant* (who considers sensory knowledge versus intellectual knowledge, and the 'thing in itself' versus the 'thing within me'), phenomenology, historicism, the inclusive view of Weber* (which combines historicism and positivism), the contributions of Gadamer*, Ricoeur* and many others.

Walter Landor, founder of the consultancy Landor Associates, said that 'products are made in factories, brands are made in the mind'. His words express well the differences and connections between external reality and the inner world of consumers.

The history of thought and ideas advances in a way that is simultaneously linear, dialectical and circular. It is like a spiral that points upwards. It shows us many ways of understanding the world around us. It is important to become familiar with the different approaches. They all contain some element of the truth, while at the same time each is restricted and incomplete.

Some authors have preferred the scientific method as the model for universal knowledge. Others believe that the human and social sciences need also to use more flexible methodologies which allow them to approach what they research (individuals, society, culture and the historical dimension) in a more holistic way. We agree with this latter viewpoint.

The following figure suggests how the various schools of thought interrelate.

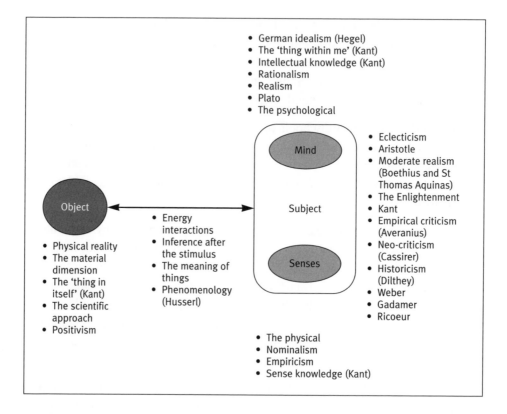

Qualitative research adopts an eclectic and relative viewpoint that is based on common sense. It is also enriched by the offerings of historicism, and currents of thought that emphasize the subjective. In reality, qualitative researchers look for an interpretation that will be intersubjectively valid (interpersonal consensus). The qualitative approach is pluralist and pragmatic.

Victor Cousin* stands out within the eclecticism of the 19th century. He reduced the different philosophical viewpoints to four: idealism, sensualism, scepticism and mysticism. For Cousin, eclecticism consists of the harmonious combination of the strong points of each of these four views of the world.

Semantics

Semantic chains arise from the relationships an individual has with objects (in the broadest sense). For example, money is a physical, material reality with many possible meanings. It can be seen as a means (of attaining enjoyment and pleasure) or an end in itself. It can be considered as an expense or an investment. It can be associated with saving, providing security and protection. For someone who plays the stock market it may mean adventure and risk; for someone who plays the lottery it is associated with chance and luck (the dimension of magic).

The reality that interests us lies not in physical things, but in our relationship with them. Consumers are not bound to things (physical products for consumption), but rather move as if they were floating in the world of meanings which emerge from their relationship with the elements around them. Ortega y Gasset* said two things are central to life, *'I and my circumstance.'* Each person is conditioned by their biological, psychological, sociological and historical circumstances, as shown in the next figure.

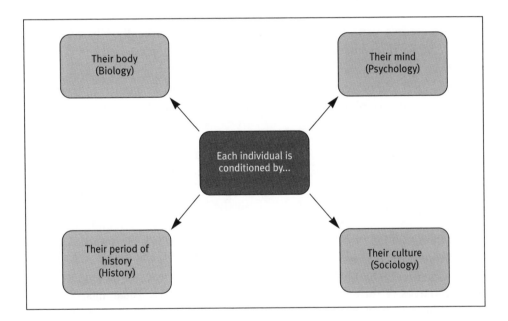

Analytical models

Qualitative research does not have an unique model of interpretation. Each project is carried out within an eclectic philosophical framework, and uses the theoretical models that best explain the information gathered and illuminate the problem. We concluded this after having worked on many, many qualitative studies, in which it was found that no model was perfect.

In their book *The Landscape of Qualitative Research: Theories and issues* (1998b), Denzin and Lincoln underline this eclectic nature: 'The combination of multiple methods, empirical materials, perspectives and observers in a single study is best understood as a strategy that adds rigor, breadth and depth to any investigation.' Our view supports the stances of methodological pluralism, eclecticism, relativism, common sense, pragmatism, historicism and subjectivism (as what is truly important to us is the internal subjective reality of consumers). The research incorporates models and theories from many different disciplines, of which the most important are psychology, sociology, anthropology and linguistics.

Group analysis

There are two ways of undertaking analysis and interpretation in qualitative studies. Some researchers prefer a single person to undertake all the different tasks from moderating the groups or interviews to analysing the material, preparing the report and presenting the results. We prefer and recommend a team process. There are several advantages if a study is conducted by a small, well-coordinated group.

The team approach comes into its own in the analysis phase, since the usual method is for each of the researchers to moderate a section the fieldwork, before the group comes together to analyse and structure the resulting information and produce hypotheses.

We believe three or four individuals is the right number for a project group, with one taking overall charge. The more heterodox the team, the better: psychologists, sociologists, anthropologists, statisticians, marketing experts; representatives of different schools of thought or theoretical leanings; a mix of demographic characteristics (age, gender, class). The more eclectic it is, the wider the experience that is brought into play, and the more open it will be to developing the most appropriate conclusions, strategies and recommendations.

The analysis meeting follows much the same process as a focus group meeting. Again the attitude of participants is fundamental, as is the atmosphere in the meeting, which must be constructive and harmonious. When different points of view are compared, the risks of subjective interpretation decline. Analysis in a group makes it possible to explore and delve deeply into different aspects, dimensions and realities of the subject.

Summary and conclusions

- The analysis and interpretation of qualitative discourse is exciting, but also difficult and complex. It brings together the methods of the social sciences and the richness of the art of interpretation.

- It is important to adopt a neutral stance, and to connect and empathize completely with the internal world of the respondents.

- Theories must not interfere with data gathering. First adopt an open attitude of unconditional listening and observation, then apply an analytical model.

- Analysis and interpretation starts when the client gives the briefing, and continues throughout the research process (the methodological design, recruitment of the sample and fieldwork).

- Although analysis is a continuum, there are three successive stages or levels: content analysis, structural analysis and interpretation. These run from the most superficial, manifest and external, to the deepest, latent and internal.

- Qualitative research does not have unique interpretive methods. It lies within an eclectic philosophical framework, and uses the theoretical models that best serve each problem. Its prime sources are psychology, sociology, anthropology and linguistics.

- We recommend group research and analysis, which guards against subjectivity and broadens the range of input to the analytical process.

PART II

CONSUMER LYFECYCLE RESEARCH

9
Research with children

ROSANA RODRÍGUEZ

Introduction

'Childhood has its own ways of seeing, thinking and feeling. Nothing is more senseless than to try to replace them with ours.'

JEAN-JACQUES ROUSSEAU*

Rousseau's thoughts from the 18th century might seem obvious to us today, but they have not yet been integrated well enough into market research practice: studies among children still sometimes use data collection tools and approaches more suited to adults. The next table summarizes some relevant differences between adults and children.

Adults	Children
Order	Chaos
Comprehensible codes	Incomprehensible codes
Social rules	Their own individual rules
Calm	Movement
Known	Unknown
Rational	Fantasy

We can treat childhood as the period from birth until 12 years of age. Among those who have explored the psychology of this life stage are Freud*, Vygotsky*, Piaget* and Erikson*. Two points they make are of real importance in conducting research involving children. First, a child is not a small adult, but someone who perceives and communicates with the world in a different way. And second, children's interests, tastes, motivations and needs change rapidly.

Child psychologists have identified a sequence of cognitive and emotional states during this phase of life. By cognitive development is meant the capacity of a child to understand what they are told and to use language in an informative way. Piaget was the first to show how human beings progress from concrete thought to more adult abstract thought. His ideas have since been modified but are still relevant. A young child takes information literally, accepting all external stimuli as 'real', without any previous processing. Growing children learn to process external data in a more complex and personal way; and to distinguish reality from fantasy more clearly. They acquire the ability to think abstractly, and talk about concepts when no tangible stimuli are present. This change is gradual, and each child has their own pattern of growth, but in general children do not acquire any ability to think abstractly until around the age of nine, and their cognitive development continues beyond this age. It is essential to understand the stages of cognitive development in order to choose the most suitable research techniques. (See next figure)

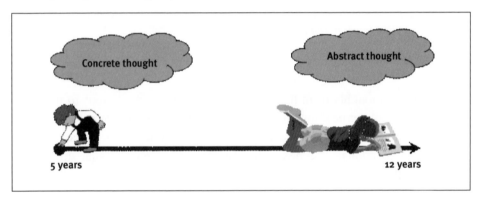

Children's viewpoint

When working with children, it is also important to consider their emotional development. Children's needs differ at each stage of their growth, in a sequence which is universal, although different children progress at different rates. Psychologists, educational theorists and other professionals have long recognized how important it is for children to satisfy three basic emotional needs:

- **Safety.** They need to feel secure, and to find reassurance when faced with uncertainty, anxiety or stress. All interactions with children must take place on the basis of trust.

- **Independence**. Paradoxically, children also want to feel independent – free from control by others, with their own personal space.

- **Control.** Children of all ages swing between the illusion of omnipotence and the reality of their limitations and dependency on others. Control means having power over their own life and surroundings.

In many studies we have found these concepts to be useful in understanding children's reactions to products and advertising. They are also helpful for analysts who face the challenge of interpreting and working with children's discourse. They are built into Millward Brown's Kidsmap analysis framework, described later in this chapter.

Qualitative research with children

Working with children is often difficult, uncomfortable or disconcerting. Their conversation is chaotic, superficial and not very concrete (adults may feel they are not being told anything). They are not as disciplined, ordered or calm as adults; they don't stay still or do as they are told, and their energy levels can overwhelm us. Nevertheless, it is possible to conduct research with children if an effort is made to understand them and certain guidelines are followed:

- Do not expect rich verbal discourse; children express themselves more and better in, for example, drawing and role play. The information obtained requires more interpretation than that from adults.

- Children's limited capacity for concentration means they need regular changes of activity and new things to stimulate them. (Vary the pace every 20 minutes.)

- Preparation for focus groups with children must be more exhaustive and the questioning more concrete. Include exercises, activities and different types and styles of game. They must always be suitable for the age group. It is highly likely that not all everything planned will be used. However, experience shows that improvization does not usually work well.

- Moderators must change their mindset and attitude. Patience is indispensable.

- It is important to develop our ability to listen, because information from children can seem contradictory. It is helpful to observe non-verbal communication.

- Always pay close attention to group dynamics: be alert for signs of tiredness, boredom or 'chaos', and switch activity. Use activities such as throwing paper balls in the air for a few minutes to vent energy before going back to work.

- Children should not be left alone, and should always be guided in their activities. If not, they may become confused and run wild.

- It is very important that children understand what they are doing and why. We have to encourage them to help us, by explaining very clearly what we are doing and how important their contribution is.

- Moderators should place themselves at the children's level, both physically (sitting at the same height) and psychologically (listening to their language and adapting to it). This helps create the required atmosphere of closeness and trust. Maintain a balance between authority and permissiveness; avoid attitudes that are either dictatorial, or too informal and intimate.

- The setting is key: it should be safe and fun, especially for children aged under nine.

- In general, girls are more unhurried, their language level is higher and richer, and they are more crafty and subtle. They respond better to activities that require a degree of concentration, and have higher levels of emotional intelligence. Boys are less thoughtful. Their verbal language is less rich and they may become hyperactive. They need movement and constant control by the moderator; a 'muscular' type of activity.

Major variations are also found in how children behave depending on their age. Research usually focuses on the age bands from seven to nine, or 10 to 12.

Those aged between seven and nine:

- Have very high energy levels, especially boys.

- Are still unable to follow instructions; they have not yet assimilated adult codes of sociability or rules governing behaviour.

- Are only able to talk about the 'here and now' (what they are touching, eating or seeing, not what they could touch, eat or see).

- See adults as highly important and significant, a source of security and admiration.

- Need to establish a good relationship with the moderator, who must adapt to their level. As an adult and parent substitute, moderators arouse respect. There is rarely any conflict.

- Are usually more timid at the start of focus groups, because they tend to replicate the teacher–pupil relationship.

- Have no conversation or discourse, merely individual speeches.

- Need to feel physically free and be able to move around. Seating should be informal: cushions on the floor are best.

- Can go out of control if they do not understand the moderator's instructions, are asked to talk too much, constantly asked to explain *('Why?', 'What else?', 'Why don't you like it?'),* required to think as a group *('What do you think about what he said?'),* asked to perform abstract exercises, or an activity runs on too long without a change.

Children from 10 to 12 years:

- Are pre-adolescent, and adolescence is increasingly occurring earlier.

- Are more hostile to their surroundings.

- Are starting to identify more with their peers.

- See as role models not authority figures or their parents, but older siblings or acquaintances, or 'heroes' (often in sport or music).

- Are starting to have ambivalent relationships between the sexes.

- Are starting to accept social norms.

- Begin to produce group discourse.

- Have more defined roles in groups.

- May acquire leaders in groups.

- May focus more on other members of the group than on the moderator.

- Are beginning to challenge rules.

- Need movement (especially the boys) and oppose adults (the moderator); these are the greatest problems.

- Can break rules (perhaps through mockery or apathy), and conspire (for instance using laughter, or opposing other respondents or the moderator).

- Girls usually opt for a more adult form of conflict, such as questioning the moderator or attacking the other members of the group. Boys' opposition usually takes the form of wild behaviour and anarchy (clowning and joking).

The following figure shows how boys and girls develop from birth to the age of 11 years.

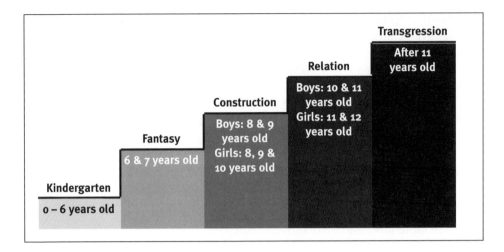

Types of boys and girls

The classification of respondents' behaviour on chapter 3 applies to adults, not to children, where a different classification is appropriate (see next figure). If children's focus groups are to be successful, we need to be able to identify these groups and know how to deal with them.

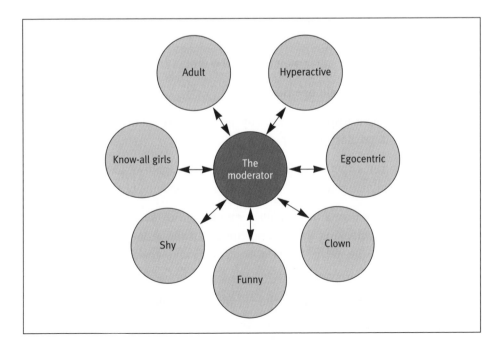

Hyperactivity is more common among younger children. These children have difficulty keeping still and quickly show signs of boredom. If you notice such problems, introduce a change of activity, if possible involving physical movement. Work to keep these children's attention, for example by constantly asking them questions.

Egocentrics are the child version of the adult narcissist. Then tend to talk in the first person, just when someone else in the group was about to speak. They usually negate or reject the opinions of the other children. Challenge these children, while pointing out their attitude and behaviour: for example *'You always want to be the first to talk,'* *'The others don't have to think the same as you'* or *'You aren't alone here, there are other children.'*

Clowns are more often boys than girls. They are immediately recognizable because they say silly or senseless things, and the other members of the group laugh with or at them. Laughing with them reinforces their behaviour. Dealt firmly with this type of behaviour as soon as it appears: for example, *'It's great to have a good time, but no stupid things.'*

Funny respondents are a less stupid, more witty version of clowns. They tend to be the group leader. The others laugh with them. Their role is usually positive and constructive, provided they do not dominate attention. Watch them, and deal with them firmly if they go too far in the clown direction.

Timid boys and girls rarely speak, and when they do, speak quite softly. They never speak first. They do not move very much and are not very proactive. They respect the moderator's authority and have a helpful attitude. They should be made to feel secure, and invited to take part. When they do join in, they should not be interrupted. Their individual contributions are usually good.

Very insecure children may need the support of the moderator. If the group is divided into smaller sub-groups it is important not to put them in the same group as the leaders.

Know-all girls play the role of leader, expressing their opinion about everything and believing they know everything. They question and argue with the moderator. Display a firm attitude of positive and constructive authority. It is better not to look at them when speaking, to avoid reinforcing their behaviour.

Adult boys and girls forget they are children and use adult expressions and vocabulary. They often focus on regulations and norms: what is correct or incorrect, suitable or unsuitable. Try projective exercises to get them to remember their inner child, and encourage them to express their feelings.

Qualitative research with children is as difficult as it is satisfying. To be successful you must not only possess a thorough understanding of market research, but be an expert on children and their behaviour. It calls for the adaptation of procedures designed for adults.

The KidSpeak™ methodology

Millward Brown has developed a specific methodology for working with children, KidSpeak™. It is a working philosophy based on observation, contact and acceptance of the child's world, as well as methodologies designed for different stages of the research process:

- methodological design
- fieldwork
- the interpretation of results.

Girls tend to mature earlier than boys, so it is better to work with single-sex groups, or if mixed groups are needed, with girls one or two years younger than the boys. Same-sex groups should be segmented as much as possible by age or school year, with a maximum of two years' difference between the participants. This helps ensure more uniform and consistent discourse – the children are at the same life stage and share not just academic knowledge but a circle of friends.

Some stages are of key importance in the development of children:

- 6 years
- 8 years
- 10 and 11 years for girls
- 11 and 12 years for boys.

When studying younger children (aged four or five) the reassuring presence of their mothers is necessary, so duo (mother–child) interviews are held. Mothers mediate between the interviewer and their child, 'translating' their language. At this stage of childhood, children have problems with the level of language used.

With six to nine year-olds, selecting pairs of friends for duo interviews works really well. The friendship makes the children feel safe, strong and helps develops an atmosphere of trust, which is very useful for the moderator. Children in this age group may find group participation difficult.

For children between 10 and 12, the most effective methodological tool is a minigroup of peers, composed of two pairs of friends. They feel freer and more relaxed with their friends, and these small groups make it possible to understand reactions and individual behaviour, group and social phenomena, and prevent the conflicts which are typical at this age, especially between boys. They also help prevent some individuals from feeling inhibited.

The ethnographic approach (observing children for example at home or school: see chapter 5) works well for all ages. Children feel comfortable, and the time taken to warm up and adapt is shorter. It is possible to gain first-hand knowledge of children's realities (their room and possessions) and to observe what they are unable to tell us. It is especially suitable for younger children, or when the study objectives mean a longer time is needed to gather the required information.

Fieldwork with children

'Children's games are not games as such ... but rather their most serious activities.'

*MONTAIGNE**

In research with children, the venue is almost as important as the moderator. It must make the children feel comfortable and safe; rooms designed for adult use may be too formal. The room should be as pleasant and familiar as possible (using for example colours, cushions, posters, toys and school things).

The discussion guide is also of fundamental importance, and must always be made as much fun as is possible.

- **Drawing** is often used by children to communicate, and is also a test of their skills. Teachers, developmental psychologists and psychoanalysts consider it to be a way of gaining access to the deepest and most hidden part of children's minds.

- The **balloon test** is a prompted extension of drawing. A child is given a very basic picture, showing a child and something related to the research topic – perhaps a television, some toys, a story book – and is encouraged to write or draw in the blank 'balloon' spaces (a projective technique: see chapter 6).

- Similarly, **collage** is especially useful when the moderator wants to probe the children's imaginations more deeply. They are asked to work in pairs and given a large sheet of paper on which to create a situation or object using images cut from magazines, painting and writing. This produces information at both a cognitive and an emotional level.

- **Telling stories**, spoken or written, is an exercise that is individual and verbal. Children are asked to invent a story about the topic. Imaginary projections are the key to understanding their symbolic and emotional involvement with the topic.

- **Role playing** is a drama technique used in groups. Respondents are asked to act out pre-set roles related to the topic. How the children interpret the role is the key to understanding how they respond to the topic. The dynamic created by dramatization offers additional information to that available from individuals.

Care must be taken when selecting the stimulus material for groups. It should be suitable for the cognitive skills of the age group. This generally involves ensuring that:

- Children are never exposed to an excessive amount of material, because they tire more easily than adults. Their ability to concentrate is directly proportional to their age. Children under eight can concentrate for about 10 minutes, after which they should take breaks and rest, move around the room, play with toys or have something to eat.

- Visual stimulus materials (boards, story-boards, videos, cards and so on) should be used, especially with children under eight who cannot yet write or read fluently. Visual items provide a concrete stimulus.

- Any language used should be simple, direct, in short phrases, using words the children themselves use. It can be supplement with non-verbal explanation to show the use of space and so on.

The interpretation of children's discourse

Interviewers must be trained not only in the analysis of results, but in how to interpret the different non-verbal materials generated. Among the key factors are the choice of colours and use of space, and how symbols are used. Sometimes children are asked to relate brands to archetypes such as witches, wizards, princesses and animals. Their choice reveals what values the child associates with brands and their attitude towards them.

For example, the following figure shows an advertisement for Nike sports shoes created by two nine-year-old English girls. They picked the cartoon character

Roadrunner to personify the brand and its users, and projected the values of quality and success (speed and being unreachable).

'I wear Nike gym shoes in order to run fust, thus nobody will never catch me!'

The interpretation and analysis phase within the KidSpeak approach uses the Kidsmap analytical model (see next figure). This identifies four emotional territories that describe the children's basic needs. They help explain a great deal about their preferences, motivations and reactions.

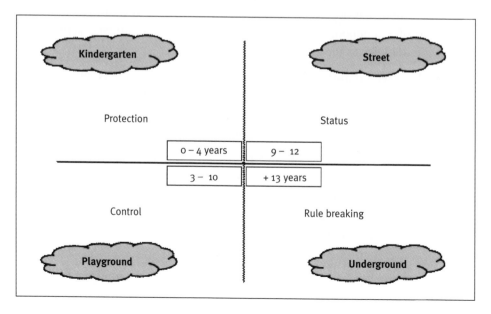

A child in the *kindergarten* stage is immersed in the maternal world. The mother is the filter through which they get to know the world, and she determines almost all purchasing decisions and behaviour.

During the *playground* stage, children explore the world and share their knowledge of it, first with their family, then with their peers. They start to question their mother's vision of the world. They begin to influence shopping decisions, and in certain cases (ice cream, soft drinks, snacks and sports clothing) make the decision themselves.

In the *street* phase, the child moves away from family values and acquires the dominant values of their peer group. Interests and purchasing behaviour are largely determined by the group, and are subject to fashion.

Lastly, in the *underground* stage, children reinforce their personal and individual world view. Interests and purchasing behaviour tend to be set by the individual.

Kidsmap works as a frame of reference in the analysis of results. It helps us to understand the degree to which a specific offer, brand or product connects with its target group, and fits the child's emotional territory.

Summary and conclusions

- Those conducting qualitative research with children need specialist knowledge about the degree of psychological maturity and limitations of each stage of childhood, and must adapt techniques, stimuli, the setting and methodologies to the age and sex of the children.

- Working with children is always difficult. Their discourse is less rich, and they must be allowed to use other forms of expression. The group dynamic should be made as much fun as possible, as play is their most important and natural activity. Ethnographic techniques are particularly useful.

- The KidSpeak™ approach and philosophy was developed by Millward Brown to make working with children fluid and effective. It offers guidelines for study design, fieldwork and the analysis of findings. It includes the Kidsmap framework for analysis based on the different stages of a child's emotional development.

10

Research with teenagers

MAR ÁLVAREZ

Adolescence is a bridge that is hard to cross

This is a very special life stage. Adolescence is generally said to last roughly from the ages of 13 to 17, but seems to start earlier than it did in previous generations. The pre-adolescent stage is increasingly considered as having its own identity.

Adolescence is like an earthquake: it completely reshapes children's minds and starts to set the foundations for their mature personality. Of course there are major bodily changes including sexual differentiation, but our main concern here is with cognitive and personality issues. During adolescence, boys and girls lack an identity that helps organize and give structure to their personality. This causes instability. Adolescence is often experienced as a real crisis, disorganization, a descent into chaos, a revolution. The existing framework of reference and of belonging, the family, expands considerably. It changes the rules in the game of life, in values and lifestyle. A new horizon emerges, of friends and a peer group. Parents cease to play the role of heroes, and are replaced by celebrities, often from the worlds of sport and music.

Teenagers are a complicated target group

In the past, market researchers worked with teenagers as they did with adults, typically using conventional focus groups or in-depth interviews. This did not work well. Moderators had serious difficulties gaining access to the internal world of teenagers, in order to gather the rich data needed for a good research report.

Teenagers do not feel comfortable in the laboratory. They feel uneasy and strange outside their natural habitat or ecosystem: their room, their friends' rooms, the park or shopping centre. More specifically, they find the laboratory threatening. It is a place where they are studied, where everyone is looking at them. This often makes them feel shy, reserved and trapped, which in turn leads to passiveness and sometimes to cynicism. Although they are with other teenagers, they do not know them. This key factor hinders the group dynamic: adolescents still lack sufficient social skills to handle such situations.

Because their internal world is so confused, teenagers are resistant to explaining their opinions, attitudes, motivations and barriers, which means qualitative researchers often come up against obstacles when working with them. Because their psyche is still being created, they prefer to conform to the opinions, attitudes and motivations of their friends.

Moderators in turn struggle when conducting focus groups with teenagers. They are uncertain what attitude to display. If they try to behave like one of the group they are not credible. If they use a paternal tone, the dynamic works poorly. If they use their authority, they lose their connection with the group. They sometimes lose control of the group dynamics and start to think the respondents do not want to help, are mocking them, or are simply unable to work well together. This can lead to frustration all round, but fortunately changes in working practice and new research techniques make working with teenagers today a more positive and fruitful experience for both parties.

Ways of working with teenagers

One general suggestion: whenever a moderator is working with adolescents, they should assume a straightforward and professional attitude. It is important to connect with teenagers on the basis of clarity and transparency. We should not fall into the trap of being paternal or pretending to be a teenager. We should be direct and empathetic.

Digital (online) focus groups work well for teenagers. Adolescents feel very at home in the virtual world of the Internet in general, and with Messenger in particular.

Millward Brown has given the name Teen Connections to the set of learnings, techniques and methodologies we use when working with this group. It includes ethnographic groups, affinity groups and work with trendsetters.

The ethnographic approach and teenagers

The ethnographic approach was introduced in chapter 5. Ethnographic studies of teenagers usually take place in for example their room, a park or shopping centre: somewhere they feel comfortable, and respond in an open, natural, spontaneous and relaxed way. The most successful focus groups tend to be of friends – say, four pairs of friends making a group of eight. Because they already know each other they feel more confident talking with the researcher. Ethnographic interviews of pairs of teenage friends also work better than separate solo interviews.

Teenagers are highly sensitive to new trends (in for example clothing, music and slang). They quickly adopt change to differentiate themselves from previous generations. This target group is a barometer for new fashions. They are like a magnifying glass: they connect with something new that interests them, include it and magnify it to the maximum, spreading it to their friends (the technique of viral marketing).

Five groups are usually identified on the basis of their attitude to innovative products and services:

- innovators

- early adopters

- the early majority

- the late majority

- passive individuals (laggards).

The process by which a trend is adopted follows the normal distribution, with the innovators and laggards forming the smallest sections of the population.

We have successfully held groups with teenage trendsetters to learn about and predict the direction of their tastes and preferences, for example for mobile telephone services, handset designs and Internet services. A special recruitment screener is used to ensure the respondents are innovators and early adopters: that is, opinion leaders within their peer groups. Interviews with experts or social opinion leaders – for example DJs, managers of musicians, and journalists – can be used to complement the point of view of the teenagers.

Summary and conclusions

- Teenagers feel comfortable in the places where they spend their free time, and very uncomfortable in social settings and research laboratories. Ethnographic group and interview approaches are particularly suitable.

- The researcher should treat teenagers in a way that is clear and transparent. Avoid being paternal or trying to be like them.

- Teen Connection is Millward Brown's series of learnings, techniques and methodologies for working effectively with teenagers. It includes the ethnographic approach, affinity groups and research with trendsetters.

- Teenagers respond best in pairs and groups of friends.

- Focus groups with teen trendsetters (innovators and early adopters) are especially suited to detecting new social fashions and trends.

11

Young Europeans
(international case study)

PEPE MARTÍNEZ

Objectives

In 2003 Millward Brown sponsored an international psychosociological study of young people across Europe.

The core objectives of the study were:

- to examine comprehensively and in depth the lives of young people in Europe
- to identify which brands were most important to them
- to identify their expectations of these brands
- to learn their preferences regarding advertising campaigns.

Methodology

Qualitative research was undertaken in cities in ten countries across Continental Europe: Portugal (Lisbon and Porto), Poland (Warsaw and Poznan), Spain (Madrid and Barcelona), Czech Republic (Prague), France (Paris), Hungary (Budapest), Italy (Rome and Milan), Turkey (Istanbul), Germany (Frankfurt) and Russia (Moscow and Voronezh).

In each we held two three-hour focus groups comprising a mix of free spontaneous discourse and projective and creative techniques, and ten one and a half hour ethnographic interviews using the participating observer technique. Approximately 300 people took part, and the sample was:

- half women and half men
- aged from 18 to 25

- middle and upper-middle class
- university students and graduates.

Starting point

Each country has a different history, culture, psychosociological context, level of socioeconomic development and language, and these differences were reflected in our samples.

In France, institutions lacked credibility and young people were becoming marketing and advertising savvy. Internet use was spreading fastest here.

German young people saw the labour market as highly competitive. They worked primarily to make money; most would have preferred to win the lottery. They lived with their parents and were very interested in economic policy.

Young people in Portugal, Spain and Italy were very similar. In Italy, four types emerged: adolescents, adults, hedonists and traditionalists. They sought support from, and refuge in, their family. Spanish young people considered themselves free, but still lived with their parents. They were keen to delay having children. In Portugal young people lived for the present, were very optimistic, and enjoyed socializing.

Polish young people reflected their country's schizophrenic situation: experiencing economic recession, high unemployment and few opportunities, but optimistic about entry into the European Union. Hungarians were similar, but less worried about the economy. Family and contacts were important in job-hunting, and male and female roles were changing.

The Czechs stood out for their cultural richness. Mature, eager to leave home, they still talked about the social revolution of 1989 and the fall of Communism, and had many doubts about the European Union.

Russia was undergoing major political and economic change, including women's emancipation. People were poorer than elsewhere, and great social differences were apparent.

Turkey still showed the after-effects of the earthquakes of 1999 and 2000. Young people felt economically insecure and wanted jobs; any job. The trend was towards Europe and away from Islam.

There were many similarities in lifestyle, main values, desires and worries. Globalization, the new media landscape and broader Internet usage make people's hopes and dreams increasingly uniform. Eastern Europeans see themselves reflected in the mirror of the West (not just Europe but the United States and Japan), and are eager to catch up economically.

Lifestyle

The 18 to 20-year-olds were closer in spirit to adolescents; those aged 21 to 25 more adult, though much continuity was apparent. They wanted to set themselves apart from teenagers, whom they saw as immature, radical, extremist and lacking in control. In essence, they wanted the advantages of adulthood but not the obligations (especially not children). It was fashionable to be young, and they wished they were even younger.

They lived in two very different worlds, one of leisure and one of study and work. In their free time they sought joy and fun, drinking heavily and socializing, but they took study very seriously. Hyperactive, they were involved in sport, music and going out. They did not leave home, but wanted adventure and travel. They were in constant contact with their friends, both face to face and using mobile telephones (SMS and calls) and the Internet (e-mail, Messenger, discussion forums and chat rooms). Their lives were technology-heavy, and they spent a lot of time looking at screens. They experienced everything instantly, and were focused on media, sharing information, and being the first with the latest news and trends. Brands played an important role in the rumour dynamic.

These young people saw image as more important than internal values. They took care of their appearance, did sport to keep in shape, dressed comfortably and informally, and talked a lot about clothing brands. In Germany plastic surgery and anorexia were significant issues.

Values

These young people had no time for traditional values: political ideologies, religious beliefs, traditional marriage. Economically they were insecure, with much unemployment and temporary work contracts. They did not experience earlier generations' rituals of transition into adulthood (conscription, leaving home, marriage). Their motto was not Descartes' *'I think, therefore I am'*, but *'I change, therefore I am.'* Attracted by innovation, flexibility and adaptation, they tried to avoid routine, monotony and tedium.

Of brands, Zara exemplified fast-changing fashion, Nokia speedy technological changes. They wanted a different experience each day:

'Every Saturday I have to go to different establishments.' (Italy)

'Everything moves really fast: we're constantly renewing, there is not enough time for things to stagnate.' (France)

They were open-minded, with few prejudices, inclined to say what they thought. Tolerant and respectful of dissidence, they sought social and cultural mixes. They considered themselves free and independent, and tended to select the best from each theory, discipline, viewpoint or attitude.

Self-realization was a priority. They were highly competitive, egocentric, ambitious, and had a strong desire to stand out. The individual came before the social. There was little commitment to social questions, which were thought too theoretical and distant. They felt small in a very large world. Realists rather than idealists, they were very much in tune with the 'micro' (close, near, real and tangible) and had disconnected from the 'macro' (the distant, abstract or theoretical). They saw themselves as unable to bring about change.

The consumer market offered them a comfortable bubble; they were more consumers than citizens. They were attracted by money, a good standard of living; willing to be seduced by brands and immersed in the exciting ocean of marketing, advertising, sponsorship, offers and promotions. At the same time, they were more sensitive than ever to the strategies and the credibility of marketing messages; they were open to everything but believed nothing.

These young people focused on communicating and on action, rather than on thought, ideas or emotion. In the focus groups, we asked, *'If young people were a planet, what would it be like?'* Replies mentioned bright colours, fun, parties, music and shops; fragmented worlds without their own identity:

'A chaotic world, without any goals.' (Germany)

'Lots of water with lots of islands; only a few are close to each other. The rest are spread out all over the place.' (Germany)

We also asked them to make collages, and next figure shows one from a focus group in Czech Republic.

The main symbols of youth were mobile telephones, computers, sports, sex, contraceptives, the body, beer, alcohol, cars, action and adventure films, music, brands, fast food and television.

Collage, Czech Republic

In general, in 2003 young Europeans wanted to graduate so that they could get a good job, make enough money and enjoy a high standard of living. They did not think of rebelling against the established system, but rather wanted to join it to obtain status and prestige:

> *'A good life in the future means having a lot of money, a bank account and a good car.'* (Russia)

They also wanted to be successful in their chosen profession, to attain a good social position and enjoy a satisfying and pleasurable relationship with their partner.

They wanted a job connected with their university studies, and looked for satisfaction and self-fulfilment in their profession, rejecting work that was routine and monotonous:

> *'Being able to work in something that you really like.'* (Russia)

They also wanted free time for leisure activities and entertainment, for their relationship with their partner, and over the medium to long term, to spend with their family.

Young people in Turkey were more economically insecure than elsewhere, and felt under strong pressure from their parents to get a job as soon as possible. Expectations for work were very basic:

'I'm not too ambitious, I'd like a job and my own home.' (Turkey)

They highlighted the importance of creating a positive climate for relationships: with themselves, their partners, friends, family of origin and future family. In Hungary, Russia and Turkey the traditional differences between the sexes were still apparent, although women wanted equal opportunities. Elsewhere, this was a unisex generation.

Most young people wanted children, but the later the better, since this was seen as the end of youth, a major responsibility and commitment and a great renunciation of individual life. Women's target age for having children was around 30; men's was 35.

Concerns

Uncertainty and insecurity predominated. They feared not finding their place in the social pyramid; feared failure, isolation, solitude and being left outside the system. They identified with symbols such as question marks and traffic signs for danger.

In western countries we found them less tolerant of frustration, because they had grown up in a bubble without any restrictions, and now feared losing their current standard of living.

They worried about choosing the wrong degree course, and in Russia in particular, about being expelled from university. Everywhere they worried about finding the right job:

'I don't want to work in a factory for the rest of my life.' (Czech Republic)

Psychologically they feared not finding their own identity among so much uniformity. There were felt to be no new ideas. The current model of society is conformist. Although this generation has not gone through an ideological revolution, they thought there was too much individualism and a lack of commitment.

'We young people of today aren't great dreamers.' (Spain)

Worried by war and conscious of 9\11 and its aftermath, they expressed opposition to armed conflict and identified with the symbol of peace (the dove).

In Spain, Germany, the Czech Republic and Russia the problem of drugs was underlined. Genetic experiments were mentioned in France, because they aroused fear of the unknown. They also expressed worries about disease (for themselves or their family).

The outlook

In the Hegelian* model of the dialectic, this is an era of synthesis. Young people at the start of the 21st century accept and enjoy most of the current social system; they are not a generation that questions and rebels. But we detected a desire for the system to improve, for an ideological revolution that would give rise to a paradigm shift.

The eurobrands

In the 20 focus groups and 100 ethnographic interviews, approximately 200 product or service brands aimed at young people were mentioned spontaneously. In the Czech Republic and Hungary the old 'communist' brands were still fairly strong. Twenty-five international brands stand out: we have called these the 'eurobrands':

- First level: Coca-Cola, Nike, Nokia and Sony.
- Second level: Adidas, Puma, Levis, Heineken and BMW.
- Third level: Zara, H&M, Reebok, Bacardi, Bacardi Breezer, Absolut Vodka, Smirnoff, Smirnoff Ice, McDonald's, Vodafone, Siemens, Mercedes, Volkswagen, Smart, Mini and Peugeot.

Coca-Cola was mentioned spontaneously in all ten countries. Points made included:

- A formula that is unique and secret.
- It has a long history, but remains synonymous with youth.
- A universal standard for soft drinks.
- A seductive brand.
- Constantly active in advertising and sponsorship.
- Projectively associated with jeans, a shirt, informal and sports clothing.

Nike too was mentioned spontaneously in all countries:

- Its products are different from its competitors': new, high quality, well designed, a wide range.

- Its logo is both simple and effective. It has become symbolic (the maximum level of abstraction).

- Its claim is provocative. 'Just do it' conveys action, success, a challenge.

- Its striking advertising centres on sporting heroes and is highly visual.

- It is thought to be expensive.

- A negative point was the media claim that it used child labour.

- Projectively it is an apartment, high-class and well designed, with light-coloured furniture (IKEA style) and very roomy.

Nike's rivals Adidas and Puma were mentioned spontaneously in approximately half the countries. Adidas had no uniform image. It was thought of as a rising brand that is trying to revive the 1970s, except in the Czech Republic, where it was seen as declining. Puma is undergoing a rebirth of sorts, and stands out most strongly for the originality of its new models of sports shoes.

The third brand mentioned spontaneously in all countries was Nokia:

- Good points were its high-quality handsets (strong and long-lasting), design (appearance, elegance, simplicity and modernity), wide range of products and accessories.

- Its software is highly intuitive and easy to use.

- It stands out for technological innovation.

- The claim 'Connecting people' conveys communication.

- Projectively it was compared to the *Matrix* films, an aspirational executive, a modern glass-clad building.

Sony was mentioned spontaneously in seven countries: Spain, France, Italy, Germany, Poland, the Czech Republic and Russia, with comments on its:

- high-quality equipment

- attractive designs (modern, futuristic, silver)

- many product categories

- long history (reliability, trustworthiness and guarantee)

- innovativeness

- broad target group.

It was compared to a loft in New York, with designer furnishings and a minimalist style.

Heineken, Levis and BMW were mentioned spontaneously in approximately half the countries. Heineken was undergoing a process of rejuvenation, and was associated with fun. Levis evoked authenticity and the mythical symbols of the wild west, cowboys and the gold rush. The BMW brand was highly aspirational for young Europeans because of its high-quality German technology, offer of sports elegance, an image of power, masculinity, prestige and status.

Zara was the only Spanish brand in the ranking:

- It emerged strongly in Spain, Portugal, France and Turkey.
- It understands young people's desire for novelty.
- It offers modern designs.
- It offers good value for money. It is highly accessible for young people.
- It is a good example of efficacy and practicality.

Key factors for a brand aimed at young people

To connect effectively with this target group, a brand must construct a marketing mix that they find consistent and appealing at several levels: the concept, product, packaging (a young design), advertising, sponsorship, price, offers (promotions and gifts) and distribution (where young people go).

At a conceptual level an ideal brand has to be:

- Like a mirror. It has to enter their psychological, sociological and linguistic worlds, adapting to their motivations and needs. Credibility is important, and care must be taken to avoid artificiality.
- Original. Young people seek differentiation among so much uniformity.
- Aspirational, offering status, prestige and an elitist personality, with class.
- Innovative, dynamic and creative, constantly renewing and launching new products.
- Proactive. Young people want a brand to be like them – always active.
- In fashion, modern, a trend-setter.

At a product level it has to offer:

- Quality. This basic characteristic gives rise to trustworthiness and guarantee.
- Design. The aesthetic dimension is very important.
- Variety. A brand should offer security and the feeling of peer-group belonging; the specific product should offer identity, personalization and differentiation. The range of choices is highly relevant.
- Technological advances.
- Versatility. For example, Nike is positioned as a sports and casual clothing brand.
- Simplicity and ease of use.

Appropriate sponsorship opportunities are in universities, at concerts, sports and cultural events and at young people's parties. Events organized jointly by brands with compatible images are highly acceptable. At a strategic level the ideal is to combine television with sponsorship and events organization. Television communicates universally, and yet conveys the international, the desirable, the mythical. Sponsorship and events bring brands down to a local level, reaching individuals and contributing to viral marketing, which is crucial: consumers increasingly see their peers as more credible than brands.

Young people are very aware of how marketing and advertising work. Brands therefore have to be credible, authentic, honest and helpful. A social role is a plus; negatives include the arrogant, aggressive, media-saturating and the image of colonization.

Key factors for an advertising campaign aimed at young people

The advertisements mentioned most often were:

- Peugeot 206 (India, the elephant)
- Nike campaigns
- Heineken advertising
- Carlsberg advertising
- the 'Chihuahua' spot for Coca-Cola.

It is important that all the elements in the campaign – the situations, characters, language, lifestyle, motivations and dreams – stem from young people's culture. What worked best with young Europeans was:

- ingenuity: people complained of realism and conformism, and were attracted by creative solutions, imagination and ideas
- fun and humour, identification with the leisure and not the work part of their lives
- music
- dynamism
- impact and surprise
- challenges, adventure, risk and provocation
- photography (images and bright colours)
- famous people (especially sports heroes).

Young people in Turkey mentioned the rivalry between Coca-Cola and local brand Cola Turka. Coca-Cola set its campaign in the Taksim area of Istanbul, where young people go for bars and restaurants. Cola Turka responded with a humorous ad featuring a North American actor drinking its product, claiming that even Americans prefer it.

Summary and conclusions

- In 2003 Millward Brown researched European youth, including the brand and advertising campaigns they found most relevant.
- Long-standing national differences are being eroded by globalization.
- Young Europeans study hard and play hard. Hyperactive, they live with their parents but want to travel. Friends and technology are important. They are narcissistic, insecure but not rebellious, ambitious but inclined to live for today.
- The study identified 25 eurobrands with strong images among the young and wide penetration.
- To succeed with this target market, a brand needs high-quality aspirational products and a marketing mix that reflects their tastes and psychology.

12

Young couples and families in Europe and Latin America (international case study)

PEPE MARTÍNEZ WITH JOSÉ RAMÓN ARTETA
AND ADOLFO FERNÁNDEZ

Research objectives

This chapter outlines a qualitative macro-study Millward Brown conducted in 2005 of young couples with and without children across Europe and Latin America.

Our main aims were:

- to conduct an in-depth study of couples aged between 25 and 35 years – their lifestyle, values, desires and fears

- to determine the most important factors influencing their consumption: changes and trends, the most important categories, brands and advertising campaigns

- to compare our findings across countries, and to look separately at couples with children and those without.

Methodology

We conducted the research across 18 countries (and 20 cities), five in Latin America (Argentina – Buenos Aires, Brazil – São Paulo, Chile – Santiago, Colombia – Bogotá, and Mexico – Mexico City) and 13 in Europe (the Czech Republic – Prague, France – Paris, Germany – Frankfurt, Greece – Athens, Hungary – Budapest, Italy – Rome and Milan, the Netherlands – Amsterdam, Poland – Warsaw, Portugal – Lisbon, Rumania – Bucharest, Slovakia – Bratislava, Spain – Madrid and Barcelona, and Turkey – Istanbul.

Our sample of approximately 500 households were:

- aged from 25 to 35 years
- heterosexual couples who live together
- young couples with partners working outside the home and no children ('dinkies' – double income, no kids); and young families with children, with one or both parents working
- broadly middle class.

We held two focus groups in each country, one for dinkies and one for young parents, both with eight to ten respondents, half men and half women, lasting three hours. We also held ten ethnographic interviews with couples in their homes (half dinkies, half young parents), each lasting one and a half hours.

In the focus groups we encouraged free and spontaneous discourse and used projective and creative techniques. The participating observer technique was used for the ethnographic interviews, paying special attention to brands present in the home.

Starting point

As expected, we found cultural differences between the 18 countries. However, we found greater differences overall between the dinkies and the parents than within each group across countries. Because of the immediacy and wide reach of today's media, there was high uniformity across countries in values and the direction of change.

We chose to concentrate our analysis on aspects and trends the different groups have in common. Where they arose, only particularly marked differences are commented on.

Dinkie couples' life is very much an extension of their youth, dominated by hedonistic enjoyment. This life stage used to be transitional, but is now increasingly important in its own right. When children arrive, life changes. Couples move from narcissism to caring for others. They take on responsibility and commitment, and they need to plan. Expenses rise, and they give up things both individually and as a couple.

Just how those opinions, experiences, values and desires change depends on the moment of history. Society is not static and eternal, but a dynamic and changing living organism. The generations of the 1960s and 1970s focused on work and bringing up their children. The family was the centre of their universe. Life today is very different: the individual now takes centre stage.

Major cities in the 21st century

The pace of life has accelerated enormously. Many of our respondents were in constant motion, and victims of stress and anxiety:

'The city sucks you in and absorbs you, you don't stop.' (Argentina)

Life in large cities is constantly evolving and new values are coming to the fore. All of this leads to uncertainty, instability and a feeling of chaos. Individuals feel they have to work hard to attain a good standard of living.

'I disappear very early in the morning and get back home at night.' (Brazil)

We uncovered two basic dimensions of life:

- Urban 'hell': everything to do with work, effort, public space outside the home, relationships with 'others', monotony, crowds and lack of safety (criminality and terrorism).

- 'Heaven': leisure, enjoyment, home, the personal and private world, family and friends, spontaneity, authenticity, and the personalization, safety and trust which arise from culture.

The trend is towards effort–reward reinforcement. Work and everyday activities are compared to a battle. Leisure and free time are becoming an increasingly basic need. People valued both the home and vacations. 'Cocooning' is important – the home wraps and comforts those who live there. Many couples would like a home cinema system. Through films, viewers enter a world between reality and the imagination. The main aim of vacations is to rediscover nature or discover exotic cultures:

'You work so hard so that later you can do what you want, go out for dinner, travel ...' (Spain)

Dinkies spend their time on:

- work (this takes up most of it)
- education (to get promotion and make more money)
- housework (although some have outside help)
- shopping (for food, personal care and cleaning products)
- leisure (individual and with their partner).

> *'I think that it's very important for him to do activities which he likes, without me.'* (Netherlands)

Parents with young families spend their time on:

- work (again, most of their time)
- education (less time than dinkies)
- their children, including the logistics: washing, school, etc.
- housework
- shopping (for similar products)
- leisure (usually as a family).

Changes and trends

This generation is strongly individualistic. The challenge they face is to live with their partner and build a family without renouncing their individuality or their right to lead their own lives:

> *'Not forgetting that you have to live your own life.'* (France)

People are hedonistic: they seek enjoyment, fun, quality of life, sensuality and sexuality. We saw evidence of a strong impulsiveness; people want everything instantly. Shopping centres and hypermarkets are the new earthly paradise, seducing and tempting with an enormous range of products and brands. People want money and the goods it can buy; they often use credit cards and loans:

> *'Now we can choose.'* (Romania)

> *'Spend, spend, spend, it's as if shopping were all that interested us in life.'* (Netherlands)

They also worship technology, which offers them:

- functionality
- convenience
- enjoyment
- image and prestige (through brands)
- modernity (being in fashion).

At all levels, this generation attempt to bring their 'real I' as close as possible to their 'ideal I':

- They try to keep in shape and healthy.

- They seek well-being and relaxation.
- try to be attractive and seductive.
- Socially, the impression they give is important to them.

This is a big market for personal care goods and services, in the widest sense.

Their dreams and desires centre on:

- achieving financial stability
- progressing at work to make more money
- getting on well with their partner
- leisure (travel)
- having a bigger, well equipped and furnished house
- owning a better car.

Dinkies' main wants are an interesting job, a larger flat and a sports car. Families most often want a good future for their children, a house with a garden in the suburbs, and a luxury car.

The worries and fears of this generation centre on instability and fragility (of their jobs, finances, relationship and so on), disease and death (affecting them or those close to them). Dinkies feel they have their lives under control, but fear both lack of control, and routine and monotony. Families worry about giving their children a good education and making sure they don't get involved in crime; many over-protect their children.

We asked participants in the focus groups to make collages. Their choices of imagery focused on:

- sexual equality and the role of women
- a crossroads with many alternatives
- money, credit cards
- mortgages
- lack of time
- again, technology.

This generation has made the transition from tradition to modernity. The traditional family had a fixed composition, was authoritarian, and centred on the ideas of duty and sacrifice. Today's families are more democratic and flexible, less structured. Parents' relationships with children are more equal. They try to convey the values of hard work and honesty. The idea of 'homes à la carte' has emerged: people choose from a range of different types of family. Women's independence has been a key factor. Because women now work outside the home, men have a role in the private space, sharing housework and childcare. Men's attitude to personal care has also changed, and the concept of a 'metrosexual' man has emerged.

But while families have evolved, dinkies are the main drivers of change. For them, postponing having children, and limiting their eventual number (often to just one), enables them to consolidate their relationship with their partner and satisfy their individual needs. Some dinkies choose to have a pet but no children: we saw this particularly in Hungary, Romania, Greece and Turkey.

The home also takes on a new meaning. It is more informal, with open spaces and less furniture, comfortable but functional and easy to clean. IKEA has understood the requirements of these new households.

We asked respondents in the focus groups about the home of the future:

- It will be very technological, with housework aids, great audiovisual equipment, remote control technology, intelligent systems and voice-activated apparatus.
- Serviced flats were mentioned more often by dinkie couples: small city homes with shared leisure and keep-fit facilities.
- Families' dream was still for a large house with a garden in the suburbs.

Consumption

Shopping has become a hobby. Consumers save money on utilitarian items like home cleaning products but splash out when they can for holidays, leisure and technology, when prestigious brands are significant. This dual approach, with the same people taking economy and gourmet stances, presents challenges for market researchers.

Dinkies are more impulsive and often buy on the Internet. Families are more cautious shoppers, seeking out specific brands for their children more than for themselves.

The categories respondents saw as most involving were:

- technology
- food
- soft drinks

- personal care products
- leisure and holidays
- clothing/fashion
- financial services
- products for children (for those who have them)
- cars
- home furnishings
- home appliances
- products and services to boost well-being (sports clothing and equipment, gyms, massages and spas).

We shall consider just three of these.

Technological items must look good, be well designed, comfortable, innovative and fashionable. These people value compact, portable equipment for individual use.

> *'If you don't follow the trends in technology, then you're excluded.'* (Netherlands)

There a number of different, but not mutually exclusive, trends in food:

- healthy foods, natural, bio, light, cholesterol-free and so on, and fresh food especially for children
- functional food: practical, fast, ready-cooked meals, frozen products and so on
- fast food at restaurants, for pleasure
- gourmet food and wine (at home and restaurants), primarily for dinkies.

In financial services they look for stability in a climate of uncertainty. Banking and financial institutions must provide support, transparency and individual service as well as speed. Respondents mentioned most often mortgages, loans, health insurance, life insurance and online banking.

The 36 megabrands

Approximately 300 brands were mentioned spontaneously in at least one of the 18 countries, but 36 stood out for their wide and successful market penetration. We identified three groups:

- First level, mentioned in all or most countries: Sony, Nike, Coca-Cola and Nokia.
- Second level, mentioned in approximately half the countries: IKEA, Philips, Adidas, Volkswagen, Levis, Nivea and McDonald's.
- Third level; with less spread:
  - technology: Microsoft, Siemens, Whirlpool, Bosch, LG, HP and Panasonic
  - cars: Mercedes, Peugeot, Audi, BMW, Skoda and Opel
  - food: Danone, Nestlé and Nescafé
  - for kids: Chicco, Pampers and Lego
  - hygiene: Dove and Johnson & Johnson
  - washing: Ariel
  - auctions and Internet : eBay
  - clothing: Puma and Zara.

The brand archetypes model discussed in chapter 17 can be useful in analysing these brands further, but here we use another Millward Brown model, BrandDynamics™, which focuses on the strength and potential of a brand.

BrandDynamics™

BrandDynamics allows us to explore the relationship between consumers and brands. It provides:

- a complete picture of the brand's current competitive position and brand loyalty
- a profile of key strengths and weaknesses in relation to competitors
- a precisely quantified evaluation of future growth potential.

Its tool is a survey questionnaire. BrandDynamics studies have been carried out in more than 70 countries and our database contains more than 50,000 brand observations. This allows detailed data mining to shed light on some of the key building blocks of marketing. We look here at the idea of a brand life cycle and the core facets of successful brands.

The brand life cycle

Our growing database revealed eight clusters of brands across different markets with common characteristics on two key dimensions: first, familiarity, and second, energy and momentum, which we call voltage. It has turned out to be a very good predictor of future trajectory. Brands with high voltage are more likely to gain share in the future than brands with low voltage.

- **Clean Slate**: few consumers know what these less well-known brands stand for.
- **Little Tiger**: niche brands, known best to a specific demographic or attitudinal group.
- **Specialist** brands often occupy the middle ground: they are reasonably well but not universally known.
- **Classics** are major brands, well known, with a significant user base, respected and appreciated but not with Olympic status (see below).
- **Olympic** brands are huge, universally known, highly popular brands, not just respected but often loved.
- **Defender** brands in the middle ground hold their position but lack real distinctiveness and find it hard to stand out.
- **Weak** brands are moderately well known but people don't feel they have much to offer.
- **Fading star**s are also known, but many people feel they have lost their relevance and distinctiveness.

We analysed 3,500 brands and discovered the following brand life cycle (see the next figure).

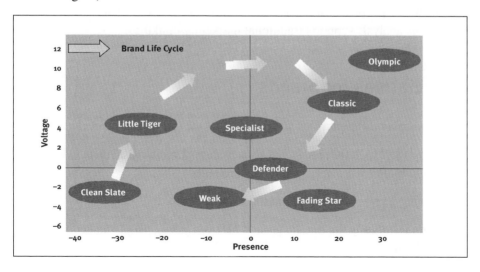

For example, Sony and Coca-Cola are Olympic brands in many countries. So are Nike, Nokia and Microsoft. Olympic brands have the risk of becoming Classic or Fading Star. In some European countries Puma has gone from Olympic to Classic to Fading Star, although it is trying to climb back. IKEA is a Specialist brand evolving into Olympic.

What makes a strong brand today?

Our research showed four clear drivers of brand success:

- Strong business basics. They must be available where people want to buy, at a price they are prepared to pay and that allows the business to make a profit.

- Great brand experience. Only truly exceptional delivery can produce truly exceptional results.

- Clarity: a clear positioning and set of values. Good brands all stand for something.

- A real sense of leadership. This can be through innovation in the brand experience, or in marketing activity and visibility.

Brand success in the future

Our model and analysis enable us to predict whether a brand will grow or decline. Brands that grow must convert people from active familiarity to endorsement; people must seen them as different and have some affinity with them. This analysis supports traditional marketing thinking.

Expectations for brands

Brands play different roles at each stage of the consumer life cycle:

- Teenagers look for brands that are new, aimed primarily at them, which help them build their own psychological identity.

- Young people look for successful aspirational brands they can relate to.

- Dinkies occupy the middle ground between young people and couples with children.

- For couples with children, emotional ties with brands become less important. Brands are like business partners that guarantee quality and a 'good buy'. When buying for their children, however, they look for the best and care less about price.

Brands are more important in categories that consumers find more interesting (such as cars, technology, entertainment, clothing, fashion and personal care) and less so for utilitarian products (household cleaning products, washing products, household equipment, electrical appliances). Store or own-label brands have improved in quality and offer acceptable value for money:

> *'Lots of people are trying to save money when shopping; 'geiz ist geil' (cheap is in).'* (Germany)

Consumers want products and services that counterbalance the growing complexity of modern big-city life, that:

- make life easier
- are functional and practical (without affecting their appearance)
- are easy to use
- save time, effort or space
- are convenient
- offer comfort
- help to enjoy life
- suggest an escape from reality.

Expectations regarding advertising

During the focus groups we asked about advertising campaigns. Of the 130-odd advertisements mentioned spontaneously, most were television ads. The range was wide, and sometimes people remembered seeing an ad in a particular medium but couldn't recall the specifics.

Those campaigns with the highest levels of awareness were for Coca-Cola, Nike, Citroen, Peugeot, Heineken, Toyota, Pepsi, Skoda, Johnnie Walker, Dove, Axe, Master Card and Doritos. The advertisements that work best:

- use humour (are fun, intelligent, ingenious or ironic)
- have strong music (different, distinctive and catchy)
- have high production values
- echo the lifestyle, values, needs and desire for modernity of this age group

- have a surprise factor
- go straight to the point, offering clear, credible information about the product and its benefits
- have a high emotional content
- feature animals, an attractive landscape and the like.

While dinkies are attracted by dynamism, movement and action, young families prefer to see children in advertisements.

A comparison of young people, dinkies and families

We combined the results of the dinkies and young families research with that from a separate qualitative study on young people aged 18 to 25. The next table highlights the main differences.

Young people (18-25)	Dinkies (25-35)	Families (25-35)
▶ Being young is in	▶ An extension of youth	▶ No longer young
▶ Cars are key	▶ Their home is the key factor	▶ The child is the key factor
▶ Live for the present	▶ Live for the present	▶ Thinking of the future
▶ Live with your parents	▶ Live with partner	▶ Life as a family (child-centred)
▶ The group of friends	▶ Construct the relationship well	▶ Family responsibilities
▶ Improvisation	▶ Improvisation	▶ Planning
▶ Spontaneity	▶ Spontaneity	▶ A certain routine
▶ Optimism	▶ Optimism	▶ Realism
▶ A restricted economy	▶ More money	▶ Expenses multiply

Fourteen brands connected with all three segments: Sony, Coca-Cola, Nokia, Nike, Adidas, Puma, Levis, Zara, BMW, Mercedes, Peugeot, Volkswagen, McDonald's and Siemens.

Summary and conclusions

In large cities with a fast pace of life, people feel under a lot of pressure. In this climate of instability and uncertainty, values are changing. Home, leisure, and holidays are important safety valves.

- The 25 to 35 generation is in transition from tradition to modernity. Women's roles have changed, and men too have had to reposition themselves.

- The major change factor is the arrival of children.

- Brands are important, though less so for families than for dinkies. Our research identified 36 megabrands that connect internationally with this group.

- Millward Brown's BrandDynamics™ model can be used to predict changes in market position.

- We also contrasted the respondent groups with younger consumers. Although there are differences apparent, some brands connect with all three market segments.

13

The financial goals of the middle-aged in the Netherlands (Delta Lloyd case study)

HENK SCHULTE

The start

Early in summer 2006 Millward Brown Netherlands was approached by Delta Lloyd, a large all-round insurer which offers a range of life and indemnity products, and banking services. Its marketing intelligence department was tasked with bringing its management board, marketing and PR professionals closer to their consumers. The brief was:

- Involve board members and top marketers: make them think about target groups.

- Research and insights must be impactful, surprising, yet realistic.

- Show them how our consumers think, act and decide.

Fascinating, but how were we to answer it? A traditional approach wouldn't work – we needed to push the limits of creativity. It felt a little like asking Picasso to take a photo with a Polaroid camera, Ozzy Osbourne to perform dressed in white, or Johan Cruyff to agree with a discussion partner.

The methodology: brainstorming

We began with a brainstorming session. We agreed we had to design a study in which the consumer took centre stage, and chose a project name: 'Delta Lloyd goes streetwise'.

In total we carried out three Streetwise projects, with younger consumers, small and medium-sized businesses, and people aged 45 to 55 (the focus of this chapter). We developed a small multidisciplinary project team: a business development director, a digital expert and a qualitative client service director. Together, we designed a research approach that was interactive and multimedia. We knew it would create impact, and we would be able to present the results enthusiastically and convincingly.

We agreed on the basic principles:

- interactive: three-way traffic between Delta Lloyd, Millward Brown and consumers
- multimedia: meetings with consumers via the Web, in-home discussions, on-street interviews and qualitative brainstorming sessions
- actionable insights: qualitative research, supported by hard facts and desk research.

Qualitative research was clearly the start point, but it was clear the client expected more than a few projective techniques and collages.

Next, we had to design a framework, a research menu we could use with any target group. We developed a grid to help us understand, interpret and delineate the consumer – one that not only sketched a profile of the target group, but was also capable of sharpening and reinforcing, or adjusting and restructuring, the brand, the portfolio and Delta Lloyd's communications.

The methodology: defining the research scope

Next, we set out to define the research scope: what issues were most relevant to consumers, and how were we to bring the target groups to life?

We defined providing insights as:

> Creating brand keys, product keys and communication keys.

To create actionable insights, we first had to learn about the target group. The information available from desk research – omnibus data and government studies – was quantitative, top-level and very generic. We wanted to delve deeper, to get underneath their skins and discover:

- what they feel, think and consider when buying insurance and financial services
- what they strive for, who inspires, influences and motivates them

- which values and norms they live by, and where they come from
- who shaped those values, when, and who were their opinion leaders.

We came up with an enormous battery of questions, which we then had to cluster and classify. We quickly agreed that inspiration and aspiration were the two most important areas of interest:

- What inspires the target group?
- How do they spend their leisure time, and which media do they use for what purposes?
- How do they communicate, and in which social environments have they lived and do they live now?

In addition, we wanted nuanced insight into the aspirations of the target group, in both their social and individual lives:

- What do people strive for in career development, education and finances?
- What do they want to achieve and what financial goals do they have?
- What concerns and challenges lie ahead?
- What certainties and uncertainties do they live with?

Certainties and uncertainties were important because these form the basis of our client insurer/bank's marketing strategy.

These questions and clusters were developed into the model in the following figure, onto which we mapped and characterized the different target groups. We agreed with our client that some elements might not be covered in it, but we felt it was good enough to help generate the insights and keys we needed.

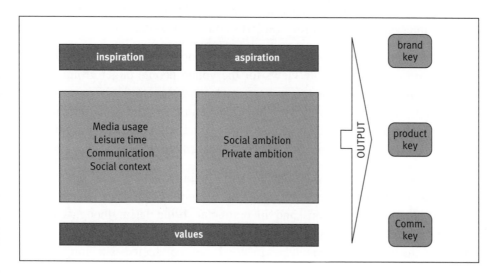

Methodology: the building blocks

Although the core of the project was qualitative research, we put it in context by conducting a thorough quantitative research exercise and an intensive desk-research study. This allowed us to validate our findings and provided the authority we needed for our presentations.

We decided that Delta Lloyd's objective for the middle-aged target group could best be achieved if we physically introduced the company to them, not through traditional group discussions but on their home ground. So we spoke to 24 married couples: in their homes, doing their shopping, and busy with their hobbies (sports, cycling and fitness). In these relaxed atmospheres, our respondents had time to reflect and think before answering questions, and their opinions were not influenced by others, as can sometimes happen in a group discussion.

In the Netherlands, social conformity and saying what you think others want to hear are largely things of the past, but there was still some risk that respondents might want to please the interviewer. The listening families provided a reality check, challenging some of what was said.

Successfully conducting research that involves challenging and corroborating respondents' comments requires considerable maturity and skill. Researchers must command authority, be empathetic and able to relativize. It is often said that measuring is knowing, but when it comes to qualitative research, understanding is knowing. It is also important to put things in context. You can't talk about life with people in their forties and fifties if you have no knowledge of their history. Given this, we decided to use a researcher of a similar age to the respondents. All in-home interviews were recorded on VHS and DVD.

We also wanted the views of as many other people as possible. We had had a good response with street interviews for the young people target group, so we used the same approach for this group, conducting short interviews across the Netherlands. Some discussions were brief; some took an interesting turn and the interviews lasted as long as 20 minutes. These street interviews also provided the supporting audiovisual we needed to give impact to our debrief.

But these tactics were side dishes to the main meal. To meet our client's objectives, we needed a series of qualitative group discussions which would allow us to contrast opinions and in particular, bring latent thoughts to the surface. In addition, premises that had surfaced during the desk research phase could be researched extensively. In total we conducted six long group discussions, three in Amsterdam and three in the provincial city of s'Hertogenbosch. The group discussions were watched by the client on a closed-circuit TV system.

The principal aim of these groups was to map out what had shaped this generation: the times in which they grew up, their cherished memories, the attitudes and values they had inherited from their parents, and still embraced and projected onto their children and partners. We dwelled at length on insurance matters and banking services, and explored their financial aspirations, thoughts about the future and vision of society.

To avoid any possible laboratory effects, we also organized two sessions in more relaxed café surroundings, in Rotterdam and 'sHertogenbosch. With a snack and a drink, we talked well into the night about the same topics. As well as new insights, these sessions served as validation and confirmation of the office-based group discussions.

To increase the client's direct involvement with the target group, we organized a series of online group discussions too, on three successive Wednesday evenings. They were facilitated and moderated by our staff, and the client was able to chat with the target group, ask direct questions and respond to ideas.

The following figure summarizes all this activity.

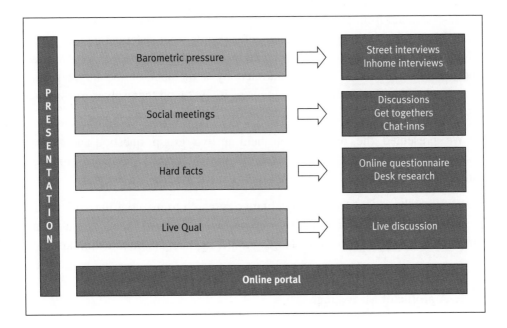

Because our approach embraced so many different methodologies, rigorous and continuous supervision was required. A team of two research managers was responsible for project management. The development director and qualitative client service director maintained client contact and were closely involved throughout. A small, well-organized team is essential in wide-ranging projects like this.

The sample

In the Netherlands there are approximately 2.6 million households of people aged between 45 and 55: 300,000 one-person, 1.3 million two-person, and a million of more than two people. We decided to focus on the average Dutch person, with a yearly income between 30,000 and 45,000 €. We included single people, those in two-income families, empty nesters, and families with children living at home. In short, we spoke to Mr and Mrs Average.

The findings

To present our findings in a surprising and impactful way, we decided to conduct a full-scale debrief in an environment that exuded the atmosphere and character of our target group: Lelystad, a large shopping outlet village. We rented a café-restaurant from ex-international footballer Aron Winter, and invited all of Delta Lloyd's board and top marketers, plus people from sister companies ABN-AMRO Verzekeringen and Ohra Verzekeringen. Around 20 people were sent an audiovisual invitation – a DVD narrated by a member of the target group. Arriving by chauffeur-driven limo, the executives found themselves transported into the world of Mr and Mrs Average.

We presented the results, then held a live group question-and-answer discussion. To maintain interest after the presentation, a password-protected online portal was created to house all the research models and insights.

We used the output from the qualitative research to map out the aspirations, attitudes and values of the target group and what inspired them. The ultimate output was funnelled into a brand key, product key and communication key.

The presentation flow we adopted was:

1. A profile of Mr Average.

2. Inspiration and aspirations.

3. Expectations of the future.

4. Relationship with financial and insurance matters.

5. Live group discussion with target-group consumers.

6. Insights and conclusions.

7. Brand, product and communication keys.

We used a mix of slides to present the qualitative insights and the desk research, enhanced with visual material and quotations from the group discussions, chat sessions and in-home interviews. The street interviews were made into a short film.

Here are some of our findings.

Mr Average

The target group were born between 1950 and 1960, grew up between 1960 and 1970, experienced their 'wild' years between 1970 and 1980, and settled down between 1980 and 1990. Clearly, their youth influenced what they are today:

'Even now, Abba provide the cheerful note in my life every day.'

'The O'Jays get my hips loose. Without them, I would still be a stiff, pious plank of wood.'

'My first Puch moped remains a milestone in my life.'

Music and technology are particularly important to this group. They saw the rise of the computer, the turbulent 1960s and the prosperous 1970s. From punk to disco, from cigarettes to joints, from hot pants to orgies, the sexual revolution, and particularly in the Netherlands the burgeoning of soft drugs, for this group there were hardly any boundaries. Society changed so quickly that it forced them to make choices, when often all they really wanted was peace and quiet. This created unrest and caused instability.

Fast forward to 2006, and their children were going off to war in Uruzgan and Afghanistan. The quality of education was declining and health care was becoming unaffordable.

The respondents were strongly influenced by consumer and related organizations. Middle-class people of this generation typically drive a mid-range car, camp in France or on the Costa del Sol, complain about but are not interested in politics, the environment or the economy. Only 30 per cent have an interest in religion and less than 10 per cent practise one. Though not intellectual, 55 per cent of them subscribe to a national daily newspaper. In many ways traditionally minded, they have nevertheless embraced the World Wide Web:

- 85 per cent have an Internet connection.
- 84 per cent use online banking.
- 57 per cent compare products and services online.
- 47 per cent make purchases via the Web (books, CDs, travel and insurance).
- 94 per cent are online every day, and 96 per cent regularly download information.

Cycling, jogging and Nordic walking, computing, gardening and doing odd jobs are their principal leisure activities. This is an active generation, which is still far from being burned out. Happiness, health and friendship are the values most important to them: the nuclear family and the extended family (including close friends) being the most important sources of inspiration, alongside work and education.

They aspire to discover the world. Some go backpacking to the ends of the earth. Anticipation (information evenings and travel guides) plays an important role in this. They bring souvenirs back home, and compile splendid photo albums, some of which we were shown.

Our respondents mostly had reasonably well-accrued pension funds, and worked on staying healthy. In 1991, 39 per cent of 45–60 year-olds smoked: by 2004 it had dropped to 26 per cent. They use olive oil instead of margarine, and have switched from white bread to wholemeal, and replaced spirits by red wine.

At the same time, the pace of social change makes many of these people feel insecure:

> *'In the past, everything was clearer, more homogeneous. There are now so many different cultures, people and trends that I sometimes wonder whether I can still follow it all.'*

> *'I'm only 56 years old, but I see things changing so fast that I don't recognize them any longer. For example, the neighbourhood where I used to live doesn't at all resemble what it once was.'*

> *'In my youth, everything was much clearer and less hectic. Nowadays, I sometimes have trouble keeping up with the daily rhythm of life: we have to do so much. In the past, at least you knew where you stood; now, we just have to wait and see what's going to happen. The future is more uncertain.'*

People react to this by trying to find a suitable identity and a social environment to link themselves to. They are looking for solidarity and security – an excellent seed bed for an insurance company. It is no coincidence that Delta Lloyd's strapline is 'Nothing is certain'. We live in a transitional world, and this older generation recognize these changes and can place them in context.

Insights and conclusions

Because of client confidentiality we cannot divulge our detailed recommendations, but below is a general summary.

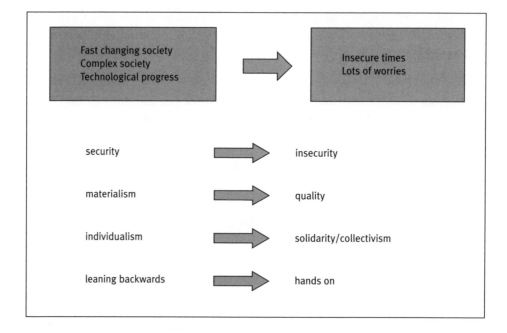

Brand key

- Focus on the values of security and reliability. Although these are very obvious insurance values, they have to be there.

- Removing worry is important. Don't bother this group with the problems they are likely to face. Instead, position Delta Lloyd as the brand which knows what it's talking about and takes the worries off their shoulders.

- Be honest and authentic. Don't exaggerate and don't promise what you can't deliver.

- Be their guide. Show them the way, and link their third phase of life to relevant brand characteristics. Position yourself close to them as a brand, and show your capacity for empathy.

Product key

- Tailor-made products and customization are not issues for this target group. They are looking for security and solidarity, and mass-market offers make them feel safer.

- Be transparent and clear. It is better to offer this target group a limited portfolio rather than a range of products with too many variances.

Communication key

- Taking this group seriously is essential. In the 1980s and 1990s, they too often received promises that were not fulfilled, even by established brands. Under-promise and over-deliver, rather than over-promise and under-deliver.

- Credibility is essential in the insurance industry. Delta Lloyd should not be led too much by the 'zeitgeist', but should bring its core values into line with current values and norms. The 'spirit of the times' is often short-lived, but a strong brand lasts forever.

- Communication is too often directed at young people; the older generations feel overlooked. Seniors are the largest population group in the Netherlands and the one with the greatest purchasing power. Yet they are rarely addressed in the advertising we see and hear today.

14
Older people in Western Europe (international case study)

ROSANA VALVERDE AND JORGE BENITO

Introduction

During 2006, Millward Brown used data from a major quantitative study by its sister company TGI (Target Group Index) to look at trends among those aged 55 and over. We focused on Germany, France, Spain and Great Britain, using TGI's data to conduct a segmentation exercise, then later undertaking a qualitative study in Spain, to explore in greater depth one of the typologies that emerged. Our study is a good example of a 'quali-quant' collaboration.

The objectives of the quantitative study

The main objectives of the original study were:

- to look at how demographics are evolving and investigate the trends among older people

- to understand their different forms of behaviour

- to analyse in depth the key values of different segments, including attitudes to shopping, brand selection and life in general.

Methodology

For over 30 years, TGI has been carrying out surveys on consumption of products and services. The respondents also provide information on their free-time activities, lifestyle, views on consumption in general and media usage habits. TGI studies are currently carried out in over 60 countries, interview 700,000 consumers a year and collect data on 500 products and services as well as on 5,000 brands per country.

This single-source quantitative study:

- included segmentation based on 70 attitudinal statements
- covered individuals aged 55 and over
- used a quota sample based on geographical area, family role, sex, age, class and size of household of 20,493 men and women
- was carried out from October 2005 to December 2006 (in France, Germany and Great Britain) and from January to December 2006 (in Spain).

Demographic data were in line with the general population, and media data were weighted to each country's national audience study.

Seniors today in Western Europe

The proportion of older people has been growing rapidly in Western Europe, so this market is increasingly important. Their habits, customs and spending power have changed dramatically over their lifetimes. They have greater spending power and better health than previous generations. They are far from being homogenous, and marketers need a range of strategies to engage the different segments.

Today's 55–65 year-olds are the 'baby boomers', conceived at a time of economic and social stability directly after the Second World War. Previously the population age structure had resembled a pyramid, but this period of soaring birth rates, together with longer life expectancy caused by better living conditions, and falling birth rates more recently, has resulted in a more cylinder-like age distribution.

Life expectancy in the European Union is increasing by an average of three months every year. By 2050 it is estimated that approximately 52 per cent of the population will be aged over 50.

Implications

For many years marketing concentrated on young people as the source of inspiration for new trends. But their relative importance is waning, and they have less cultural impact on society than they did from the 1960s to the 1980s. Older people are becoming the source of new trends. Many are in good physical condition and undertake a wide range of activities. Learning skills peak at 50 and not at 20, as used to be thought. The fear of growing old is strong at age 40, after which it declines. Plastic surgery is increasingly acceptable, and older people are happy to use new technology.

Among the products and services designed to meet the needs of older people are Windows Vista, the 'Simply Vodafone' mobile telephone handset, cruise-based vacations and cosmetics for those with more mature skin, although this group also buy many products for which they were not the original target market.

A segmented target group

From the TGI data we identified six types of over-55s:

- **Energetic hedonists.** Experimenters who love change and novelty, they like to stand out from the crowd and be influenced by advertising, are materialists and not very price-sensitive.

- **Conventionals.** This group do not like change, and prefer to follow clear rules, habits and traditional customs. They appreciate reputation and the status quo. They look for bargains and prefer to plan.

- **Cosmopolitan adventurers**. Their values fit a search for personal growth, change and new challenges. They like to enrich themselves culturally, keep up to date and be well-informed about current events.

- **Traditional homely**. These have a strong sense of duty, morality and obligation. They believe in the traditional family and in hierarchy, and have rather conservative values. Found in the lowest socio-economic group, they seek comfort over style.

- **Anxious nostalgics.** Concerned with their health and well-being, they are the oldest group and concentrate on prevention. They prefer the past, are prudent financially, look for quality and plan their purchases.

- **Provincials of the world.** This group is less open to advertising – they want to feel free and be able to express their opinions. They can be hard for marketers to reach. They appreciate other cultures but also like the local, family values and hospitality.

A simpler two-part typology groups these into:

- **Traditional**, composed of the conventional, the homely traditional and the anxious nostalgic. They represent 62 per cent of older people in these countries.

• **Modern,** composed of the energetic hedonists, cosmopolitan adventurers and provincials of the world. These make up the remaining 38 per cent.

Spain has a more traditional older population, with 39 per cent anxious nostalgic and 24 per cent traditional homely. In Great Britain more than half the population has a modern orientation, including many provincials of the world. France and Germany have similar splits between moderns and traditionals (with more of the latter), but a different split between the anxious nostalgics and the traditional homelys. Although the proportion of traditionals is highest in all four countries, indications are that the proportion of moderns will increase in future.

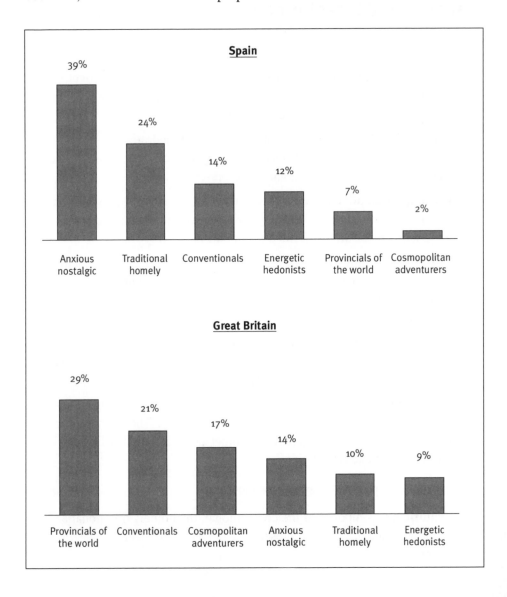

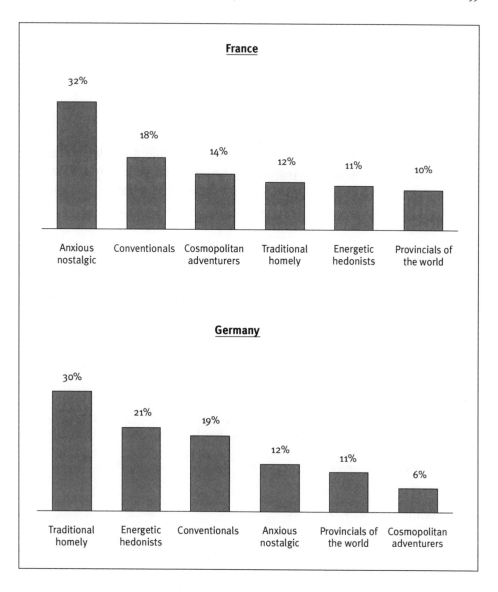

The energetic hedonists

These represent 14 per cent, 9,957,000, of the senior population in Europe. Most are found in Germany: 21 per cent of its total senior population, spread equally across the variables of sex, economic level and age.

Their mottos for life are:

'Carpe diem.'

'If you look good, you feel good.'

'Fun and fashion.'

'Shop till you drop.'

'The family comes second.'

Thirty-eight per cent say they like advertising, while a similar percentage admit it helps them when shopping. They are not very price-sensitive and are highly impulsive shoppers. They buy on the basis of style rather than product quality, and packaging is very important to their product choice.

Conventionals

These make up 19 per cent, about 12,852,000 of the older people in Europe. They are characterized by their belief that money provides peace of mind and security, pride in their family and slight insecurity about the unknown and the future. They need to see faces and places they know, and are averse to change and uncertainty.

In Great Britain, where they are most common, they represent 21 per cent of the target group. They are as likely to be men as women, and are spread across all ages and income levels. Their mottos for life are:

'It is better to go unnoticed.'

'Enjoy life in moderation.'

'Prevention is better than cure.'

'Money is security.'

'Debts are a curse.'

Their attitudes to shopping are defined by high price levels, interest in planning (74 per cent claim to handle their money well), quest for a bargain, and enjoyment of shopping in general (45 per cent, above average, enjoy buying things).

Cosmopolitan adventurers

Cosmopolitan adventurers make up 9 per cent or 6,556,000 of this age group. The youngest type, aged mainly from 55 to 64, they have a medium to high income level and include as many men as women. More common in Great Britain and France, they like a life that is full of personal challenges, and to learn new things. Their mottos for life are:

'Happiness is discovering new things.'

'Life is an adventure.'

'The art of living.'

'Knowledge is power.'

'Don't imitate, innovate.'

'The enjoyment of technology.'

They appreciate quality and comfort: 54 per cent are prepared to pay more for a product that makes their life easier. Not brand loyal, they are happy to try new things and are very good recommenders. Not especially interested in appearances, only 5 per cent said product packaging influences them.

Traditional homely

These make up 20 per cent, about 14 million, of the sector. Duty and obedience are important to them. They are most commonly found in Spain and Germany, more likely women, mostly over 75 and the least well-off type. They tend to follow rules and respect authority. Their mottos for life include:

'Father knows best.'

'A woman's place is in the home.'

'Follow rules, not your heart.'

'Shut up and obey.'

'The family comes first.'

'Home sweet home.'

When shopping, they avoid risk and seek comfort, never style; are very price sensitive but still find it hard to make ends meet. Marketing communications reach this group but do not affect them much; for example, 55 per cent rarely notice whether an event is sponsored.

Anxious nostalgic

This type represent 20 per cent or 15 million people in this European age group. They need to feel secure and find security in looking back on the past.

They worry about their health and are financially prudent. Most common in Spain and France, they are more likely to be women with a medium income level, and are the oldest type (from 85 to 94). Their mottos are:

'Prevention is better than cure.'

'A bird in the hand is worth two in the bush.'

'A penny saved is a penny gained.'

'Count the calories.'

They prefer to plan purchases, choosing more on the basis of quality than price. They prefer products they know, particularly from their own country.

Provincials of the world

These make up 15 per cent, more than 10 million, of the group. It is important to them to be open to other countries and cultures, as well as close to their family. They are not influenced easily, and are sceptical about marketing and advertising. Most common in Great Britain, they tend to be men with a medium to high income level, and in the lower age range (between 55 and 64). Their main mottos in life are:

'Think globally, act locally.'

'Be yourself.'

'Be careful! We're being manipulated.'

'I like exotic things as much as what is familiar.'

They tend to plan their purchases, and value product quality more than image, appearance or social value: 74 per cent like to own good-quality things.

The value of brands for each segment

For the energetic hedonists:

- Appealing brands values invite them to live on the wild side, show off and boast.
- Use intense, fast communications, lots of colours and images, and express rebellion and narcissism.
- They are especially sensitive to promotions of high-end products, exciting events and competitions.

For conventional consumers:

- Brands should win the respect of their family and friends.

- Underline the authority of the brand, its history, know-how, experience and value for money in communications.

- Coupons, discounts and loyalty programmes work well.

For the cosmopolitan adventurers:

- Brands should invite them to explore and experience the richness in life.

- Effective communications break with routine, promote quality of life and sophistication, and allude to culture.

- Joint promotions (with other brands) appeal to this group.

For the traditional homely consumers:

- Brand values should connect with staying at home and saving money.

- Advertising should use traditional role models and emphasize low prices.

- This segment is the most sensitive to promotions, above all discounts and two-for-one offers.

For the anxious nostalgic consumers:

- Brands should make them feel safer and free from health problems.

- Messages about security, support, trust, protection and health are the most effective.

- Free samples work well, as do coupons and offers on familiar brands.

And last, for the provincials of the world:

- Brands must allow them to be themselves without feeling manipulated.

- Avoid conventional types of advertisement, and emphasize authenticity, originality, unselfishness. Communications should be 'anti-status'.

- Effective promotions connect with humanitarian and environmental causes, and do not encourage impulse consumption.

The qualitative phase

Millward Brown Spain's subsequent qualitative study was of the energetic hedonists. They currently account for 12 per cent of Spain's older population, but all three of the modern segments are expected to grow.

Two focus groups were held, one in Madrid and one in Barcelona. Each one:

- lasted for two hours
- had between eight and ten respondents of the energetic hedonist type, aged 55 to 70
- comprised half women, half men.

We saw at first hand that these people are indeed full of energy. With their children grown up they are free to spend time on themselves and their partner. They want to enjoy doing their favourite activities more often, and do new things they never had the time to do before. At a stage of personal rediscovery and in good health, they do not yet experience drawbacks in growing older:

'I feel satisfied – I want to enjoy life to the full.'

'I've been doing what I want for the last five years.'

'You only live once and have to make full use of your life.'

'At night we like to go to a fashionable restaurant, then for a dance and a drink, and enjoy ourselves.'

'On Sundays we enjoy organizing family reunions.'

Most were still in paid employment, but free time was becoming a more important part of their lives. They were mature, self-assured and materialistic. They could buy a vacation home, new car or boat, and still dreamed of winning the lottery:

'My hobby is sailing, and my aim is to sail around the world.'

They enjoy shopping and are attracted by brands, and influenced by advertising and promotions. They take great care of their appearance, like buying products, and are attracted by style and design.

'Saturday is the best day for shopping. It fills me with energy to see all these people looking for fashionable brands.'

'I like going to see what people are buying and how they dress to go out.'

'I admit that I like exclusive clothing brands, that I like to look as good as possible.'

They also like change:

'What I like is to change things at home all the time …. I soon get tired of seeing everything look the same. I start off wanting new curtains and end up changing the whole room.'

And they like to travel the world, enjoying other cultures, countries and cities:

'Last weekend we went to Prague for three nights, and next month we're going to Ibiza.'

'I've travelled a lot in Europe; now I'd love to go to exotic countries.'

Solo leisure activities included:

- at home: reading, listening to music, DIY, Internet, television, writing, painting, playing the piano
- in natural settings away from home: cycling, fishing, sunbathing, walking on the beach, sailing, flying
- outside the home in the city: gym, dance classes, swimming.

And social and family activities included:

- at home: get-togethers, talks and gatherings
- outside the home in natural settings: travelling, walking, going to parks
- outside the home in the city: going to the cinema, the theatre, exhibitions and museums, concerts.

They are fascinated by technology, and their attitude to it is very positive and open. Used at work and in leisure activities, it makes their lives easier, adds to their prestige and helps them feel part of the wider society:

'Technology is a friend who helps me.'

'It offers me social inclusion.'

'It makes me feel young.'

'I'm looking at a new alarm system; I've got one already but it's obsolete. Now new ones are coming out that warn the water company if you have a water leak, or calls the fire service in case of fire. They're digital.'

'I like it a lot because I practise with my daughter too, as she is the expert.'

'It really helps with work, I do lots of things directly from my PDA.'

Energetic hedonists buy well-designed technology products from good brands, and are not particularly sensitive to price. Male and female attitudes to technology differed. Men talked of computing, mobile phones, the latest developments in cars, and home leisure products: home cinema, hard discs, DVD recorders, MP3, computers (desktops and laptops), scanners, printers, digital cameras, PDAs and plasma screens:

'I've downloaded lots of music in MP3, I've got thousands of songs.'

'Right now sailing is great, you take your GPS on board.'

Women were generally less technologically minded, but appreciated electronic home appliances.

We were interested in respondents' attitudes to retirement. These energetic hedonists saw it as something to look forward to:

'Joy ... jubilation.'

'Enjoyment ... free time.'

'Freedom.'

'The beach ... happiness.'

They tended to downplay the more depressing side, emphasizing opportunities rather than tedium and routine. They were attracted to celebrities of their age who continue to work, enjoy good health and express joy and lust for life, including Paul Newman, Robert Redford, Concha Velasco and Lola Herrera.

Summary and conclusions

- Millward Brown carried out a major quantitative segmentation study in four European countries, and a follow-up qualitative study in Spain, both based on the over-55 age group.

- Six typologies were identified: energetic hedonists, conventionals, cosmopolitan adventurers, traditional homely, anxious nostalgic and provincials of the world. Marketers need different tactics to attract consumers of each type.

- The Spanish energetic hedonists were studied in depth through qualitative research. They enjoy shopping, are attracted by advertising and promotions, and value leisure time and travel. They are not price-sensitive and are fascinated by technology.

PART III

QUALITATIVE TO SOLVE
CONTEMPORARY
MARKETING ISSUES

15
Media planning

PEPE MARTÍNEZ

The new media ecosystem

In recent years the media landscape has changed significantly, with many more television channels and the emergence of new media including mobile phones and the Internet. The number of potential points of contact (touch points) between brands and consumers has multiplied. Media agencies are developing creative new ways to attract consumers' attention, and new technologies offer alternative platforms for brand communications.

In this changing environment advertisers are rethinking their media plans. With their agencies, they are reviewing whether channels that worked in the past are as effective today.

Until now, the concept of a 'contact' (GRP) has been enough, and advertising efficacy has been measured quantitatively: the number of GRPs received by a hypothetical average consumer. However, in this new media landscape we need to take into account of the *quality* of contacts as well as the quantity.

The quality of a connection

To explore how different touch points resonate with consumers we have to know how an individual *feels*. We have to understand the meanings a certain channel has for them, their relationship with it and their needs in that environment. Given current levels of media fragmentation, marketers need to take advantage of every point of contact to ensure a connection that is both real and effective, and has a positive influence the next time the advertised product or service is purchased or used.

The following figure summarizes a target's mindstate and exposure to media at different times of the day.

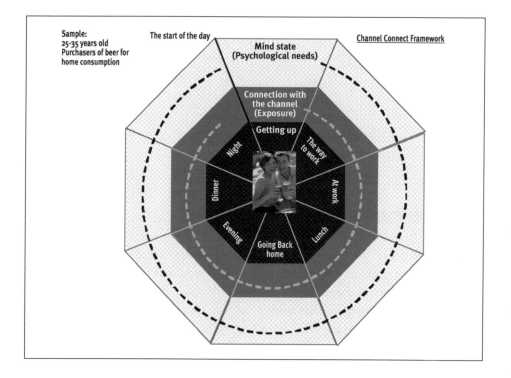

ChannelConnect™

This qualitative methodology developed by Millward Brown helps marketers and their agency teams identify how to make the best use of advertising channels. The approach places consumers at the core of a media plan, ensuring that marketers communicate the right message, in the right way and at the right time.

Its objectives are:

- to identify the points at which consumers and brands interact, where marketers can communicate in the most credible way

- to discover the times of the day and the week when the target group are most receptive to brand messages

- to discover new communication opportunities

- to define how best to convey the brand communication idea to engage consumers in the most effective way in each place and at each time.

ChannelConnect's philosophy and areas of focus are expressed in visual form in the following figure.

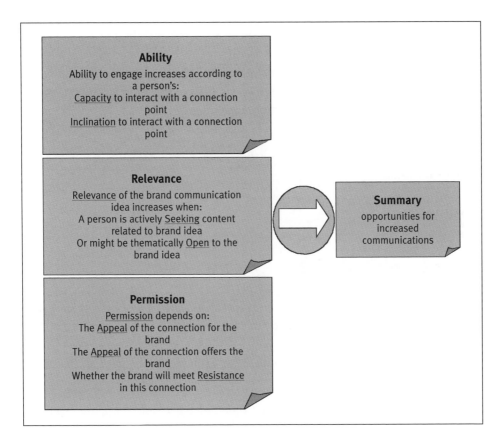

ChannelConnect identifies the connection points target consumers are more able and inclined to engage with in their daily lives; the ones that are relevant when people are in open or seeking modes. It also identifies the contexts that are most credible, differentiating or problematic. This enables us to identify the key stepping stones to increasing communications engagement. It is used to research not specific campaigns, but rather how consumers relate to the communication channels in the context of the idea that the brand intends to convey.

It does not research media consumption habits (when, what, where and who), but rather how and why communication channels interact and are consumed. It does not research consumer attitudes to a brand or its image, but rather where, how, and to what degree the brand connects with consumers. And it seeks not to evaluate creative work, but rather to identify the ideal context in which the message should be presented to amplify communications engagement.

Methodological design

ChannelConnect™ is based on a thoughtful study design and the careful selection of respondents. It can use a range of qualitative techniques, tailored to the needs and aims of the brand in question, including:

- ethnographic diaries

- focus groups

- ethnographic interviews.

Ethnographic diaries

Before they attend focus groups, all respondents keep a diary for at least four days (two weekdays plus Saturday and Sunday), in which they answer the questions:

- Where are you? Who are you with? (For example: in the gym, in the car, at home, in a shopping centre.)

- What are you doing? (For example: watching television, shopping, walking, reading.)

- How do you feel? What is your mood? What are your psychological needs? (For example: relaxed, anxious, tired, sociable.)

- What advertising channels are you watching, reading or listening to right now? (For example: television, radio, a newspaper, a magazine, the Internet, a billboard.)

The next figure shows the structure of an ethnographic diary.

Day of week	1. Where are you? Who are you with?	2. What are you doing?	3. How do you feel? (mood)	4. Which media or advertising channels can you see or hear at this time?
1. Breakfast (Getting up)				
2. On the way to work				
3. Morning				
4. Lunch				
5. Afternoon				
6. Traveling home				
7. Dinner				
8. Night (before going to bed)				

We ask respondents to photograph advertising material that has caught their attention, and to take 'projective' photographs that reflect their mood. This aids our understanding of how they interact with media and whether they are in the right frame of mind to receive a message. We also ask them where and when they think about concepts that specific brands try to convey, such as 'performance'. They use their own digital camera or mobile phone camera, or if they do not have one, we supply a disposable camera.

On the basis of the information from the diaries we identify the moments in the day when consumers' relationship with advertising channels is most intense and relevant.

Focus groups

The focus groups explore in depth the relationship between the target group and the media. They analyse which media channels are more or less effective in connecting with consumers. We ask respondents questions designed to bring out what they think and feel, and use brainstorming techniques to search for ideas on new target group connection opportunities.

Together the diaries and focus groups allow us to identify the days of the week and times of day when respondents will be most receptive to the brand's communications.

Once we have analysed the diaries and completed the focus groups we may conduct ethnographic interviews (a technique discussed in chapter 5).

Ethnographic interviews

In these interviews we accompany those taking part in the study on their most frequent journeys (on the underground/metro, by bus, on a suburban train, by car or on foot, whatever), at the most representative times of day and on different days of the week. (The locations and times are identified through the diaries and focus groups.) The purpose is to talk openly and spontaneously with respondents about the channels they encounter, and the advertising campaigns that run on them. The technique provides real-time emotional and cognitive reactions to the contact points.

Team work: marketing, media, creative and research

Effective qualitative research of this type calls for several groups to work together:

- the marketing team responsible for the brand, product or service

- the media planning team

- the Millward Brown research team

- often too the advertising agency.

At the start of the study an initial meeting is held to share all available information about the product and brand. All data are important, especially those that relate to the media. A quantitative review of this information is usually conducted before the main qualitative study.

The teamwork and synergy between the different professionals who work on nurturing and growing the brand helps to develop a more effective and strategic perspective. A workshop is held at the end of the study with all the parties involved. It aims to turn the insights that have emerged into a new communication strategy and media plan for the brand, using existing channels more effectively and/or suggesting opportunities that have not yet been exploited fully.

ChannelConnect and marketing

This new methodological approach provides opportunities for the marketing department to improve competitiveness and differentiation. Because the new plan takes account of consumers' lifestyles together with the degree to which they are receptive to brand communications, return on media investment improves. Advertising campaigns also become more impactful as we are able to identify the most effective place and time for them to run. Last, this approach creates a working style that is inclusive and up to date. The client's marketing department, the media planners, the ad agency and the market researchers work together, placing the consumer at the heart of the planning process.

Summary and conclusions

- To adapt to the evolving communication channel landscape, advertisers are re-evaluating their media plans.

- Marketers need to be aware of the quality as well as the quantity of the connection between advertising and promotional material and its target group.

- ChannelConnect is a qualitative methodology which helps advertisers and their agencies understand the dynamics at work. It offers in-depth understanding of consumer lifestyle and motivations, as well as an understanding of how consumers interact with brand communications. By identifying when, where and how a brand is best able to connect with its target group, it contributes to more effective touch-point choice.

16
Point of sale

BÁRBARA GUINOVART

Research at point of sale

For many years marketing focused its efforts on building brand image, advertising campaigns and media plans. The aim was to create high levels of brand preference and generate consumer demand. Little or no attention was paid to activation at the point of sale. Display shelves were seen as no more than the final setting where the forces created by consumer preferences are played out.

A lot of work studied consumers as the *audience*. The time has now come to centre on consumers as *shoppers*. Point of sale touch points must be understood if products and brands are to be supported properly.

Each product category and each sales display has its own rules, but there are some common factors. Merchandising rules are important; but it is also important to know the roles played by packaging (the pack itself as well as the label), the different varieties of a product, price, price sensitivity, offers, discounts, promotions and advertising at the point of sale, and so on. To gain a good understanding of all these issues we can use a qualitative research technique know as *accompanied shopping*.

From viewer and consumer to shopper

We have seen a focus on viewers (those exposed to advertising campaigns), and a focus on consumers, and the consumer profile of specific products. A lot of work is now taking place around the shopper. The aim is to better get to know and understand who buys what, and all aspects surrounding the moment of purchase – the 'ecosystem' of the final purchase.

Often the viewer, shopper and consumer are the same person, but not always: for example, parents buy products for their children. It is important to understand the dynamics of the relationships between: viewers, consumers and shoppers, and between shoppers and their choice of purchase.

Accompanied shopping

In this technique the researcher (who is often an expert psychologist or sociologist) goes with the shopper to make a purchase: for example in a traditional food store, supermarket, hypermarket, clothing store, petrol station shop or mobile telephone shop. The shopper is asked to forget they are being observed, behave as normally as possible, and shop just as they usually do.

In a supermarket or hypermarket the shopper may be asked to buy products from three categories they usually purchase, one that is the subject of the study and two dummy categories, to ensure their behaviour is as natural and spontaneous as possible.

The researcher can act as either a passive or a participating observer, making remarks or asking questions.

Immediately after the purchase has been made an in-depth interview is conducted, perhaps at a café close by, in the shopper's home or the research company offices. The aim is to explore the influence of each element in the buying environment and the role it played in the purchase decision, while the experience is still fresh.

An example

The researcher's observation at point of sale can be unstructured, staying alert for any element of importance, or more structured, using a protocol or a grid to record the information. This example is of an open observation accompanied shop to research yogurt. It is based on the researcher guide drawn up before the activity.

Introduction

The researcher meets the respondent at the door of the hypermarket where she usually buys her yogurt. She introduces herself by name and company, and the consumer is also introduced by name. The researcher explains, 'We are going to go in to buy biscuits, yoghurt and cooking oil. Please shop as you usually do, in a natural way. I will accompany you and observe what you do. Later on, we will talk at your home about the shopping trip.'

Accompanied shopping

The interviewee does the shopping. The researcher observes the process and takes notes about factors that might play a role in, and influence, the purchase: for example shelf position, offers and promotions, shapes and colours of packs and labels, advertising at the point of sale. Useful prompt questions are:

- What do they look at?
- What do they pick up?
- What do they read?
- How long do they take?
- Which brand do they buy?
- Which product (type of yoghurt) do they select?
- What amount do they buy?

In-depth interview

The interview makes use of spontaneous reactions and free discourse, plus prompts as necessary to ensure all the issues are covered. This includes the role and relative importance of factors that influenced the shopper before she reached the store (brand image, advertising, channels/media, word of mouth, experience of the product and so on) as well as the in-store experience. Prompt questions might include:

- *'Which brands were on your shopping list, and why?'*
- *'What would lead you to exclude a brand from the list?'*
- *'Which brand did you plan to buy when you arrived at the store? Did you actually buy it? Why or why not?'*
- *'Why did you choose the brand you bought?'*

- *'What did you think of when you were choosing?'*

- *'Which factors were most important?'*

- *'What other factors were important when you bought yoghurt on other occasions?'*

- *'Lastly, is there any other factor that would influence you to buy one yoghurt brand instead of another?'*

Variants of accompanied shopping

Several variants of this technique may be used depending on the client's objectives.

- Individual video supported shopping (reality research). The shopper is asked to wear a video camera while shopping. Footage taken during the shop is used as stimulus for a follow-up in-depth interview.

- Intercept interviews. Respondents are not pre-recruited, but intercepted at the point of purchase after they have made a relevant purchase, and asked questions.

- Immersion approach. Here, the client accompanies the shopper, with or without a qualitative researcher. The insights form part of a later workshop.

Summary and conclusions

- Point of sale used to be considered of secondary importance to building a strong brand image, using advertising campaigns and media plans. Today, it is seen as an important activator in its own right.

- Factors that can have a decisive influence at point of sale include merchandising, packaging, different varieties of a product, price and price sensitivity, offers, discounts, promotions and in-store advertising.

- The accompanied shopping technique provides a good qualitative understanding of the purchase decision. It can comprise passive or participant observation, and is usually followed by an in-depth interview with the shopper.

17

Brand essence (international case study)

PEPE MARTÍNEZ

In search of lost archetypes

In 2003 Millward Brown undertook a global qualitative research study to develop an analytical model that would allow us to determine the positioning of a brand in a specific country, and at the same time compare its positioning across different countries or cultures. The aim of the research was to identify the most fundamental typology of archetypes, the different types of relationship between a consumer and a brand.

Methodology

The study was undertaken in 14 countries across five regions of the world, as noted in the next table. Two two-hour focus groups, each with an average of eight respondents, were held in each country, so this was a very large qualitative study.

North America:	1. The United States
	2. Canada
Latin America	3. Chile
	4. México
Europe	5. Denmark
	6. Spain
	7. The Netherlands
	8. Poland
	9. The United Kingdom
	10. Sweden
Asia Pacific	11. India
	12. Japan
	13. Thailand
Africa	14. South Africa

The sample were:

- half men, half women
- aged from 25 to 40
- middle and upper-middle class
- with an active and creative lifestyle
- brand-driven rather than price-driven
- at least 50 per cent graduates.

At the end of the study, we constructed a model of ten basic archetypes, as shown in following figure.

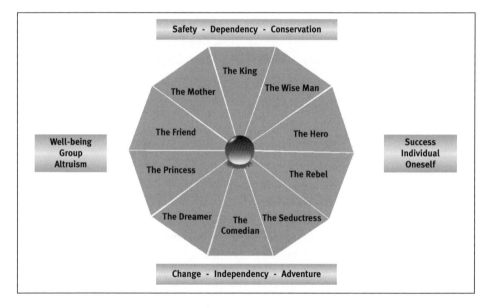

As can be seen from the next table, each archetype has a shadow, which is its negative counterpart.

Archetype	Shadow
1. The King	1. The Tyrant
2. The Wise Man	2. The Charlatan
3. The Hero	3. The Villain
4. The Rebel	4. The Anarchist
5. The Seductress	5. The Femme Fatale
6. The Comedian	6. The Madman
7. The Dreamer	7. The Fantasist
8. The Princess	8. The Witch
9. The Friend	9. The Traitor
10. The Mother	10. The Stepmother

The power of the archetypes

Archetypes are symbols that are especially important for human beings. For example, the Hero is the archetypical model of bravery and courage. Archetypes are universal references – their meaning remains constant across time and space. What may vary is how the archetype is represented.

The great myths, legends, stories, literary works and films contain archetypical characters (the Hero, the King, the Traitor, the Wise Man, the Princess, the Stepmother and so on) who move the audience because they connect with the deepest part of their psyche. Archetypes symbolize the fundamental relationships human beings have with their surroundings. Carl Jung* developed the concept of the collective unconscious, by which he meant the existence of a set of primitive symbols that is shared by all human beings, expressing values that go beyond the rational dimension. For Jung, the archetypes link us to unconscious ancestral symbols, to primordial images.

The ten archetypes and their shadows

1. The King

- Symbols of the King include God, Zeus, Jupiter, Theoden (*The Lord of the Rings*), a lion, a gold crown, a sceptre, the colour gold.

- The King represents strength, potency, power, leadership, authority and order.

- Brands that correspond to this archetype are admired by consumers (due to their power). They are also felt to provide protection, safety and trust.

- The shadow of the King is the Tyrant, represented by the devil, Saturn (who devoured his children), a shark, the trident, the colour black. The Tyrant is the symbol of a monopoly, despotism, control, egotism and arrogance. This shadow arouses submission and anger in consumers.

2. The Wise Man

- Symbols of the Wise Man include Merlin, King Solomon, Gandalf (*The Lord of the Rings*), Einstein, a scientist, a wizard, an expert, a craftsman, a book, a telescope, a microscope and an owl.

- The Wise Man represents wisdom, intelligence, knowledge (know-how), technique, technology and intuition.

- Brands that correspond to this archetype are admired by consumers (because of their wisdom). Thanks to their friendly, human tone, they instil the desire to learn and a sense of well-being.

- The shadow of the Wise Man is the Charlatan, who represents hot air, empty talk, fraud, and makes it look as if he knows things he doesn't. Compared with the owl, which symbolizes the spirit of the Wise Man, the parrot and parakeet best express the Charlatan.

3. The Hero

- Symbols of the Hero include Ulysses, Aragorn (*The Lord of the Rings*), Theseus, Rambo, Spiderman, Superman, a sword, a bow, a laurel wreath.

- The Hero represents self-confidence, bravery, courage, daring, charisma, an adventurous spirit and success in the face of adversity.

- Consumers identify with brands that correspond to this archetype – they create a desire to overcome obstacles and problems. These brands are usually highly aspirational and admired.

- The shadow of the Hero is the Villain, who represents narcissism, envy, imitation, copying and weakness.

4. The Rebel

- Symbols of the Rebel include Robin Hood, James Dean, Steve McQueen (in the film *The Great Escape*), a wild horse.

- The Rebel represents opposition to established values, renewal, originality and differentiation.

- Brands that correspond to this archetype offer the market a change. They have new values and bring a new paradigm. They stimulate consumers' unconscious motivations.

- The shadow of the Rebel is the Anarchist, represented by chaos and the lack of any clear direction. The extreme of this shadow reflects social exclusion and criminality.

5. The Seductress

- Symbols of the Seductress include Venus, Aphrodite, geishas, the Song of the Sirens (*Ulysses*), Cleopatra, Marilyn Monroe, Eowyn (*The Lord of the Rings*), a black panther, a magnet, a woman's red lips, a glass of wine, a fan.

- The Seductress represents irresistible attraction, persuasion, temptation, sensuality, intelligence, cunning, subtlety, elegance and mystery.

- Brands that correspond to this archetype offer consumers a unique and hedonistic experience, stimulating them and arousing their desire. They also offer them variation and change.

- The shadow of the Seductress is the Femme Fatale, represented by a vampire, a bat, a snake, a viper, a praying mantis, a whip, Mata Hari. The Femme Fatale symbolizes manipulation, deception, control of another person, destruction and the dark, hidden and perverse side of life.

6. The Comedian

- Symbols of the Comedian include Charlie Chaplin, the Marx Brothers, a joker, a fool, a clown and a clown's red nose.

- The Comedian represents the fun side of life, play, humour, joy, amusement, happiness, laughter, jokes and jests.

- Brands that correspond to this archetype create a relationship of cooperation with consumers, through fun, play and humour; these brands always show the positive side of things.

- The shadow of the Comedian is the Madman, who represents ridicule, lack of control and disconnection from reality.

7. The Dreamer

- Symbols of the Dreamer include the Little Prince, Alice in Wonderland, the world of Disney, the sky, clouds, a butterfly.

- The Dreamer represent the flight of the imagination, travelling into fantasy to create possible worlds. Here, we are in the territory of creativity, originality, dreaming and fiction. This is a utopian world.

- Brands that correspond to this archetype offer a reality that is enchanted and magic, full of fantasy and imagination.

- The shadow of the Dreamer is the Fantasist, who symbolizes a complete lack of limits, eccentricity or exposure to total chance. The Fantasist also suffers, as does the Madman, from a major inability to connect with reality.

8. The Princess

- Symbols of the Princess include Isolde, Dulcinea, Sissi Emperatriz, Arwen (*The Lord of the Rings*), Snow White, vestal virgins, swans, the colour pink.

- The Princess represents beauty, external (physical) as well as internal (values), perfection, purity, light, clarity, goodness and inspiration,

- Brands that correspond to this archetype stand out for the 'goodness' of their image and their good product characteristics.

- The shadow of the Princess is the Witch, represented by a witch's hat, a broom, the colour black, Cruella de Vil – she symbolizes diabolic power, evil, revenge, ugliness (physical and psychological) and fear.

9. The Friend

- Symbols of the Friend include Sancho Panza, Obelix, Lassie, dogs and the links that form a chain.

- The Friend exemplifies company, closeness, support, loyalty, nobility, honesty, sincerity, authenticity, simplicity and sympathy.

- Brands that correspond to this archetype are very close to consumers. They empathize well with them, satisfy their main needs and talk their language. These brands are very reliable. Users feel that these brands understand them – these are brands they can trust, brands that make them feel safe. Such brands see their purchasers as 'partners'.

- The shadow of the Friend is the Traitor, who symbolizes falsehood, deceit, hypocrisy and lies. While the Villain is more about imitation and copying, the Traitor is more about a lack of credibility and trust.

10. The Mother

- Symbols of the Mother include a woman breastfeeding her baby, a cow giving milk to its calf, a female kangaroo with her baby in her pouch, Romulus and Remus and the she-wolf, Mother Earth, Nature, the colour green, Mother Teresa of Calcutta.

- The Mother exemplifies unconditional love, care, nutrition and feeding (psychologically as well as physiologically), life, sustenance, devotion, generosity and growth.

- Brands that correspond to this archetype offer consumers protection, safety, warmth, well-being and comfort.

- The shadow of the Mother is the Stepmother, symbolized by Snow White's Wicked Stepmother, a carnivorous plant, poison, the colour purple. The Stepmother represents egotism, coldness, envy and emptiness.

Archetypes, brands and marketing

Archetypes offer a graphic, simple, clear and intuitive language by which the essence and rhetoric of a brand may be understood. The model allows us to gain a better understanding of the deepest essence of a brand and how it relates to consumers. By discovering a brand's archetype we can see whether its communication is relevant, consistent and credible, and whether it has clear associations and a personality that is differentiated from its main competitors.

Once we know the archetype of a brand we are better able to define:

- Its positioning.

- The consistency of the different elements in the marketing mix (such as advertising, packaging and promotions).

- The future strategy of the brand. The archetype framework is an inexhaustible source of inspiration when seeking ideas for brand development.

There are many ways of assigning archetypes to brands. A brand may correspond perfectly to a single archetype or shadow, be halfway between two archetypes, or be ambivalent, based simultaneously on an archetype and its shadow. The model is sufficiently practical, flexible and dynamic to enable us to be precise when determining the archetype(s) and/or shadow(s) that define the essence, positioning and communication of a brand.

A successful brand generally has a strong relationship with its consumers because it is based on a positive and appealing archetype. Weak brands have no clear association with an archetype, or may be associated with a negative archetype, or one that is already dominated by a stronger brand.

Not surprisingly, when we work using the brand archetypes model, positive archetypes are used more often than negative ones or shadows. This is because brands always try to have a positive and appealing relationship with consumers.

Extended focus groups (lasting from three to four hours) are used to discover the archetype of a brand. They explore the brand image at several levels:

- **At a rational level**: at first, the brand's best-known side emerges. This information is superficial and predictable.

- **At an emotional level**: subsequently, more significant consumer brand experiences emerge. At this point its main values and differentiating characteristics are revealed.

- **At a symbolic level**: projective and creative exercises are used to reach a deeper level, and get to the essence of the brand.

The archetypes model is not used directly with the groups, but at the analysis stage, when the projections obtained from the groups are studied, and the archetype that best fits the brand is identified.

Sony's archetype

In 2005 Millward Brown carried out a qualitative study on young couples and families in Europe and Latin America, outlined in chapter 12. Sony was mentioned spontaneously in all the 18 countries covered, and its image was fairly consistent across all of them.

Sony was felt to have a long history and a solid reputation. It was considered to provide a great product experience in multiple product sectors associated with technology. It stood out in the present for its quality, technology, design, range of products, good service and trustworthiness. Young families have strong emotional ties to the Sony brand. In terms of the future, Sony was seen as an innovative brand at the cutting edge, which invests in R&D. In projective terms it was seen as:

- a man, mature, Japanese, a worker, intelligent, successful and friendly

- a futuristic house, technologically advanced, with a minimalist design, very bright, in which materials such as glass and aluminium predominate, a modern loft.

At the time of our research, Sony maintained a perfect balance between two positive and complementary archetypes: the Wise Man and the Friend. Within the territory of the Wise Man, Sony appropriated advanced technology, avant-garde design and know-how. It was felt to be an aspirational brand in the context of technological products. Within the territory of the Friend, Sony was felt to adapt technology to meet consumer needs. It moves closer to users, placing itself at their level – it talks their language. The brand offers them a guarantee – it can be trusted. Its products are also considered to be easy to use. Had we been asked to recommend a future strategy for Sony, we would have advised it to use its marketing to maintain the balance between these two archetypes.

The Nokia archetype

Nokia was mentioned spontaneously in the group discussions in 12 countries (11 in Europe and one in Latin America). Its main characteristics were ease of use (simplicity), intuitive software, quality, variety (of models, ringtones, prices and so on), design, innovation, leadership and a strong advertising image.

However, we detected some major changes at this time to Nokia's image. In the Czech Republic and Turkey, for example, the quality of its products was thought to have fallen. In the Czech Republic, the brand was starting to be seen as too mass-market, losing its aspirational personality. In other countries, Nokia's competitors were launching new handsets with innovative designs that users found attractive.

The Nokia brand had originally been positioned positively as the archetype of the Wise Man. It represented specialization in the mobile telephone sector, with wisdom, intelligence and know-how. It also connected with consumers through its ease of use, closeness and support as the Friend, giving it a very similar position to Sony. However, when we did this research, we uncovered an imbalance between the two archetypes that represented the brand. The Friend archetype was becoming increasingly important (the brand was becoming mass-market) and it was simultaneously becoming weaker in the territory of the Wise Man. This was a risk, because the brand was ceasing to be aspirational, and felt to be losing its leadership in technology and design. Should this have continued, it would leave the space for the archetype of the Wise Man empty – a major danger if a competitor were to move in.

Our advice to Nokia would have been to work to recover the balance between its two archetypes, by strengthening its image as an aspirational brand with state-of-the-art technology and innovative designs. (It should be emphasized that this study took place in 2005.)

Other brand archetypes

Nike was seen to be closest to the archetype of the Hero, which it represented in the sports world. Consumers associated it with leadership, a lifestyle, youth and modernity, quality and success in sports. Its advertising campaigns with famous sports personalities were top of mind. Its slogan 'Just do it' fitted well with the Hero figure. But Puma was seen as challenging for this positioning in several countries.

Coca-Cola and McDonald's were positioned between two archetypes: the King (strength and leadership) and the Seductress (attraction, irresistibility, the world of pleasure).

IKEA corresponded to the archetype of the Rebel, due to its inclusion of new trends, its differentiation and originality.

Microsoft was positioned between the archetype of the Wise Man (technology, innovation, intelligence, wisdom, specialization and know-how) and the shadow of the Tyrant (because of its monopolistic business approach). Brands rarely occupy negative or shadow territories.

Nestlé connected with consumers on the basis of warmth, protection, care, safety and guarantee, so it centred on the archetype of the Mother. Danone, in contrast, stood out for innovation, technology and intelligence applied to the development of new refrigerated products: closest to the territory of the Wise Man.

Nivea and Dove were positioned between two archetypes: the Mother (care and protection) and the Princess (natural beauty, internal values, the properties of their products and the quality of their formulae). Nivea was probably closer to the Mother and Dove to the Princess.

The brand images of Lego and Disney centred on the archetype of the Dreamer (imagination and fantasy were their chief asset).

Summary and conclusions

- Each brand has a particular view of the world, a way of thinking, together with certain values, and each has its own way of connecting with consumers. All of these elements come together to create its essence.

- Archetypes are symbols that are especially important for human beings. Archetypes are universal references – their meaning remain constant across time and space. What may vary is how the archetype is represented.

- The brand archetypes model allows us to discover the true, in-depth essence of a brand. The archetypes and their shadows provide a language that is symbolic, graphic, simple, clear, intuitive and practical. We can check out whether a brand's essence and language are relevant, consistent, credible and motivating, and determine whether it has clear brand associations and a personality that is differentiated from its competitors.

- The ten basic archetypes are the King, the Wise Man, the Hero, the Rebel, the Seductress, the Comedian, the Dreamer, the Princess, the Friend and the Mother. Their ten shadows are the Tyrant, the Charlatan, the Villain, the Anarchist, the Femme Fatale, the Madman, the Fantasist, the Witch, the Traitor and the Stepmother.

18

Communication efficiency (Renault case study) (Spain)

PEPE MARTÍNEZ

Background

When Renault introduced the Megane Scenic to the Spanish market, it was the first medium-sized people carrier, targeted at over-30 couples or modern families who wanted something slightly different. Later, Renault Spain decided to try to attract a younger target group: employed men and women aged between 25 and 35, living alone independently of their parents. It developed a new advertising strategy and asked its advertising agency to create a new campaign.

The concept it came up with was called 'Amish'. The agency turned it into an animatic, a rough version that comprises a series of drawn images and an audio track (words and music). It is a simpler, faster, more economical way of testing an idea than making the final film. Renault then approached Millward Brown Spain and asked us to carry out qualitative pre-test market research on the Amish animatic.

The animatic

The next figures show frames from the animatic.

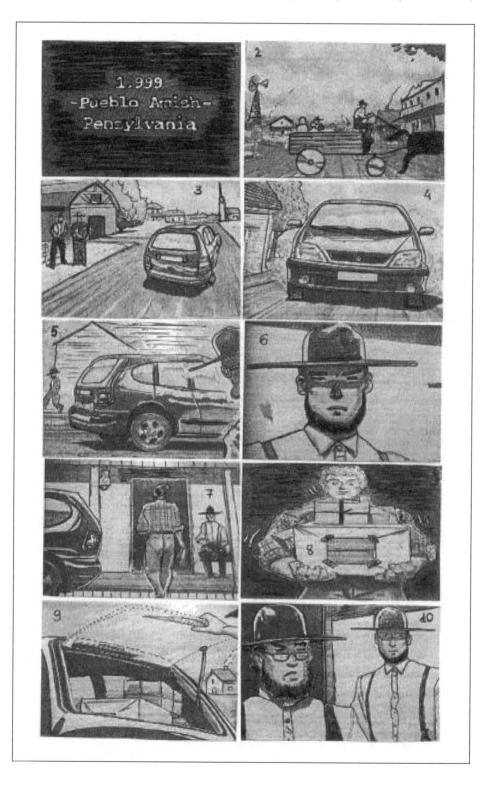

The action takes place in Pennsylvania in 1999. We are in a town occupied by the Amish sect. Its inhabitants still live as they did in the mid-19th century. The town's residents watch a Renault Scenic drive into the town. They are against progress and indifferent to cars.

The Scenic stops in front of a shop. Its driver gets out and goes in. A young Amish man sitting there looks at the car with interest. The driver comes out, puts his purchases in the car and closes the rear hatch door. He starts the car and drives off.

The shopkeeper comes out and reproaches the young Amish for allowing himself to be tempted by progress.

A few days later we see the young Amish man heading to the shop from another Scenic, parked in the same place as the previous one. He goes in, and after a while comes out with his purchases. The shopkeeper follows him, clearly disappointed, even angry with him for having succumbed to temptation.

The young man places his purchases in the car and closes the rear hatch. When he drives off we discover that what we thought was a Scenic is in fact a traditional horse-drawn Amish wagon, modified to look like a Scenic. As the 'Scenic-wagon' drives away, we see, in the foreground, the original Scenic driving down the street. A voiceover says, 'New Scenic. Evolution is contagious. Scenic. Evolutionary.'

The animatic we tested included music. A video with a fragment of the film *Witness* starring Harrison Ford was also shown (this too is set among the Pennsylvania Amish). If our pre-test showed the idea to have potential, the final ad would use the same style as *Witness*.

Research objectives

The main aim of this study was to pre-test the campaign, determine its potential and likely degree of advertising efficacy. More specifically, we wanted to determine:

- the degree to which the advertisement would have impact
- the advertising style (the way it connects with viewers)
- its originality
- its level of appeal

- comprehension of the story and the main messages

- how the 'personality' of the Renault Scenic came across

- the target group for the ad and the car

- the image of the Renault brand based on the execution

- possible ideas for changes and improvements (if it proved suitable).

Methodology

We used four focus groups to test the animatic, two in Madrid and two in Barcelona, each with between eight and ten respondents and lasting for two hours.

Two of the groups (one in each city) had Type 1 participants:

- half men and half women, aged 25 to 35, upper middle class, singles living alone, all in work, owning their own car and intending to change in the next six months to a car in the middle to upper segment.

The other two groups were Type 2:

- men aged 30 to 40, upper middle class and living with their partner; with children or planning to have them, all in work, owning their own car and intending to change in the next six months to a car in the middle to upper segment.

Subsequently, of course, we analysed the data obtained, structured and interpreted it, and presented the results to Renault..

Results

The film Witness

We showed the movie to respondents after presenting them with the animatic. Most had seen it at a cinema. They remembered it fairly well, and recognized Harrison Ford and the lead actress, as well as the Amish culture and values, although they did not use the name Amish.

In the free and spontaneous discourse during the groups, respondents mentioned that the Amish are craftspeople who reject technological progress, live anchored in the past, have their own rules and regulations, keep their distance from the rest of the world, respect others, and demonstrate a spirit of comradeship.

Responses to the animatic

We showed respondents the animatic twice over. It was impactful because of the originality of the Amish setting, the humour, the cinematographic style, the shot at the end of the 'Scenic-wagon' (the high spot of the advertisement) and the final claim, 'Evolutionary'.

The advertising style was described as: *'striking', 'high impact', 'surprising', 'different', 'original', 'innovative', 'funny' and 'nice'.* The creative idea was very positively received in all four groups.

The structure of this ad was based on an axis that ran from non-evolution to evolution, as shown in the following table. The Amish context works well because of the strong contrast between it and the values Renault wished to associate with the Scenic.

Evolution	Non-evolution
Change and novelty	Traditional classic values
Modernity, fashion and ephemeral	Eternal, perennial
The young Amish man	The older Amish man
The Renault Scenic	The conventional cars
A medium-size people carrier	Typical cars

In the animatic the Amish people represent the world of non-evolution. Symbolically they stand for conventional cars, in contrast to the Scenic. The older Amish man represents values associated with 'no progress'. The ad positions the Scenic as if it was the first car ever invented. Its young owner represents the new target group of buyers. Potential owners identify with the young Amish man and his irresistible temptation. The three people are perfectly characterized and each one plays a fundamental role in the advertisement.

Respondents described the young stranger as:

• aged between 30 and 35

• single and independent

- in the upper middle socioeconomic group

- dynamic and active

- has an adventurous lifestyle and likes travelling; he is thought to be passing through the Amish town

- a role model who triggers a rethink of Amish values (and by extension, of motivations and attitudes to cars on the market).

The young Amish man:

- was thought to be more or less the same age as the stranger

- aroused empathy in viewers because his conflict reminds them of other difficult life situations

- is seen as caught between desire for the car and the rules of his community

- resolves his conflict in a way that was found delightful, funny and striking

- represents openness to change and interest in everything new and revolutionary; he efficiently plays the role of the motivated purchaser and viewers can identify with this.

Lastly, the older Amish man:

- was sometimes thought to be the father of the younger Amish man; other respondents thought he was his grandfather, or an unrelated acquaintance

- represents tradition, rules and control, and symbolizes the most typical, traditional and conventional car

- is against evolution, not unlike the attitude of many drivers to the new-concept cars that were being launched in 1999.

Respondents suggested this character be shown as being tempted by the Renault Scenic, either at the end of the advertisement or in follow-up advertisements.

The car plays a central role in the advertisement and animatic. It and its features were felt to be very relevant. It creates genuine desire which translates into purchase interest. Respondents found these features the most striking:

- its newness; respondents realized it was a relaunched Scenic

- the openable rear hatch window

- its lines, especially the rear, together with the references to the new front

- its size, roominess and volume, and versatility (suitable for the city or countryside, passengers or load)
- the new younger target group
- the colour (red in the animatic): respondents suggested a bright, modern and young colour, perhaps yellow.

Respondents thought the two target groups (thirties couples and families, and younger singles) were quite compatible.

The music was well liked: it was felt to be young and informal, suitable for the images and storyline, and fitted the uninhibited personality of the young characters.

The 'Evolutionary' claim ('Evolucionario') impacted strongly on the groups due to its phonetic quality and because it is an invented word in Spanish. Some respondents believed they had not heard it correctly the first time, and this made them concentrate more the second time the animatic was shown. Semantically the word is associated with evolution and revolution, and gave the impression that the car really is innovative.

This campaign had a positive effect on the image of the Renault brand, which was described as:

- the pioneer
- innovative
- creative
- evolving
- renewing itself.

Transactional analysis

The transactional analysis model proved to be a very helpful way of analysing this advertisement. It was developed by Eric Berne* in the early 1950s, based on observations in group psychotherapy. Berne recognized the influence of his teachers, Paul Federn* and Erik Erikson*. A branch of the psychoanalytical theory of the personality, transactional analysis has a social approach and studies the ways in which we communicate with and relate to other people. Although it originated in the context of psychotherapy, it is now applied to, for example, counselling, companies and organizations (consultancy, organizational culture, team work, intra- and inter-departmental relationships and so on), social work, education, training, market research and marketing.

Transactional analysis distinguishes between three possible states in a single individual: the parent, adult and child. It defines an ego state as a system of emotions and thoughts that is accompanied by a set of behaviour patterns. These ego states are manifested internally (in what we think and feel in a situation) as well as externally (in what we say and do).

When we interact as a **parent**, what we have inherited from our parents, and our sense of duty and obligation become important. The parent aspect is made up of everything we have introjected from culture, traditions, rules and values through the social medium in which we grew up.

When we interact as a **child** we give free rein to our desires, impulses, needs and emotions, to our expressiveness, affectivity, spontaneity, creativity, enthusiasm, liveliness and intuitions. The child always tends towards what we would like to do.

When we interact as an **adult** the most mature part of our personality comes into play. This involves independence, autonomy, authenticity, common sense, reason and good judgement, the unique and different being we have inside. The adult takes into account the needs of both ourselves and others, and also takes the environment into consideration. The adult tends to make the most suitable decision on all occasions.

The three characters in the animatic map well onto these three roles: the older Amish man plays the parent, the stranger the child, and the younger Amish man the adult (see the next figure).

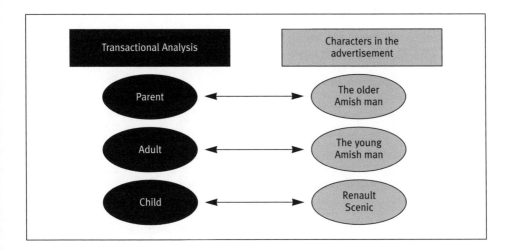

Viewers identify with the young Amish man. They found his conflict interesting, and the tension increased noticeably as the advertisement progressed. They expected a fight or an argument, for the young man to be subjugated and forced to give up the car.

The way the story is resolved is of fundamental importance. The humorous solution relieves the tension between the different forces in the ad, and takes the viewer into the worlds of fantasy and imagination..

Conclusions and recommendations

Our conclusions from the focus group information were:

- The campaign will be impactful.

- The target market is likely to react very positively.

- It puts across well the message that the Renault Scenic is a new concept in cars.

- The advantages and unusual features of the car – its lines, its rear window, its roominess and visibility – are covered effectively.

- The ad is felt to be motivational by the new target-group. It increases interest in the Renault Scenic.

- The ad will make the Renault brand appear more innovative – indeed the Scenic was one of the models that has led to the greatest evolution of Renault's image in general.

- The ad is easy to understand. No negatives emerged.

We advised Renault that the creative idea of the Amish animatic could be used effectively to relaunch the Renault Scenic. In making the final film, we recommended that they:

- take care with the contextualization of the Amish town

- choose the cast and convey the characterization carefully

- take care with the acting, as this advertisement is based on what the characters do – their movements and their looks, gestures and attitude

- make the scene showing the 'Scenic-wagon' the core of the advertisement

- ensure the car and its different features are clearly visible.

Renault followed our recommendations, and the Amish advertisement was first broadcast on 13 September 1999. Because TV ads are very short, detailed shots of the young stranger were cut, but his presence is implied by the presence of the car (see the following images).

Advertising post-test

In October that year we conducted another study to check whether the Amish advertisement was working as planned. This advertising post-test used the same methodology as the pre-test: four focus groups with the same sample characteristics.

At the start of the groups we asked respondents to name all the TV car ads they could recall, to check whether the Amish advertisement would be mentioned spontaneously. We grouped those mentioned into advertisements that:

- used movie references or famous people (as the Scenic ad did)

- used humour (including two Scenic ads, the Amish campaign and the previous advertisement, 'Widows')

- centred on the features of the vehicle.

The Amish ad was mentioned in a completely spontaneous way in all four focus groups, making it clear that the campaign was impactful and resonated with viewers.

The groups were now asked about this campaign in detail. They recalled the style, context, characters, story, product (the Scenic) and brand (Renault). The advertising style was particularly well liked. Its most characteristic features were:

- the cinematographic look and feel

- the music and absence of speech, which meant that viewers had to concentrate to discover its message

- the conflict-based storyline and the humorous surprise ending.

Respondents commented:

'I like the visual style of the ad, I really like the colours.'

'The ad is well-made, it is nice and striking.'

'You see the ad and it isn't one you'd surf away from, because you think that it's a film or something like that.'

'It's different, because it tells you a story, a story about evolution, in comparison with how backward that society is, that community.'

'It's an amusing ad. It's an ad that you remember, especially because of the final scene of the wagon, which is the humour of the ad.'

'It hooks you, he gets what he wants.'

'It's really good.'

'It's very expressive.'

The music was also liked a lot, seen as young, modern and dynamic, and well suited to the car. The context (Amish culture) was easily identified and interpreted correctly, and the characters' roles were understood, as were the values they represent:

It was understood that the young Amish man was intended to show that the target group for this car had broadened:

'When the older man turns away, and the girls or women do too, then only the boy looks at it, it seems that they want to advertise above all for young people aged from 25 to 35 years old. They want to tempt young people. They want to change the tradition of the Mormons.'

'I'm not married, but I like this car, I like its lines ... and I also like going to the countryside and driving around in the car. This is a car that is good for everything.'

The product plays a very central role, and viewers noticed that it was a new Scenic:

'You understand that it breaks with what's old, that it is amazing, it has new lines, a revolutionary line, and the ad says something like 'evolutionary'.'

'It must be that they have brought out a better one or something like that, and that is why they're advertising it again.'

'The image of this car is a bit like that of the ad, that it evolves.'

'It's for people who need something intermediate, who don't need a people carrier, but not a tiny car either. It's roomy, but not as expensive as a people carrier.'

The Scenic execution had a positive effect on Renault's overall image. The brand was felt to be advancing and evolving – the ad modernizes it and makes it seem more dynamic. It gives it a personality that is young, innovative and pioneering.

We recommended to Renault that they continue to use this advertisement.

Summary and conclusions

- In 1999 Millward Brown Spain to carried out a qualitative advertising pre-test on an ad for the Renault Scenic with an Amish setting.

- We used a focus group methodology, and the transactional analysis model to interpret the information.

- The advertisement was very well received, and put across the intended messages clearly. We recommended to Renault that they use it, which they did.

- Later that year we carried out a qualitative advertising post-test, using the same methodology. It confirmed that the advertisement had been a success.

19
Ethnic communication (case study) (Italy)

Mimma Novelli and Monica Spinola

Starting point

In 2003 Millward Brown Italy conducted a qualitative study with immigrants. The main objective was to analyse the responses to advertising communications in Italy by people from different ethnic groups, cultures and languages.

Introduction

Immigrants necessarily react to the media and promotional messages of their host society in a way that reflects demographic factors such as their age, income group, family composition and occupation. They watch television, look at billboards and are exposed to displays in supermarkets and shopping centres. Therefore, they come across products and services which integrate the graphic and linguistic codes of their new country. But they interpret them according to their original cultural and social norms.

How does this interpretation and integration process take place? How and at what levels do the communication codes of the host market connect with different cultural perceptions? These were the broad questions we were trying to answer. More specifically, we asked:

- What important elements do immigrants take from advertising communications?

- How is this reflected in their consumption choices and behaviour?

- What can be done to communicate more effectively to these new targets?

And more specifically still, we explored:

- What are their criteria for enjoying or disliking an advertisement?

- What are their means of comprehension and approval?

- Which elements from the execution do they accept or reject?

- Which types of communication do they feel closest to? Which types are best at generating identification, and which ones generate most aspiration?

- How does advertising fulfil their needs and desires? And how does it impact on their behaviour?

Our procedure

We first looked to select samples to enable us to tackle this very broad subject. We segmented Italy's immigrant population according to a number of criteria, and chose three communities, all among the most numerous ethnic groups present in Italy, and from three geographical areas of origin: the Maghreb (Tunisia and Morocco), Eastern Europe (Albania and Romania), and the Far East (Philippines and China).

The research design consisted of two steps: 12 group discussions and 18 ethnographic interviews.

Step 1: Group discussions

Within each selected community, we carried out four group discussions in order to understand how immigrants talked about advertising, how they perceived it, and what role it played in their life. The groups were composed of:

- men or women (not mixed), all possessing residence permits

- working, studying and/or with a home in Italy for at least four years

- subdivided by age:

    - children and pre-adolescents, aged 11 to 14

    - late teens plus, aged 16 to 20

    - young single adults, aged 20 to 25

    - adults, heads of household and mothers, aged 25 to 40

- located in Milan and Treviso.

These groups were moderated with the help of a 'cultural mediator' of the same mother tongue and culture as the community. The discussions started with a phase of spontaneous reconstruction (what type of advertising they had in mind). This was followed by deeper exploration of the advertising landscape of their country of origin, then they were shown a selection of Italian advertising campaigns and their reactions were sought.

Step 2: Ethnographic interviews

For direct observation of how advertising was perceived by individuals, we carried out ethnographic interviews. We chose from each community:

- family units of at least three members (father, mother and at least one child of school age)

- individual men and women aged 20 to 30, half single and half with a family not living with them in Italy

- located in Rome and Treviso.

The interviews were conducted into two phases: one in the respondent's home (in the evening, while preparing the meal, during and after dinner, and with the television always switched on), and the other away from home (for instance doing the shopping, picking up children from school, in meeting places, going for a walk, visiting shops).

Self-perception and self-image

The respondents expressed a common need to systematically define their personal identity, family identity and social identity at two distinct levels: one, their country of origin with its peculiar culture, values and traditions, and two, their home country reality and values. This bipolarized image led to a feeling of subordination which varied among respondents depending on their ethnic group, age, level of education and socioeconomic situation, and length of residence in Italy. However, across all the communities there were three common frames of reference:

- attachment to their origins (place, culture, habits and rituals), and feelings of pride, detachment or simple nostalgia

- their present life in Italy and living and working conditions, at which they all looked with realism and strong concern for practical planning (particularly young people and fathers for their children)

- the recollection of their journey from their home country to Italy, acting as a symbolic and emotionally charged bridge through space and time.

They also showed a common ability to repress their emotions with reserve and modesty, despite the shared perception that they were living in a place between two worlds that could easily transform into a 'land of nowhere'.

When asked to think about Italy, the respondents primarily focused on tangible facts:

- economic well-being

- free public services

- women's emancipation in the family, at work and in public institutions

- limited family size

- fast pace of life.

They all mentioned differences in values between their home and host countries, but there were significant variations in attitudes towards them:

- closed and impermeable among some ethnic groups (especially Filipinos)

- more defensive among adults

- more curious among young people (especially Maghrebis and Romanians)

- conflictual if projected onto children, especially younger ones born and raised in Italy

- often curious but tinted with anxiety among women (especially Romanians and Albanians).

Immigrants also shared the need to unify their composite and somewhat contradictory world, preserving their own values and original culture, reconciling the two different cultural systems, but keeping distant from the values of the host country for fear of complete assimilation. Their integration was mostly practical: working in Italy, speaking the language, being among Italians, having children who go to school in Italy. This did not require them to change or question their home values and habits, which were maintained within their family cell and the migrant community.

The relationship with their origins

All the respondents had found ways of maintaining a strong bond with their home country:

- in their leisure time (at specific meeting places such as churches, bars, restaurants and nightclubs)

- in their food habits (cooking home recipes, using ingredients bought or sent from relatives back home)

- in their rituals (respecting both religious and other conventions)

- in their homes (interior decor, ornaments, and physical layout, sometimes including an area for prayer

- above all through media (see the next page).

This sat alongside leisure interests, relationships and other involvement with Italians, at levels and with focuses that varied:

- more interaction at the workplace for adult men

- only in terms of appearances (Filipinos)

- common aspiration and desires among Romanian and Albanian women

- more women-to-women interaction among Maghrebi mothers due to the priority given to their maternal role

- systematic interaction for all mothers as the result of stronger involvement in their children's education.

A common characteristic observed in all the interviewees was prudence, reflected in:

- the attention paid to their own identity, individual and collective – their origin, self-confidence, role, image and external situation

- the realism with which they assessed their situation, avoiding deep evaluations and implications

- the gradualism with which they reconciled their reality and their expectations.

The surroundings: actors and roles

For the respondents, the mass media acted as a screen through which they grasped Italian culture. Advertising was the place where the host culture was 'on stage', and brands acted as identificational elements. Retail outlets were the place of action.

The media

They used the media in a wide-ranging and diversified way, apparently more so than native Italians. Their media include press, television, radio, billboards and didactic publications, particularly the free press, fulfilled the need for contact and knowledge (for instance, Maghrebi women put great store by 'embroidery' magazines), and sources of information on practical issues like paying national insurance. For news and information from their home countries, they relied on satellite TV and some ethnic newspapers: for example there is a Philippine newspaper distributed by the church.

They selected television programmes that were compliant with their home values (which rejected excessive eroticism, sensuality or feminine nudity) and adapted to their level of language skills and education. All the men mentioned sport, and other common preferences in style and content were for:

- simple satire that is entertaining and simultaneously helps them further understand and criticize the Italian culture (such as *Striscia la Notizia*)

- romantic programmes, drama or reality television series (such as *100 Vetrine, Stranamore, Verissimo*)

- programmes targeted at young adults (*Amici, Zelig, Camera Cafè*).

Immigrants are a multifaceted and demanding media target, who watch television programmes in a critical and active way to serve several purposes: observe, learn, be entertained and be informed.

Advertising and brands

Advertising and brands are seen as a place of emphasis, seduction, transgression and imaginary adventure, functions that are perceived as dominating informational content. Most looked at them with both attention and suspicion. They also expressed an overall perception of excess and overwhelming materialism, which was transformed into cultural arrogance.

They particularly rejected Italian advertising that included, in terms of representation:

- everything connected to the private sphere (sexuality and the body)
- aggressiveness, crudeness, violence
- deviant behaviour, switching of gender or family roles even if portrayed in a humorous way
- the improper use of animals
- double meanings, allusions, plays on words (perceived as irritating and too difficult to understand).

And in terms of content:

- untruthfulness, effects not borne out by experience (with for example detergents)
- too many actions and performances that create illusions
- the call to buy (*'as if you had to obey'*).

On the other hand they appreciated, and expressed a desire to see, in terms of content:

- precise information
- elements that make it possible to learn and understand
- simple, didactic and straightforward demonstrations.

And in terms of contexts:

- situations that activated positive emotions (endearments, family scenes)
- harmony and cleanliness
- polite tones, light humour, comical aspects that can be understood by children
- images that make one dream or hope, and that show openness towards other people.

Respondents also compared Italian advertising with the advertising landscape of their home countries. The main similarities were because of global brands. They perceived differences in tone, style and content. Their home-country advertising usually:

- lasted longer than in Italy

- frequently used spokespeople

- contained different expressive codes: respect for women, for family roles, basic narrative styles, soft and reassuring emotional atmospheres, absence of deviant or anxiety-inducing behaviours, use of simple and immediate humour

- did not feature alcoholic drinks, condoms, intimate products and the like.

In summary, there was particular appreciation of two types of Italian advertising. The first can be categorized as 'family advertising' (predominantly of food), which was accessible and easy to understand, placed the product in the foreground, came across as emotional and empathic, non-discriminating and universal, used a visual and verbal language that did not create perceptual or linguistic difficulties, took place in realistic and identifiable contexts, and showed the product in its usage context (on the plate, at the moment of consumption). The second was 'entertaining advertising' in which the spokespersons were famous and familiar, stories were told in instalments and followed with curiosity, there was simple humour, fantasy (surreal contexts, personalities, and pretexts to enable people to accept the particular setting without touching on deep values) and the products were central.

There was common rejection of advertising that showed narrative or symbolic distortion – of roles, values or emotions, whatever its objective (to attract attention, create involvement or seduce). This created a strongly defensive attitude. Advertising without any relevance of tone, particularly regarding important themes and ones of greater tangible interest (money, communication, the family) was also rejected, and so was advertising perceived to have deceptive or untruthful content or promote excess.

Retail outlets

Retail outlets are places of action, a mode that fitted particularly well with the pragmatism of these respondents. They are also the place where advertising is or is not validated. Immigrants go there for leisure purposes, and also to reason, reflect, measure up, and decide whether to buy. It is at the retail outlet that the brand materializes.

The respondents saw a brand as accessible if it got the basics right, guaranteed functionality, was affordable and its price reflected the value they attributed to the product. It was seen as inaccessible if it was too expensive and also if it 'communicated other things' and 'to other people' (because it was associated with values that differed from theirs, did not express clear promises, or imposed a type of world that was different and distant from their own). The brand acted as a parameter for assessing their belonging to the codes of the Italian system of consumption, and an element of identification that made them seem and feel either more or less Italian.

Summary and conclusions

- Although there is much quantitative knowledge about immigrants, there is far less knowledge about how they perceive the world in which they have arrived.

- Being an immigrant is a transitional state, not a definitive one. There is a clash between the desire for stability and belonging (especially after the instability, fear and difficulties that often accompanied the decision to emigrate) and the desire to retain one's original identity. Respondents showed pragmatism and prudence, favouring observation over involvement, rational assessment over emotional commitment.

- Because of its broad reach, advertising offers a convenient route to immersion in the host society, and a touchstone for the level of integration and the host country's values.

- Immigrants favour advertising with which they can identify, and which is not in conflict with their existing values and cultural norms. They reject advertising that does not seem relevant to them, that is difficult to understand, and when elements of the mix are culturally unacceptable to them.

- The retail outlet is the place of action, where people put into practice their choices and rejections. The brand acted as a parameter for assessing their belonging to the codes of the Italian system for consumption, and an element of identification that made them seem and feel either more or less Italian.

20
Targeting doctors (Eli Lilly case study) (Spain)

Enrique González

Introduction

Much market research, both qualitative and quantitative, involves pharmaceutical products. Researchers work on gathering and analysing input from doctors (GPs and specialists), distribution channels (pharmacists) and patients.

The Millward Brown Spain pharma department has considerable experience of working with major pharmaceutical companies. This has shown us just how complex it is to conduct qualitative research with the medical profession. Moderating a focus group or in-depth interview requires more effort than for other types of respondent. Moderators have to approach the research in a particular way; they need to know their facts and have a good knowledge of medical words and jargon. They also need to know how doctors think, feel and relate to their patients and to pharmaceutical companies.

Doctors find it hard to separate their professional from their personal lives. Most of their discourse centres on being a doctor, which dominates all their other life roles. It can be difficult to move them from a super-rational level of discourse, and from discussions in which they sound like encyclopaedias. We believe focus groups and in-depth interviews with doctors work best when we get them to bring their other roles into play, they look for explanations that are more real and are based more on experience, and different facets of the medical professional emerge – the cognitive and emotional levels, as well as the level of 'true beliefs'. Doctors need to commit themselves to the subject and task in hand, before they put forward arguments that will help us gain a clear understanding of the dynamics of the pharmaceutical market.

We have to create a relaxed and informal atmosphere, and do everything we can to penetrate their professional armour, get them to take off their white coat and remove their tie, and allow us to see inside their persona. We need to remember there is a personal as well as an analytical side to the medical profession: doctors have feelings, empathize to a greater or lesser extent with their patients, have their own ways of dealing with pharmaceutical companies, hold certain beliefs about drug brands, and so on. We know we have done a good job of moderating a discussion with doctors when each participant discovers something about themselves during the group or personal interview.

Doctors are very comfortable taking part in meetings, talks and the like, so they can fully accept and internalize the research task. Our job is to find some way to surprise them, to make them break with routine, and move out of the role they know how to play so well.

We have found that the best way to get doctors to relax is by giving them a task: answering a short questionnaire, doing exercises (individual as well as whole-group), analysing clinical cases. These are attempts to get them to enter the world of reflection and thought through action, movement and stimulation.

The research setting

If an interview or group is held in a setting such as a hospital, surgery or doctor's office, this encourages professional discourse. Doctors keep looking at the clock, they make researchers wait, seem reluctant to deal with them, and treat them as if they were medical representatives. Psychologically, doctors are asking themselves, *'What am I going to say to this interviewer?'*

Working on our terrain (say, our office or a hotel), the situation is different. Doctors have accepted the appointment and really do display a more helpful attitude. In a sense, they are more of a person and less of a doctor. In this environment, they are more likely to think, *'I wonder what this is about.'* So this is the option we prefer.

Research approaches

Conversations with doctors take place at two levels, the scientific and the intuitive or unconscious. Scientific discourse is more common. Here, doctors use their authority. They are in control of the most valuable things a person possesses, health and life. They are very comfortable talking about scientific matters. Talk like this is highly predictable, and purely descriptive, rational and cognitive.

Spontaneous discourse (which provides access to the unconscious level) tends to be less common. It is unscripted and extends beyond knowledge and science.

It makes doctors feel more insecure and uncertain. Moderators have to be alert for keys in the discourse that can lead in some way to spontaneity.

The composition of the group and the group dynamic are also important. Doctors tend to have a group bond even before they arrive at the discussion venue. The moderator is seen as a threat and outsider, and needs skill and experience to guide the group successfully.

We have found that it is easier to get doctors to help us when we are open with them from the start. We have to be clear from the outset what we expect of the respondents, in both the tasks we ask them to complete and their attitude and willingness to contribute. However, if we go too far, we risk creating the opposite effect to that intended.

There are four basic approaches, shown in the next figure. The moderator must know now only how to use each technique, but how to switch from one to another as smoothly and consistently as possible.

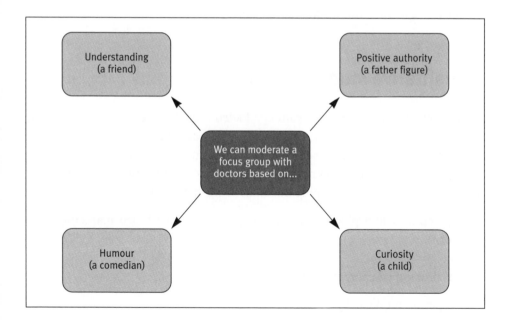

Positive authority requires a fair degree of self-confidence from the moderator. In gaining respondents' trust they also gain in authority. Authority can be won via the introduction, body language, the moderator's approach (the way they ask questions), and their way of changing the subject. The aim is to establish a relationship of equal partners with the respondents.

In the **curiosity** approach the moderator expresses surprise and a certain ingenuousness in response to the doctors, who play a teaching and demonstrating role. Doctors find this very gratifying.

With **understanding**: the moderator's archetype is a friend. The aim is to make the respondent feel that the moderator appreciates what they are saying, that nothing is being manipulated and that the information given is not being distorted. We are talking about honesty, transparency and sincerity.

Doctors in Spain have recently found themselves on the defensive with patients, pharmaceutical companies and the government. They are being forced to sign agreements and to accept responsibilities. This is why they find it hard to open up and feel nervous.

The last approach involves **humour.** The moderator plays the comedian to facilitate contact with the doctors: joking, being affable and taking things with a certain cynicism (but always in moderation). If the doctors are happy to play this game and come to joke amongst themselves, we enter a new dimension. It can be therapeutic and cathartic for the participants.

A qualitative study for Lilly

In 2006 Millward Brown Spain conducted a qualitative study for Eli Lilly, with the aim of understanding how doctors relate to and interact with the Internet. In recent years, the Internet has become an increasingly important commercial tool. Pharmaceutical companies now use it as one of the main ways of maintaining relationships and keeping in contact with specialists.

The options in a pharmaceutical company's Internet-based marketing plan include:

- a virtual medical representative

- ordering products by e-mail

- taking part in virtual congresses.

Before exploring the potential for virtual services, the client wanted to know how the medical profession use the Internet, what they think of it and what motivates their use.

Research objectives

At a diagnostic level, we wanted the most accurate picture possible of:

- the use doctors make of the Internet
- their relationship with it
- what they think of it
- its strong and weak points in terms of their jobs and their everyday practice
- any differences in attitude between those in the public and private health care system
- usage habits
- hardware.

For the future, the aim was to determine the key factors and scenarios that would encourage doctors to make more use of the Internet:

- the current situation and the likelihood of future use
- expectations regarding use
- particular scenarios of likely further use
- reactions to pharmaceutical company proposals to encourage greater professional use.

Methodology

Our qualitative research included both general practitioners and specialists (in gynaecology, rheumatology, endocrinology, traumatology and psychiatry). We talked to these groups separately to avoid any clashes because of the tensions between specialists and general practitioners in the Spanish health care system.

Four focus groups were held, each lasting two hours, with seven to eight respondents. The sample was structured on the basis of:

- Age: categorized as up to and including 39, and over 40.
- Private or public practice: each group contained 70 per cent of doctors in the public health system and 30 per cent from private health care. We

believed the computer equipment available and the time they have to use it would differ, as was indeed the case.

- Location: two groups each in Madrid and Barcelona.

Results

Computerisation of the surgery

Although doctors agree that computers are useful and play a key role in modernizing their working practices, the majority had experienced problems in computerizing their surgeries or consulting rooms. All said they were unable to take full advantage of the potential of modern technology, or use it as often as they would like, because:

- Most medical centres had either no IT department or offered only a minimum level of support.
- Different medical centres use incompatible programs, making data transfer impossible.
- Few good Internet programs were available for medical purposes.
- There was also felt to be a lack of practical computing applications that really do solve problems and would motivate them to use the Internet.
- The doctors themselves lacked computing experience, not just with the Internet, but also with basic programs such as databases and PowerPoint.
- Time pressures meant the doctors had very little opportunity to improve their computing skills.

Perceptions, however, varied by:

- Age: younger doctors knew more about computing, and found it more intuitive and quick and easy to learn. Older doctors found it harder to adapt to new technologies and more difficult to understand them.
- Location: doctors in Barcelona had a greater knowledge of new technologies and used them more.
- Type of medical centre: let's the see differences.

Doctors in public health centres tended to see computerization as a control mechanism:

'It seems that they only installed it to see what you prescribe.'

Computer equipment is very basic, and doctors find it difficult to access the Internet because there are only a few connections available, passwords are required, and what can be accessed is often restricted.

Private centres provide doctors with more IT training and allow them greater access to technological resources:

'They gave us some training courses that were quite good.'

These doctors have greater access to the Internet, and the computer equipment generally includes peripherals such as speakers, a printer and a webcam.

However, because all doctors can access the Internet from home, and have found ways of getting online when access is restricted (using other computers or sharing passwords with their colleagues) there are few differences in practice between the private and public sectors. The differences usually involve how frequently a doctor can get online.

One significant factor we identified was the amount of time doctors spend using computers for consultations. Frequent usage led to faster learning as well as discovery of the broader potential of the Internet.

Doctors and the Internet at work

In doing their job, doctors now consider the Internet to be an indispensable standard tool. It gives them access to all sorts of information, and saves time, paper and space.

'It's the big filing cabinet.'

However, most respondents had had no proper training on its use, so were not able to take full advantage of online resources. They had learned by trial and error or using advice from more knowledgeable (often younger) colleagues:

'Luckily the nurses are usually on the ball and they give us a hand with this, as otherwise ...'

This is an interesting inversion: although older doctors know more about medical matters, younger ones are more expert on new technologies.

The doctors access professional and other information using:

- General search engines, mainly Google and Yahoo, for general information relevant to their everyday practice (pathologies, medicines, recent studies and so on):

  'I always have one of those general search engines open in my surgery, it is very useful. I ask the patient questions and consult at the same time: it's very practical.'

- Web pages specifically designed for the medical community: mainly university sites such as Navarra or Houston, listings of pharmaceutical substances (formularies), the interactive doctor, subscription to online journals, guides on standardized protocols and so on. For the most part, they use these to look up information and resolve queries, read interesting articles or follow studies.

- Intranet, e-mail and specialist discussion forums for professionals.

Doctors value access to large amounts of information. We were keen to find out how they felt about patients having access to this same information online. This proved controversial, and divided opinion. Some doctors believed the available information causes patients high levels of alarm, which is counterproductive for their clinical practice:

  'A patient came to see me saying that he had leukaemia, because he had seen I don't know what about symptoms on the Internet – and there was nothing wrong with him at all.'

Others, however, felt it could be positive.

  'The more patients know and the better informed they are, the better it is for everyone.'

E-mail

Eli Lilly was very keen to obtain in-depth information about e-mail use, attitudes and reasons for using it. Our doctors considered it a very convenient, easy means of communication and a good way to obtain information. They used it:

- to communicate with other doctors and departments, for instance consulting about uncertainties and patient follow-up

- to subscribe to specialist journals, to read interesting articles, broaden their knowledge and learn about new products

- to send or receive tests and analyses

- to get information related to their own discipline: congresses, discussion forums, news and so on.

That they were very busy during the day affected their choice of times for going online, which were usually:

- before they started work, just to check their mail

- during their surgery to quickly request information

- at the end of the day to resolve any outstanding questions or issues, check their mail again and answer it

- at weekends to delve more deeply into interesting aspects of their work, check their mail, take part in discussion forums and take online courses (the most advanced users).

Their online frequencies varying from several times a day to once a week, depending on their age and ease of Internet access.

Our doctors were well aware of risks and problems such as unwanted advertising (spam) and computer viruses. To counteract these, their strategies were to:

- only answer messages when they know the sender

- restrict areas of interest in journals, webpages and portals which request their e-mail address

- create several e-mail addresses to divide the information that is sent to each.

  'I have three e-mail accounts, and I give one or another, depending on what I want.'

The potential of the Internet: spontaneous creation

We held a brainstorm during the second part of the group sessions and asked the doctors, first to come up with ideas on how the Internet could be better exploited to help them do their job, and second, to evaluate ideas put forward by Lilly. The doctors made five main types of spontaneous suggestion, including some that were not as new as they imagined, or similar to the client's proposals:

• bibliography

• interaction and information about patients

• communication between professionals

• computing

• practical tools.

A **bibliography** was seen as useful to provide access to specialist documents, perhaps as a compendium of published articles, classified according to speciality and date of publication, with one index per speciality and the option of searching by subject, author and key words. The doctors thought the pharmaceutical company would create the site, although they would prefer it to be run by an impartial independent body.

Instead of subscriptions to well-known specialist journals, they suggested the pharmaceutical company could sponsor access to online versions.

To get information from talks and congresses, they suggested a compendium of summaries classified according to speciality, interest and date of publication; an index of abstracts, together with a chance to read the whole paper, if desired; and multimedia presentations – video, audio or slides, with subtitles where appropriate.

Their ideas about uses for **information flow** between doctors and various parties included:

• online consultations with central services (such as pharmaceutical suppliers and x-ray facilities) and hospitals to which they referred their patients

• the possibility of digitizing the results of diagnostic tests and sending them via the Internet (with the pharmaceutical company sponsoring the equipment needed)

• an open communication channel with patients using e-mail, for initial consultations, answering queries and the like (they suggested the pharmaceutical company might pay them to spend, say, two hours a week doing this)

- SMS reminders to patients' mobile phones to either come for an appointment or take their medication (something the pharmaceutical company could supply and manage).

Our doctors suggested the Internet could be used to enhance **communications between professionals** through:

- a communication channel for specialists in specific fields using e-mail or video-conferencing, with the pharmaceutical company financing the time they spent using it
- an online community of doctors: a discussion forum to debate questions, resolve queries and help keep up to date on new drugs (with the pharmaceutical company creating the virtual space).

When it came to **computing**, doctors wanted:

- a help desk, plus access to IT support staff (which the pharmaceutical company would pay for)
- training courses on, for example, general computing and Internet skills, medical management programs, and presentation programs for talks (with funding again being the client role).

Finally, doctors said they'd like to be able to access a number of **practical tools:**

- a library of presentations for talks, including preparation tools, templates, illustrative drawings and videos
- articles and videos on clinical skills (such as bandaging, protocols for treating different diseases and the validation of scales).

Again, the pharmaceutical company function would be to provide the content and maintain the site.

Evaluation of concepts put forward by Eli Lilly

Five concepts provided by the client were presented to the doctors in the focus groups in a rotating order. Below they are discussed in the order of appeal to the respondents (most appealing first):

Summaries of congresses

Much like the doctors' own suggestion, this was described as an online compendium of published articles, ordered by speciality and date of publication, with an index of abstracts and the option to access entire papers. It would differ from existing online services because of:

- the ability to watch a presentation on video with audio soundtrack

- the ability to download the slides used in the original presentation

- subtitles in Spanish

- an associated bibliography.

Online training courses

Doctors were attracted because this would give them a chance to organize their own time for the training. To be attractive, online courses would have to be accredited, and the content would have to be relevant and effective. Doctors felt online courses should last longer than 20 hours (this would give them a professional credit for participating), provide impartial content, and include a clearly differentiated (but equally important) theoretical part conducted online, and practical part to be attended in person, at weekends.

Respondents were happy for a pharmaceutical company to finance such a course provided it did not promote their products too relentlessly.

Educational materials for patients

This appealed as an aid to patients, provided the materials produced were truly educational, and really effective in both content and presentation. They could be used to offer patients, particularly those with chronic diseases, online information about their illness; as a preventive medical tool (covering hygiene, dietary advice and so on); and to create templates for patient records (covering issues such as obsessive behaviour, diets and harmful habits) to help patients manage their own conditions.

Patient simulations

There was less enthusiasm for the idea of pharmaceutical companies providing doctors with online patient simulations. Respondents found this concept rather confusing, and found it hard to imagine how it would work. Their interpretations included presentations of clinical cases requiring treatment, a fun medical version of *Trivial Pursuit* with questions and answers on a range of medical practices, and a 'digital actor': similarly to the training courses, the actor would exemplify different pathologies and show how they are treated.

Doctors liked this suggestion better when they could perceive it as offering both fun and education:

- It should be interactive, they'd have to answer you.

- With drawings, something that's fun but educational too.

- But without forgetting that what they say has to be true.

Information about patients and follow-up

Although this was very similar to one of the doctors' own suggestions, when they discussed it in more detail they foresaw some problems:

- It would be hard to manage: they foresaw a considerable increase in the number of patient consultations.

- The need for feedback to the patients would increase the doctors' workload.

- There could be legal problems if a patient supplied information that was not acted on correctly, and was later found to be suffering from a serious medical condition.

Summary and conclusions

- Special training is required for researchers carrying out qualitative work with health care professionals, not just to learn their vocabulary and issues, but to develop techniques to break down their professional veneer.

- Four useful moderation tactics are based on positive authority, curiosity, understanding and humour.

- In 2006 Millward Brown Spain undertook a qualitative study for Eli Lilly to explore doctors' relationship with the Internet. Although doctors use the Net, they often lack both resources and expertise, and there appears to be scope for further developments, some of which might be mediated or sponsored by a pharmaceutical company such as Eli Lilly.

PART IV

INTERESTING QUALITATIVE STORIES

21

Drinking beer at home (international case study)

PEPE MARTÍNEZ

Introduction

In 2006 Millward Brown undertook a multi-country qualitative macro-study of the European in-home beer category. It was concerned solely with in-home (off-trade) consumption, not the 'on-trade': bars, hotels, restaurants and so on. It took place in 14 European countries, among 25 to 35 year-olds who buy beer to drink at home.

Research objectives

The main aims were to identify:

- all current media touch points (as defined by consumers) among those who drink beer at home
- the meaning and importance of beer brand associations and the sources that most influence those associations
- potential touch points and opportunities for European beer brands.

Methodology

Qualitative research was undertaken in the countries and cities listed in the following table.

Western and Northern Europe
1. Germany (Frankfurt): Warsteiner and Beck's
2. Croatia (Zagreb): Ozujsko and Heineken
3. Denmark (Copenhagen): Gron Tuborg and Tuborg Classic
4. Spain (Madrid): Mahou 5 Estrellas and Heineken
5. France (Paris): 1664 and Heineken
6. The Netherlands (Amsterdam): Heineken and Grolsch.
7. Italy (Milan): Nastro Azzurro and Heineken
8. Portugal (Lisbon): Super Bock and Sagres
Eastern and Southern Europe
9. Greece (Athens): Amstel and Heineken
10. Hungary (Budapest): Borsodi and Heineken
11. Poland (Warsaw): Zywiec and Heineken
12. Czech Republic (Prague): Gambrinus and Staropramen
13. Russia (Moscow): Staryy Melnik and Tuborg
14. Turkey (Istanbul): Efes, Tuborg and Miller

The sample was of middle and upper-middle class men and women (10 of each in each country) who buy beer for drinking at home at least once a fortnight. The techniques used were:

- ethnographic diaries

- two mixed focus groups in each country with six respondents, three men and three women, lasting two and a half hours

- ten ethnographic interviews in each country, each lasting two hours: one hour in-store observing the respondent without any verbal communication, followed by an in-depth interview in respondents' homes which probed the shopping and buying process.

Discourse in the focus groups was free and spontaneous. Projective and creative techniques were also used.

Start point

The choice of brands, though wide everywhere, varies considerably from one geographical region to another. In each country we selected one city and two beer brands, one national, the other international (see the table above). Across Europe, we noticed our sample tended to prefer beer that:

- is easy to drink

- is low in alcohol

- has a smooth flavour
- is kind on the stomach
- has a conscious brand image
- is more unisex
- is relatively healthy.

Heineken was included in eight of the countries in our study, and came close to meeting these criteria.

Lifestyle

Before analysing the relationship between consumers and communication channels we needed to know the role played by different media, and how those media fitted with people's lifestyle. We used ethnographic diaries (see chapter 5) for this purpose. Respondents completed them for four days, from a Friday to a Monday, to give us a sense of both weekdays and weekends.

From analysis of the diary information we developed a ChannelConnect™ model (see chapter 15). The following figure shows what weekdays are like for Europeans between the ages of 25 to 35 who drink beer at home, and the next one shows the same target group over weekends and on holidays.

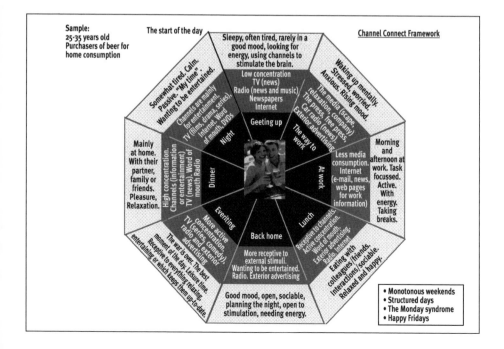

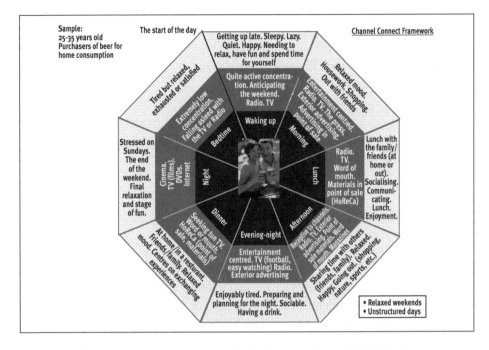

We asked respondents to include digital photographs in their diaries to express their mood at different times of the day, and of any advertising campaigns that caught their attention. The following figure was provided by a Croatian respondent who remarked, *'At the corner of Savska and Vukovarska there is a giant image of Heineken on the wall; it's the best advertising that I've seen.'*

Views of in-home beer brands

Beer tends to be seen as an informal drink midway between soft drinks and strong alcoholic drinks. It is low in alcohol, has an unique flavour, and is versatile. It can be drunk:

- by one person, a couple or a group (of family or friends)

- on both work days and holidays

- day and night

- summer and winter

- by all adults

- by all types of people

- from noon until bedtime.

Women are increasingly moving into a market that was traditionally dominated by men. In northern and western European countries, beer consumption is more evenly spread across both sexes, but in Eastern Europe gender differences are evident.

Respondents' comments showed that:

- At a physical level beer's bitter taste stands out, as do its natural ingredients and refreshing and thirst-quenching qualities.

- At a psychological level it is highly versatile and has a bipolar effect: invigorating when you are tired and relaxing when you are stressed.

- At a sociological level beer evokes belonging to a group, being together and sharing. It involves us in a social ritual, makes us think of leisure, and creates a festive spirit. It is a symbol of friendship. Projectively it is a young friend.

Although the in-home beer category has not changed much over the years, major innovations are starting to emerge, including varieties with lower alcohol content and different flavours, special beers and new types of packaging.

Purchasers are usually loyal to a beer brand. Their selection is influenced by:

- Personal experience of each brand's characteristics: its flavour, bitterness, alcohol content, foam and quality. *'Each brand tastes different'* (Spain).

- Word of mouth and preferences of family and friends. *'My friends' opinion is quite important; I may prefer Amstel, but if my friends prefer Heineken, then that is what I buy when they are going to come to my home'* (Greece).

- Brand image: personality, values and projected lifestyle. *'The image of each brand is very important for me'* (Hungary).

- Advertising campaigns, particularly television and outdoor (bus shelters, hoardings).

- Sponsorship of concerts, sports events and sports teams.

- Price. As consumption is frequent this is an important variable.

The characteristics of the product, the personality of the brand (its image, advertising and marketing activities), its price and accessibility (how easy it is to find) are key.

Consumers normally differentiate beer brands on two dimensions:

- premium versus standard: price is the decisive variable here

- classic versus modern, where the key factor is the brand image.

Placing the beer brands along these axes produces the positioning map shown in the following figure.

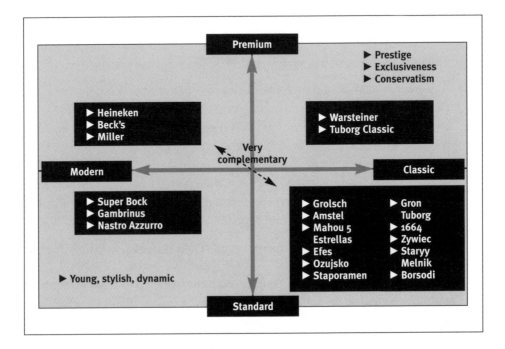

The largest group of brands studied is in the standard-classic sector, of beers more product than image-centred. They are strong, authentic and are seen as masculine, reliable, good quality, traditional. Preferences often pass from one generation to the next. Beers are often seen as local or national symbols. These brands are mass-market and close to consumers, are affordable and simply packaged, and available in all sales outlets.

Heineken, Beck's and Miller are positioned in the premium–modern quadrant. These brands are more image-centred. International, young, modern and fashionable, they have strong advertising campaigns. Their beer is smoother, somewhat 'light', seen as unisex, high quality, natural, with tradition and experience. Their image is more sophisticated and they are higher in status and price, with more elegant and attractive packs. They are also less widely available.

Super Bock, Gambrinus and Nastro Azzurro occupy the standard–modern quadrant. These brands are young, stylish and more dynamic than the classic brands. Warsteiner and Tuborg Classic are in the opposite quadrant, premium–classic: seen as prestigious, exclusive and to a certain extent conservative.

Points of brand–consumer contacts

All the contacts consumers have with a brand influence demand and purchase behaviour. The main touch points in this category are:

- personal experience of the product and pack (consumption moments)
- word of mouth
- communications: television, advertising outdoors, in cinemas, newspapers and magazines and on delivery lorries
- sponsorship: sports, music, culture and parties
- point of sale material, including ads inside and outside shops, and branded coolers
- branded materials in licensed premises: for example sunshades, beer mats and napkin holders showing a brand logo
- promotional gifts.

The respondents had usually decided on a brand before they entered a sales outlet. They tended to buy beer from the same store each time, heading straight for their favourite, and paying little attention to point of sale marketing. Brands in this category should therefore make the best possible use of every earlier point of contact with purchasers.

Sometimes, however, purchasers glance at price, discounts, offers, promotions and gifts. Beer brands must use every opportunity to encouraging switching.

In general, the beer aisle is considered to be dirty, disorganized, confused, lacking in 'magic', cluttered and complicated. The wine stand is seen as much more elegant, motivating and attractive.

Future opportunities for beer brands

ChannelConnect™ (see chapter 15) shows that for in-home beer consumption there are two key moments:

- Weekdays on arrival home after work. Here beer symbolizes the 'warrior's rest'. *'You get home and have a beer to get rid of the stress of the day'* (Turkey).

- At weekends and on holidays, for parties or get-togethers. *'To be happy, to get going when you're with people'* (Turkey).

Less significant are lunch and dinner times at home (on all days), when beer competes with water, wine and soft drinks.

The touch points most relevant to the category are:

- Television advertising. The product and the consumption experience are sensually appealing, and the ads can show this through, for instance, images of foam and colour. (However television advertising is not permitted in all countries.)

- Outdoor advertising (such as on bus shelters), again a visual medium.

- Promotional material at sponsored events.

- Point of sale merchandising.

The product cannot be shown on radio, but it can be used to announce sponsored events.

Focus group respondents suggested how beer could best connect with the target group:

- Premium brands could sponsor events, teams and sports people in the most prestigious sports, such as sailing and yacht racing, golf and tennis.

- Campaigns should be close to places this target group go (cinemas, gyms), in and outside sales outlets (such as supermarkets, hypermarkets), and for outdoor advertising, on routes home from work.

- Product placement in television series, movies and television films.

- Internet possibilities, as well as manufacturer/brand sites, include new forms of net-based advertising, with interactive games, multiple-player Internet gaming, competitions and prizes, and helping to create a community of brand consumers (with photographs, videos, blogs and so on).

- Building on the trend for branded coolers containing cold beers at points of sale.

- New forms of in-home consumption similar to those outside the home: for example, 5 to 10 litre barrels for parties and get-togethers.

- Offer free gifts such as glasses or stylish bottle openers.

- Special offers to accompany take-home ready meals (for example, *'Nastro Azzurro is the beer offered by the Tipico pizzeria when you order a pizza'* (Italy).

- Create multipacks that include standard and premium beers from the same brewer, so consumers try several different beers.

- Organize offers in supermarkets and hypermarkets with brands of chilled or frozen pizzas, savoury snacks and so on.

- Use new designs for multipacks to stimulate all five senses: use refreshing water droplets on the pack, foam, gold and yellow tones, natural colours.

Summary and conclusions

- In 2006 Millward Brown undertook an international qualitative macro-study across 14 European countries on beer for home consumption.

- There are two key moments for in-home beer consumption: on weekdays after work, and for get-togethers at weekends and on holidays.

- The most relevant touch points were seen as television advertising, outdoor advertising (bus shelters), event sponsorship and visibility at point of sale.

- Interesting and original ideas emerged in the focus groups about how a beer could connect better with a target group aged between 25 and 35.

22

Go-getters in the Czech Republic (Vodafone)

Lenka Robosova

Introduction

In 2004 the Czech mobile operator Oskar (now part of Vodafone), a client since 2001 with a creative approach to market research, asked Millward Brown to research a key target group, defined as the Go-getters. We designed one of the largest qualitative research programmes the company has ever sponsored. Our output was as unconventional as our approach.

Prior to our study, we had a description of the Go-getters market segment and knew about their consumption behaviour. What was missing was a detailed insight into their private lives and thinking, which Oskar could use to train its employees.

The context

Of the three mobile operators in the Czech market, Oskar was the smallest. It was perceived as a very flexible operator which followed new trends and focused on the younger market.

Research goals

The aims of the broad research programme were to:

- gain deeper insight into Go-getters' lifestyle, needs, goals, feelings, brands, day-to-day problems, aspirations and so on
- further define the Go-getters' segment and explore the potential broadening of this target group

- ensure that the final output could be used as an internal training resource across Oskar, for both existing and new employees

- present the results in a way that was attractive, entertaining and packed with information for Oskar's employees.

Research method

During a brainstorming session in which all members of the research team took part, we agreed on a four-phase research approach:

- pre-recruitment groups

- ethnographic interviews

- creative groups

- photo diaries.

Pre-recruitment groups

From earlier quantitative segmentation work for the client, we knew how to identify the Go-getters, Oskar's primary target group. Now we used pre-requirement groups to select typical and communicative Go-getters and allocate them to the individual research phases based on their abilities and attitudes:

- For ethnographic interviews we selected respondents who were open to talking about their private life, ambitions and concerns.

- For photo diaries we chose respondents with a broad range of interests who were creative and willing to share their daily lives with us.

- Creative group participants were selected based on the ethnographic interviews. These groups comprised the 'best of the best', those who proved most open during visits to their homes.

A total of eight short (30-minute) eight-person pre-recruitment focus groups were conducted, enabling us to select only the most suitable participants as the 36 respondents in the main study. A psychologist from our qualitative team helped with the selection process.

Our discussion guide contained the most pertinent topics for all subsequent phases:

- lifestyle: work habits, free-time activities, description of a typical day, passions and irritations

- mobile phones: their role in respondents' lives, the degree of addiction, which services they use and why

- a collage on 'Live your life as you want to' to evaluate respondents' creativity.

Ethnographic interviews

Ethnographic interviews in respondents' homes enabled us to obtain general but detailed diagnostics of the respondents' lifestyles, and understand their behaviour and motivation. We conducted 20 interviews, 16 in Prague and two each in the smaller cities of Plzen and Olomouc.

Half the interviewees were Oskar customers and half competitors' customers. Each interview lasted two to three hours, and all were recorded on video by a professional photographer. The final video report was created by a professional film editor. Help and advice from these professionals brought us high-quality output. Among the lessons we learned were:

- The moderator often prompts respondents, but verbal prompts are distracting in the final video. It is better to use non-verbal prompts such as head shaking, smiling, eye contact and gestures.

- The video works best when questions and answers flow into each other. This is difficult, and if it cannot be achieved when filming, it is better to show the question as a subtitle.

- Footage of respondents' lives was crucial to project success. The moderator looked for opportunities for respondents to pull something appropriate from their desk or wardrobe: photos of their home, their favourite pastimes, medals, their artwork, favourite websites, pictures of friends and so on. For this project, we consciously focused on any visible brand names.

First we talked briefly about the respondents' lifestyles, then we asked them to differentiate themselves from the 'average Czech'. We next used a projective question, *'If you were to select an item or a symbol representing your friends or those with the same lifestyle as you, what would it be?'* We then talked in greater depth about respondents' lifestyle and attitudes to life, looking at their photos and discussing their content. We used the adjective technique, asking respondents for the adjectives that best described themselves and their friends.

We also focused on the future, asking respondents about their dreams and goals, concerns, interests and ambitions, past successes and motivations.

Each respondent was asked to write down their five favourite brands, of any type of product, for example clothing, cosmetics, electronics, cars or beverages. This enabled us to determine the categories where brands were important. Later we talked to them about brands they knew and loved. This approach made it easy for us to get quickly to the emotional evaluation. A detailed evaluation of selected brands covered strong and weak points, consumer benefit, their relationship to the brand, motivators and reasons for liking a brand. The adjective technique was used again, and we asked them to show their favourite brand names on items in their home. This led to interesting comparisons when they came up with brands other than those they had named as favourites.

Again, projective techniques were used:

- *'If a brand were a person, what would they look like?'*
- *'If a brand were a house, what would it look like?'*
- *'If a brand were an object or a symbol, what would it be?'*

We also asked respondents how they thought their ideal brand should be developed in future, and to explain how it generates respect among its customers, and the type of advertising most suitable for it.

Next we moved to the core topic: mobile phone operators. We asked which operator was emotionally closest to Go-getters and why, and looked for an evaluation of brand attributes and attitude to customers, and for suggestions for improvement.

Oskar was then focusing on three pillars: inspiration, captivation and delight. We discussed the motives behind this strategy and positioning, and focused questions on what inspires, captivates and delights customers.

The most useful part of the interview was the final ethnographic insight we gleaned from being able to observe Go-getters in their natural habitat. Respondents showed us their home, their room, their favourite spots and any items with which they had a deep relationship (positive or negative). They also showed us their

CDs, books and even their wardrobes. In each part of the home, we looked at the item that best represented their values and lifestyle. The results were surprising, and we used the video footage to illustrate our final presentations.

Creative groups

A total of six creative expression groups were conducted with four respondents in each group. Two were chosen from the ethnographic interviewees, according to their ability to express themselves, creativity and ability to think abstractly. To gain insight into their immediate environment and social status, we asked each person to bring along their partner or a friend (a use of the friendship cells methodology, or snowball technique).

Each group lasted three hours. After a short warm-up, most of the time was given over to projective and creative techniques, social drama and so on:

- The 'If' game was played to introduce respondents to each other and the moderator (*'Imagine you could be any person you liked from any period of history. Who would you like to be and why? Now imagine you are on a desert island, and name five things you would take with you. Why these five?'*).

- A 'Sherlock Holmes' game provided more detailed insight into Go-getters' characteristics. We divided the four respondents into two pairs, and each pair was given a questionnaire to fill in: one with questions about themselves (their lifestyle, values and so on) and one with questions about the other pair, so both pairs gave answers about the same two people. The projection apparent is interesting, but the focus was on the contrast between the two sets of answers. A candle and Sherlock Holmes props (deerstalker hat, pipe, coat) created the right atmosphere.

- A photo sorting game focused on respondents' ambitions and aspirations. They had to pick from a set of photos the people they would most like to be, definitely not like to be, like to be friends with and definitely not want to be friends with, then their choices were explored.

- Collage was used to focus on respondents' aspirations and concerns for future. Using magazine pictures, they produced *'Our goals, dreams and ambitions – what we want to achieve'* and *'Our concerns, worries, frustrations – what we fear'*. We observed their interaction and questioned them on their picture choices.

A second section focused more specifically on mobile operators:

- Free association was used to explore reactions to expressions routinely used in mobile operators' marketing communications. The moderator provided the words – 'quality', 'communication', 'coverage' and so on – and gave respondents five minutes to provide as many immediate associations as possible to each one.

- Laddering helped us explore the end benefit consumers felt drove satisfaction with a mobile operator. This began with asking respondents to name the most important features in a mobile operator. Their comments were written down on a flip chart, the moderator questioned them about each one, and this became the focus for the laddering exercise. (the next figure uses a different example to show how this works.)

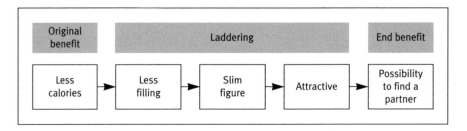

- Role play helped us understand why respondents had chosen a particular mobile operator. One respondent played a customer and the other three took on the roles of the main Czech operators, Oskar, T-Mobile and Eurotel. They were asked to act out the personality of the operator brand, not to represent its sales staff.

  - The first game focused on rational reasons for choosing an operator: the individual operators were asked to help out the customer (a woman) in whatever way they could, and the customer was able to ask questions.

  - The second game focused on emotional reasons: the respondents in their role as operators had to invite the customer out for a date.

  - The final phase is always important in games of this type. The 'customer' had to decide which operator had been most convincing, and why.

- Metaphors: this game helped us understand respondents' subconscious associations and emotional relationship with mobile operator brands, especially Oskar. We prepared six cards showing words like trumpet, spinach, wind, football, champagne. Respondents drew individual cards and completed the metaphor: *'Oskar is like a trumpet because ...'*.

Photo diaries

One of the greatest benefits of the photo diaries phase, which involved 16 respondents keeping diaries for a week each, was the enormous amount of authentic material we gathered from Go-getters' everyday lives. Their records of all sorts of daily situations helped us to further understand their relationships, needs and aspirations, concerns and worries.

Respondents prepared four types of output:

- **Photos**, of their ordinary day, taken every hour; of life moments which involved emotions – situations in which they felt joy, were particularly attracted by something unusual, felt sadness, respect, inspiration and so on; and photographs of any contact they had with a mobile operator.

- **Captions**: for each picture they gave the date and the exact time, and added where they were, what type of situation they were in, who they were with, and what emotions were involved.

- **Daily reports**: every evening, respondents wrote a brief overview of everything they had done that day. We were particularly keen to find out what pleased or displeased them, including the intensity of their feelings.

- **Overall summary**: at the end of the week, we asked the respondents to evaluate the experiment. We were also interested whether the exercise had helped them learn something new about themselves.

Analysis

Analysis took a relatively long time because we had gathered so much material. Each phase gave us an insight into Go-getters' lives from a different angle.

Given the complexity of the topic and the research goal, we used the 'group analysis' method to analyse our results. All participating moderators and the senior qualitative researchers evaluated each phase of the project, then in a day-long workshop they determined the main conclusions, the overall shape of the report, and the rough structure of the video report script.

The areas of analysis were:

- mindset: ambition and recognition, finances, freedom and independence
- relationships: partners, family and friendship
- fashion
- travel
- fitness
- music and culture: music, nightlife, culture and celebrities
- reading: books, magazine topics.

Some of the results are summarized below..

Mindset

Ambition and recognition

Go-getters are defined not by age or class but by a shared mindset – values, preferences, interests, dreams and fears. They are extremely achievement-orien-ted. They want to be better than others, if not the best; to be given recognition, and to exceed expectations.

Those over 30 came of age just as totalitarianism was coming to a sudden end in the Czech Republic. The change was so drastic that this generation believed they had to seize opportunities quickly or risk losing them. They have a strong work ethic, more so than the younger Go-getters. (This generational difference is also apparent in broader Czech society.)

Finance

Although Go-getters today are very driven and focused, they no longer repre-sent the Western yuppie archetype of the 1980s. Work is very important to them, but it is not everything and they live a balanced life. They enjoy being busy and slightly over-extended, but this comes not only from work but from trying to fit in friends, family, hobbies and fun.

Continued education is the most common shared goal. They are acutely aware of their image, and take time to manage it. They expect to be judged by how much money they make, what car they drive and so on. They don't want to be rich, simply to have enough money to do what they want. But their want-list is longer than for most Czechs.

Freedom and independence

Go-getters share the desire to be independent and free, which to them means not needing support from family, friends or a partner, and not being tied down by a mortgage or an inflexible job.

Relationships

Their friend and partner bonds are not as tight as for other segments, but family is an emotionally tight bond. They see their relationships much as they see their lives – dynamically. One commented, *'I have no problems with my boy-friend, but I'm not sure whether he's "the one", whether I'll be with him for more than ten years.'*

Go-getters don't see themselves having children before age 35, and before reaching personal milestones such as success in their career and travelling.

In the Go-getter family, individualism is encouraged in children. (In a traditional Czech family, this is not so: children are taught first and foremost to respect and obey their parents.) One Go-getter, still living at home with his parents, explained, *'Although I still live with my parents they don't restrict me in any way, I can do what I want.'*

Go-getters are social butterflies and can be very fickle in their friendships. Quantity is more important than quality. They have many different friends and acquaintances to fit with their different hobbies and pastimes.

Go-getters seek out people who share their values, rather than offer something different. They want openness and honesty from their friends, but not challenge. They do not have friends from other social spheres or different social strata. The better-off are intimidating to them; the worse-off threatening.

Fitness

Go-getters engage in sport and fitness, shopping, going to the cinema, con-certs, out to restaurants, bars and clubs, and other informal social events with friends. Almost all their pastimes are social events. However they often choose individual sports, which fit better into their schedules than team games.

Fitness centres are trendy places for Go-getters to see friends and or meet new people. A group of them often go out together afterwards to a bar or club. Tae-Bo, aerobics, yoga and weight training are the most popular fitness activities. While Go-getters are competitive in their careers and studies, very few of them engage in competitive sports. They like branded sports clothing, and also wear it for leisure activities.

Go-getting men are body-conscious, see sport as fun or as a stress reliever, and tend to get involved in collective sports and extreme sports: climbing, snowboarding, paragliding, mountain biking. For women sport and fitness is done to look good.

Processing the outputs

This included preparing the analysis text, editing the video footage, and comprehensive interactive output. It was important that the report was easy to read, well segmented, and the language was in sync with Oskar's internal corporate culture. We used music in the video edit, selected to represent Go-getters' style.

Oskar's creative department prepared *Hunger*, a fictional lifestyle magazine reflecting the Go-getters' lifestyle in its writing style, content and topic selection (see the next figure). Our input was a detailed analysis which allowed its authors to fully understand the Go-getters' personality and lifestyle.

The final output was not the standard PowerPoint presentation, Word or pdf file. To allow users to click on individual topics and move between the analysis, the video and the magazine, we prepared an off-line website about Go-getters. The home page highlighted the *Hunger* magazine. The site offered an in-depth analysis of particular topics, illustrated with video and photographs from the respondents' diaries. It also included a detailed explanation of the research methodology.

Summary and conclusions

- Millward Brown's very large study for the Czech mobile operator Oskar (now part of Vodafone) is a good example of an in-depth qualitative study of a brand's target group.

- The research phases included pre-recruitment focus groups, ethnographic interviews, creative groups and photo diaries. Both creative and projective techniques were used. The final output was interactive.

- The research happened before blogs and community websites were popular in the Czech Republic. Today, we would probably not be surprised at how excited the respondents were about sharing details of their personal life.

23

The formula for happiness (Coca-Cola) (Spain)

CRISTINA GONZÁLEZ and PEPE MARTÍNEZ

Introduction

In 2007 Coca-Cola Spain asked Millward Brown Spain to undertake an exploratory qualitative study on happiness. We used a psychosociological approach to find out what consumers think happiness is, and to determine what they believe determines each person's degree of happiness.

Objectives

At the outset Coca-Cola set up a group of experts including marketers, scientists and academics, a team from Millward Brown and a psychologist with specialist skills in analysing happiness scales. This team approach can be particularly useful in studies like this, to think about the subject and set parameters for a focus group stage, before regrouping to analyse the information it provides. The group identified 16 dimensions they felt drove happiness:

- being in control
- being able to influence an outcome
- dealing with emotions
- being totally absorbed in what you are doing
- having goals
- having self-confidence and self-esteem
- being curious
- achieving recognition
- being able to empathize
- relationships with our family of origin

- the relationship with our partner
- facing up to difficulties
- balancing time and priorities
- being able to solve problems creatively
- being optimistic
- being afraid.

Methodology

The core of the research was four focus groups, each with seven to nine respondents, half women, half men, all graduates, and lasting three hours. Two were held in Madrid and two in Barcelona. One in each city was of young people living apart from their parents and 'dinkies' (dual income no kids), aged from 25 to 35; the other was of parents aged from 35 to 45, with children aged from six to 12.

The constituents of happiness

During the free discussion, seven concepts emerged spontaneously as driving happiness, and these are discussed below:

Optimism

Idealism, optimism, realism, conformism and pessimism can be placed along a continuum, as shown in the following figure.

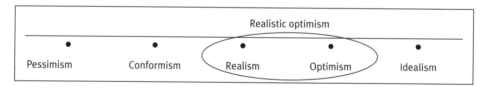

Realistic optimism, an intelligent form of optimism, was felt to be the ideal, and most closely associated with happiness:

'Optimism is good, but the important thing is realism.'

Idealism was thought to be dangerous:

> *'You've got to be careful when you build castles in the air.'*
>
> *'The bad thing is foolish optimism, thinking that everything is fine.'*
>
> *'The bad thing is not to see reality, as you may trip over.'*

And pessimism was said to prevent people enjoying life:

> *'Pessimists concentrate on the negative side, they see everything as black; pessimism incapacitates you.'*

Realistic optimism, on the other hand, is associated with:

- activity, energy and strength ('optimists want to live')
- being extrovert and sociable
- joy, enjoyment and happiness ('optimists are happier and make other people happier, too')
- taking the initiative, being brave, having goals and not being afraid
- overcoming problems
- having self-esteem and self-confidence.

Talking about optimism, our respondents said:

> *'Optimists know how to enjoy the small moments or details in life.'*
>
> *'Optimism is an attitude to life, but it is far more apparent when times are hard.'*
>
> *'Optimism is not thinking how wonderful the world we happen to live in is: the world is what it is, so let's make the most of it!'*

Having goals

Respondents also thought having goals was an important contributor to happiness. Intentions and goals express movement, evolution, hope and motivation. Having a goal is synonymous with being alive:

> *'Everyone has an aim: nobody can live without goals.'*

Lacking goals was a sign of stagnation, routine, disillusionment and depression; synonymous with death. How goals influence happiness depends on:

- lifestage, since goals change depending on age

- what the goal means to the individual

- how people try to attain their goal (the degree of commitment, flexibility or rigidity and so on)

- the type of goal: large or small, concrete or abstract, materialistic or self-fulfilment, realistic or idealistic, professional, personal or for the family

- the time frame.

Goals are directly linked to strength and energy, and make people want to live more fully. They are also associated with optimism and a high level of self-esteem. Happiness tends to be associated with minor goals set over the short to medium term:

'Short-term ones give a better return.'

'It's better to have a range of goals in different areas of your life.'

'Some people get stressed out by goals, they don't enjoy them. You have to enjoy the journey there.'

Self-esteem

The ideal is to have neither too high nor too low self-esteem. This involves a suitable dose of self-recognition. Balanced self-esteem brings us closer to happiness. Excessive self-esteem is associated with arrogance and narcissism, a lack of self-esteem with immaturity and insecurity. Both are associated with a hunger for recognition by others.

The following figure is a psychosociological picture of self-esteem.

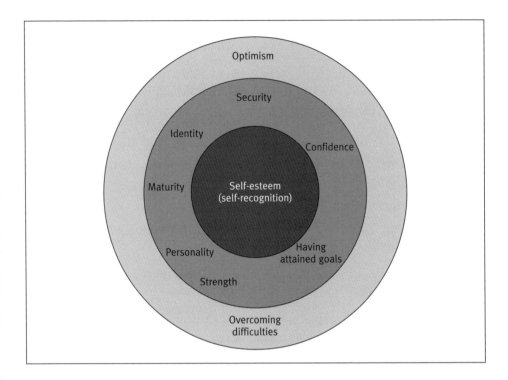

Good self-esteem is associated with security, confidence, having attained goals, having a strong sense of identity, maturity, personality and strength, optimism and overcoming difficulties. It means a person has a solid personality – a necessary foundation for personal and family life, as well as functioning well in the workplace. Respondents commented:

> 'Attaining your goals makes you feel more confident, and that raises your self-esteem.'

> 'Someone with self-esteem is more enterprising, they take the initiative.'

> 'Too much self-esteem may make somebody seem arrogant.'

> 'Self-esteem is associated with the maturing of the personality.'

The family of origin

Our birth family (in a wide sense: parents, siblings, grandparents and other important figures) has a determining influence on our lives. The respondents thought 'nurture' was more important than genetic factors. They were not experts, and did not know the degree to which personality is inherited.

A family provides us with resources that are crucial in forming our personality, how we live our life and the degree to which we will be happy. The broad nature and complexity of the family means that a wide number of factors again come into play:

- What we mean to our parents is very important, and so are the expectations they communicate to us. Their personality, the relationship between them and their professions all have an influence.
- There is the dynamic of the family and the atmosphere within it: values, education, rules and habits, and so on.
- Another factor is the number of children, their gender, and the individual's place in the family.
- It matters whether people grow up in a structured or unstructured family environment (in terms of separation, divorce, abandonment and so on).
- School is an extension of the family. Parents communicate what school means to their children, and children also have their own views. School provides values and information, and is the scene for important relationships with teachers and fellow pupils.

Relationships in couples

Six factors influence the relationship couples have with each other today:

- Women now work, so they are more independent at all levels.
- The higher level of equality within couples has led to greater self-esteem and satisfaction for women.
- Couples are no longer permanent. An effort is required to keep the relationship alive.
- Children are not the objective, they are an option. The individualistic dimension is the most important.
- Compromise now is more complex and has to be negotiated.
- The importance of sex is now talked about more openly and honestly.

To keep a good relationship alive, respondents felt that couples need:

- respect and tolerance
- a strategy of compromise; having shared goals
- shared values, interests and moments
- good communication
- to help each other
- a sense of humour
- surprise.

Couples most often fail when there is a lack of respect, disregard for the other, and in extreme cases, abuse. It is clear that our relationship with a partner is very important to our happiness. Having children, however, is no longer as directly associated with happiness as it once was.

The capacity to face up to difficulties

This is linked to self-esteem (security and strength), optimism, creativity, a person's ability to deal with emotions (seen the next section), and their ability to reach resolution:

'Overcoming difficulties makes you stronger.'

People who find it difficult to face up to problems tend to see major rather than minor difficulties. Particularly difficult life problems include the death of a loved one, divorce, separation, job loss, physical and mental illness, and abuse.

Dealing with emotions

Our emotional controller functions as a continuum, from total lack of control to absolute control. Emotional balance lies at the midway point along with emotional and social intelligence.

Those overcome by their emotions are considered to be immature, infantile, impulsive, temperamental, vulnerable, insecure and victims of emotional influence.

This state was more commonly associated with women, although gender rules are changing. Those who completely control their emotions are seen as cold. This emotional state is more commonly associated with men.

We are not given lessons in how to deal with emotions as we grow up, and there is no instruction manual. We work out what to do through experience. Someone who is emotionally well-balanced:

- can connect their internal (emotional) world with the external situation

- can integrate their emotions into their everyday life

- distinguishes very clearly between private and public settings

- feels their emotions, analyses situations and reacts, in a spontaneous way

- feels their emotions and expresses them in a suitable way.

Respondents felt more comfortable with terms such as 'including', 'channelling', 'feeling', 'expressing' and 'conveying' the emotions. They felt less comfortable with words like 'controlling', 'using' 'managing' and 'manipulating'.

Comments included:

'The emotions are like horses, you allow them to run, but rein them in when they get wild.'

'I'm very emotional and cry for any reason. I've suffered, sometimes I've felt like a little girl.'

'Emotional intelligence is in fashion, you have to have emotions, but you also have to know how to control them.'

'You have to work out how people feel, and if a feeling is going to hurt other people or harm your image then you have to stop yourself saying what you were going to say. You have to move away until the feeling has passed.'

The formula for happiness

Of the sixteen dimensions that were studied in this research, seven stand out in connection with happiness. They are the seven that were analysed above: optimism, having goals, self-esteem, the family, being part of a couple, facing up to difficulties and dealing with the emotions.

It is clear that the remaining nine dimensions (creativity, being in control of your own life, sharing out your energy and time, empathy, recognition, doing activities that you experience very intensely, curiosity and fear) are important in our lives, but they are neither so strong nor so basic as the others.

Happiness is a very complex concept. Some people believe it to be unattainable, while others see it as a momentary feeling associated with specific events. Few believe that they live in a state of "relative" happiness.

Happiness is linked to all of the levels that constitute a human being: biological, psychological, sociological, cultural and historical. To be happy biological needs must be met. Different cultures may have different views of what happiness consists of. The same applies to history: different historical times may seek different types of happiness. However, it is clear that human beings yearn to be happy, desiring it and seeking it in their own way, using their own resources.

But happiness depends chiefly on psychological and social factors. Happiness is a feeling (Psychology) and it has to be attained together with other people (Sociology). Happiness is a balanced state, in which we make the best use of the unique being inside us, the needs of others and the characteristics of the situation. At moments of happiness everyone present expresses what is "divine" inside them and shares it with others. Using marketing language, hapiness is about being "well positioned" in life.

The majority of people believe that happiness is something that comes from outside, something which either reaches you or does not. They have a passive or receptive attitude to happiness. But on the contrary, happiness is inside people, not outside them. It is within us and work is required to develop it.

If we return to the main dimensions that we identified in this study, we reach the following formula for happiness:

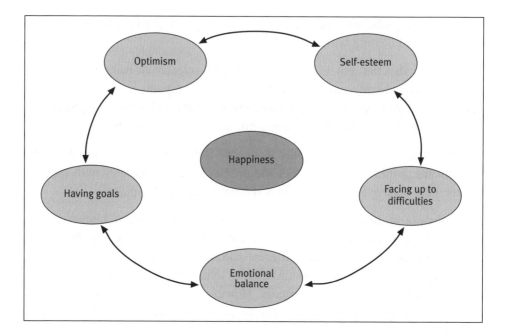

The five main factors which determine the degree of happiness we are able to attain during life is:

- Level of optimism

- Level of self-esteem

- Capacity for facing up to difficulties

- Emotional balance

- Having goals, and the nature of these

One's family of origin (and the family one forms), the couple and work are the main scenarios where we can bring the above-mentioned characteristics into play. They are also the chief ecosystems that decisively influence our state of happiness.

The formula for happiness is therefore:

Happiness = optimism + self-esteem + facing up to difficulties + emotional balance + having goals in life

Subsequent phases and actions

After the focus groups, the team of experts met again to write a questionnaire based on everything that had been learned. A major quantitative study was then undertaken, directed by Mar Areosa of the Millward Brown team in Madrid. It comprised 3,600 home interviews of individuals aged 18 to 65, on the Spanish mainland and islands. Finally Coca-Cola published a report, *The Coca-Cola Report on Happiness*, and undertook a major advertising campaign.

Summary and conclusions

- In 2007 Coca-Cola Spain requested Millward Brown Spain to undertake an exploratory qualitative study on happiness.

- Experts suggested 16 possible factors that determine our ability to be happy, and focus group respondents identified seven factors as particularly important: optimism, having goals, self-esteem, family, relationship in a couple, facing up to difficulties and dealing with emotions.

24
Images of Lech Walesa in Poland

KRZYSZTOF B. KRUSZEWSKI

Introduction: portrait of a president

Millward Brown Poland has been always active not only in market studies but in political research. A few years ago we carried out a particularly interesting qualitative study during and after the presidential campaign of the leader of the Solidarity movement and Nobel Peace Prize winner Lech Walesa.

The methodology was inspired by Pierre Bourdieu, and in particular his book *Distinction* (1986). It took a practical and empirical approach, using projective techniques such as the 'Chinese portrait'.

Classic methods for studying images of leaders

Studies of social attitudes to well-known political figures are usually quantitatively based. For many years the Public Opinion Research Centre (CBOS) in Warsaw, a government institution founded in 1982, conducted studies on Poles' attitudes towards Lech Walesa. The next table shows the results of a question about the level of acceptance of Walesa's influence on political life.

Date	Accept (%)	Do not accept (%)	Not sure (%)	N
August 1987	19.3	42.7	38.0	1493
November 1987	18.5	48.4	32.5	1498
February 1988	24.1	40.7	35.0	1497
May 1988	23.8	43.2	32.8	1489
August 1988	25.7	44.8	29.1	1477
November 1988	44.9	31.5	23.8	1494
January 1989	65.6	13.3	20.7	1500
March 1989	78.5	7.6	13.9	1497
April 1989	81.8	5.5	12.5	1493
May 1989	83.3	7.0	10.0	1495
June 1989	85.5	5.6	8.5	1496
July 1989	83.3	7.0	9.8	1498
September 1989	87.2	6.2	6.6	999
November 1989	92.8	3.1	4.1	1497
March 1990	73.7	17.9	8.0	1498
July 1990	62.0	23.6	14.6	1497
November1990	60.0	24.0	16.0	1497
February 1991	53.0	15.0	32.0	1496
June 1991	46.0	41.3	12.6	1497
September 1991	49.0	39.0	12.0	1496
October 1991	45.0	43.0	12.0	1496

This information is hard to evaluate, even against an in-depth analysis of the dynamics of the economic, political and cultural environment. Although surveys have the advantage of precise quantification, there are evident limitations. First, there is no opportunity for subtle analysis of the yes/no answers to closed questions, and sometimes it is difficult to phrase the questions without being sure what factors are most relevant. (Open questions, of course, provide answers that are much less open to reliable statistical analysis.) Second, it is difficult to prevent respondents from being influenced by the pollster and the research environment, particularly for political topics which can kindle strong emotions and cause arguments. In Eastern Europe especially, people are reluctant to give open and honest answers to this type of survey (Sulek, 1990).

An alternative method

These problems induced us to look for a new methodology, which we have used to research attitudes to a number of major Polish political figures. Qualitatively based, we believe it is a valuable supplement to classic quantitative surveys. It combines two well-known techniques, focus groups and Chinese portraits.

Focus groups are discussed on chapter 3. Chinese portraits is our term for the projective techniques discussed on chapter 6. It seems especially suited for studies of leaders' images, a very sensitive task where people sometimes hesitate to give direct answers. Instead of saying the president is a sissy, for instance, a respondent can suggest he resembles a small, vociferous Yorkshire terrier with a bow on the top of its head, his favourite occupation is cooking, and his favourite forms of entertainment are the *Dynasty* television series and reading women's magazines.

This method brings out respondents' top-of-mind associations. It provides access to the deep layers of the mind: beliefs and emotions that are unconscious and not easily verbalized, but act as important motivational mechanisms. It works particularly well in the focus group context.

The qualitative study on Lech Walesa's image

Two studies of this type were carried out on Lech Walesa's image in Poland, the first just before the first free presidential elections in November 1990, when he was known mainly as the Solidarity leader and a Polish national hero, and the second more than a year after the elections which brought him the presidency, in January 1992.

The portrait of a public figure is generally made up of a set of closely linked but dissimilar images, reflecting his or her different social roles. For example, for Polish Communist Party First Secretary, General Wojciech Jaruzelski, the image of an officer was an important element; Tadeusz Mazowiecki, the prime minister of the first non-communist Polish government, prompted the motif of an intellectual, while the image of economist Leszek Balcerowicz, the mind behind Poland's economic transformation, contained the model of a cosmopolitan scholar.

We started the Walesa study by looking for projective associations, then analysed their relative importance. Finally, a descriptive picture was built of all of the images that had been collected.

Walesa in 1990

Before the 1990 elections, we conduced 12 focus groups. Their perceptions of Lech Walesa had three main constituents:

- The dominant image was of Walesa as the charismatic leader of Solidarity, a hero who toppled the communist system in Poland.

- The second, slightly less important, image was of a politician, a presidential candidate.

- The third, relatively unimportant, image was of Walesa as a private person: husband, father and enthusiastic angler.

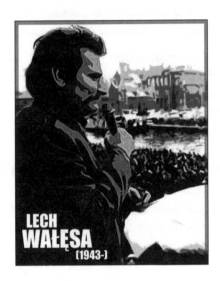

The hero

In participants' opinion, Walesa played the decisive role in overthrowing the communist system. When constructing his image, respondents said he should not leave Gdansk, the home of the workers' movement and the shipyard whose workers he led. He was seen as a modest man, reckoned to suit a small, three-roomed home and a thick sweater, turtleneck pullover and workers' dungarees. He was pictured as a strong man, and riding in a powerful all-terrain vehicle or a military armoured car. Nearly all participants said he would participate in physical men's sports such as boxing, football, wrestling or judo. For his pet, they picked a dangerous guard dog such as a rottweiler, bull terrier, German Shepherd or Dobermann, and as his favourite dish, a rare-cooked steak.

The group participants saw him as of exceptional sexual potency. For a suitable wife they had two equally popular but very different choices: Krystyna Janda, a dynamic actress and Solidarity activist, and Teresa Orlowski, a Polish-born porn star living in Germany.

The politician

Walesa had only one real rival as presidential candidate, Prime Minister Tadeusz Mazowiecki. He was described as a typical intellectual, a serious and wise man praised for his impeccable behaviour, thoughtfulness, moderation and respect for democracy. On the other hand, he was criticized as a politician for being too lethargic, inconsistent and willing to compromise.

Walesa's image was of a more strong and consistent politician. Participants saw him as living in a monumental palace in the capital city or in a large estate on top of a hill near Warsaw. The right animal for him was a strong, aggressive dog, the right car a Rolls-Royce or a bullet-proof Mercedes. He dressed the way a future president should, often hunted, and only watched television programmes about politics.

Few doubted his political might, but many, especially Mazowiecki's supporters, feared his despotic tendencies. These worries were also reflected in his image. He was pictured with many domestic staff and travelling in a bullet-proof car accompanied by personal bodyguards. He combined civilian authority with command of the armed forces. Respondents saw him as someone who liked splendour and solitude, isolated from society, who would wield power alone.

The regular guy

Least important was this image of a man who spent a lot of time at home. Respondents agreed that he was full of vitality, the best proof being his eight children. The right partner for Walesa in that role was seen to be his real wife.

After returning from work, the respondents thought he would wear a loose-fitting, comfortable track suit, a sweater and cotton shirt. He was perceived as sitting in an armchair, talking with his children and wife and playing with his big dog: a Great Dane or English bulldog. They agreed that he lived in a tidy, small house in Gdansk and liked to watch television: westerns, war movies and thrillers. They also thought he would like traditional home cooking: pork chops, cooked cabbage, roast chicken.

Again, his image was of someone physically strong, practising body building, with an interest in sport. On Saturdays and Sundays they said he would often go fishing. They thought he earned enough to be able to provide for his family, and wielded power over his wife and children responsibly and consistently. He was seen as the head of a traditional patriarchal family.

These three images – of the hero, the strong politician, the regular family guy – combined to represent a promising president, someone who could put things in order in Poland, and win happiness and prosperity for her people.

Walesa in 1992

How differently did respondents see Walesa after he had spent a year as president of Poland? Two basic images made up the portrait. This time, the decisive role was played by what had formerly been the least important image, that of the regular guy.

The regular guy as president

Paradoxically, the president was seen as not so much a politician, more a private person. This time, respondents saw him living outside the city, in a village or a poor, plebeian neighbourhood. The cars that best suited his image were cheap and ugly ones: a Syrena, a 'plastic' Trabant, Nysa or old Fiat 125. They said he would wear modest worker's clothes: dungarees, an unfashionable shiny suit, the gaudy tie of an upstart, and that Polish symbol of bad taste, a dark blue beret.

Lech Walesa now appeared as a corpulent ageing man, a weak and helpless person. Now his archetypal pets were a hamster, guinea-pig, cat, bird, aquarium fish or a small dog with a shrill bark. Participants thought he needed to be partnered with a strong and determined housewife who could run both the house and her sluggish husband: actresses with this image were Bozena Dykiel, Irena Kwiatkowska, Danuta Rinn and Joan Collins playing Alexis in *Dynasty*. As for his sexual prowess, when asked how he would fare now with the porn star recommended a year earlier, the respondents from a medium-sized town east of Warsaw summarized: 'Too fat now. He couldn't handle it.' 'Hardly!' 'Come on! That woman would finish him off in five minutes!'

Now people saw him playing physically undemanding club games such as chequers, billiards and ninepins, tinkering at home and going fishing at the weekend.

The image that emerged was of a somewhat incompetent and not very quick-witted, but certainly very friendly and likable man. People saw him enjoying traditional Polish cuisine such as pork chops with cabbage, herring, beef steak, sour soup and tomato soup. Although respondents could not call Lech Walesa wise, they saw him as basically good and gentle. They thought he had a sense of humour and would often like to tell jokes. His favourite television programmes were said to be funny cabarets, *Benny Hill* and *The Muppet Show*. One participant from a focus group held in the countryside reckoned he could be friends with this character:

> *'Not too smart, not too stupid, jolly, a great guy – he could sit here now with us and chat.'*

The politician as president

There was a split apparent here, between what participants thought a president should be like, and what they perceived Lech Wales as actually being like. A head of state:

- lives in a palace or a luxurious apartment in a government district
- is driven in black or metallic limousine
- wears dark, fashionable suits, a hat, and a conservative tie
- hunts in his free time.

Talking about the real person, participants expressed their dissatisfaction with his clear lack of formal education and good manners. They argued that a head of state ought to know at least one foreign language and use his own language without making mistakes. They did not appreciate his tendency to tell inappropriate jokes.

He was now seen as a weak, incompetent and yielding politician. Participants characterized him as the 'president-signer' (pen-pusher); four groups called him a 'pawn' in the game of powerful forces, which were alien to him. He was seen as a prisoner of the legal system, Polish and foreign advisers, officials, the Church, the parliament, and first and foremost, his own incompetence.

The image now of Walesa the politician saw him living with his family outside the city in a large isolated house. Cut off from public life, he went on long walks with his dogs, and went fishing in a nearby lake. He was seen as debarred from power, only a titular head of state.

An attempt at interpretation

To summarize, before the presidential elections in November 1990 Lech Walesa was perceived as a charismatic leader, tough man and effective politician. A year after election, study participants stated that he was only a titular president, weak, sluggish and incompetent. Using content analysis on comments presented by the focus group participants, researchers at Millward Brown Poland were able to identify three main reasons:

- A the end of 1990 and the beginning of 1991 not much was known about the actions of the president. The culture of social marketing, especially public relations, was still at an early stage of development in the very new Polish democracy. Lech Walesa seemed to have vanished from the political stage. He rarely granted interviews and made infrequent television appearances; the impression was that he had been shoved aside from power.

- Both in November 1990 and later, Poles believed that wise, and above all consistent, policies could improve the country's economic situation. Few doubted Walesa's good intentions, but a year after he became president, Poland's economic position remained unchanged. People had concluded he was not capable of doing anything.

- Walesa was seen to be well suited for the position of head of the trade unions, but the role of head of state required other qualifications. A sheep dog at work is the very picture of strength and pride; the same dog in a city appears weak and poor. Now people noticed what Walesa lacked, such as education and good social skills.

The results of our studies were exploited successfully by analysts serving in Lech Walesa's advisory team. They led to some well-designed public relations exercises, and as a result the social image of Lech Walesa improved considerably.

Methodological conclusion

- Classical quantitative surveys have asked about attitudes to politicians, but it is difficult or impossible to interpret the data or measure the dynamics.

- Millward Brown's Chinese portrait methodology in a series of focus groups provided two revealing and contrasting images of Lech Walesa, before and after his election to the Polish presidency.

- The image of Walesa as president showed how the different role drastically changed people's perception of his power and success. It also paved the way to actions that would restore his prestige.

25
Mad cows in Spain

PEPE MARTÍNEZ

Background

At the end of the 20th century widespread alarm was caused by the emergence of a new disease in cattle, bovine spongiform encephalopathy (BSE) or 'mad cow disease'. A degenerative pathology of the central nervous system, it is fatal.

At the time of writing there have been 182,507 cases, 179,441 of them in the United Kingdom where the first cases were detected in 1986. More than 2 million animals have been slaughtered in Great Britain. There is a similar human disease, Creutzfeldt-Jakob disease (CJD), of which 91 cases have been confirmed, although it is not entirely clear whether or how it is contracted from cattle.

Although BSE affected other countries in Europe, including Spain, at a far low level than the United Kingdom, it had a very negative effect on beef consumption there. Sales of other types of meat such as pork and chicken increased, as did fish consumption.

Millward Brown Spain therefore thought it would be interesting to study the psychological reactions of Spanish consumers to 'mad cow disease', as well as the social phenomena to which it gave rise.

Research objectives

The main aims of the research study were to:

- carry out a complete and in-depth examination of the 'mad cow disease' problem
- determine the opinions, attitudes and reactions of consumers
- understand the psychosociological issues that arose as a result of BSE

- discover how this problem affected beef purchasing and consumption habits, in and outside the home.

Methodology

We used focus groups, each with between eight and ten respondents and lasting two hours. The research was conducted at the beginning of 2001. The sample consisted of half male and half female heads of families aged 30 to 50, broadly middle class, who usually shop for food for their household. Two groups each were held in four cities in the most populous areas of Spain: Madrid (centre), Barcelona (north east), Bilbao (north) and Seville (south).

Analysis of content

All the free and spontaneous discourse in the focus groups was transcribed, then the data were reduced and transformed. At a broad level, respondents' opinions, attitudes and experiences of BSE were that:

- it is a serious problem

- it is very alarming psychologically as well as socially

- there is major confusion about the problem

- the available information is poor and not always credible

- the problem has overwhelmed the government and scientific authorities.

Respondents saw 'mad cow disease' in the context of other problems with food, such as genetically modified rapeseed oil, swine fever, disease in Belgian chickens and salmonella. They also made associations with other types of human-made catastrophe such as Chernobyl, and the submarine *Tireless* which was leaking uranium.

The respondents knew something about BSE, and were able to outline its origination, spread across Europe, timescale, and the main theories about its cause and dangers: that it was linked to cows being fed animal waste products, and that there were particular worries about consumption of brains and entrails, cheaper cuts of meat, the spinal cord and bone marrow.

Four key agents were mentioned:

- the government (politicians and ministers)
- scientists (veterinarians and inspectors)
- cattle farmers and others working in food supply
- the media (television, press and radio).

There was confusion and differences of opinion about the part played by these agents. Largely because of perceived vested interests, the agencies lacked credibility.

Respondents felt that the media:

- gave the problem prominence
- used a sensationalist approach
- showed high-impact images such as the handling and disposal of culled animals; cow entrails, brains, blood and other body parts
- showed images of people with CJD
- raised doubts whether the authorities had covered up deaths caused by eating beef.

There were frequent references to distrust, suspicion, disbelief and worry. Some used more intense and negative terms such as fear, panic and alarm.

Opinion was divided over the impact of safety controls on the crisis. One group felt there was no safer time to eat beef, because of the control procedures throughout the food chain. Another group, however, believed there were no guarantees, because there was a lack of machinery, apparatus, laboratories, incinerators for slaughtered cows and qualified personnel (inspectors and veterinary surgeons) to perform the necessary checks and tests.

Asked about meat purchase and consumption, respondents said:

- the situation had directly and negatively affected their consumption of beef
- this had had a positive effect on the consumption of other types of meat such as chicken and pork
- the problem reactivated some previous concerns about products made from beef, such as sausages and hamburgers, chopped cold meats and mortadella

- they checked food packaging for details of ingredients in products that might contain beef, and country of origin

- they believed the sectors most affected by the problem were cattle farmers, slaughterhouses, transport, butchers, catering, hamburger restaurants, and the producers of meat by-products, preserved meats, beef broth and baby foods.

Structural analysis

Having analysed the content, we now had to structure the analysis: in other words, to move from the explicit and concrete data to latent structures and theory.

It was clear consumers were divided over this problem and there was a lot of confusion. At an emotional level they were afraid of catching CJD. At the level of desire they wanted to be able to eat beef safely. At the level of action they tried to avoid eating it. All this led consumers to develop a paranoid psychological mechanism, which in turn led to different interpretations of the problem.

Some thought the authorities were really unaware of the consequences of the disease and had left the population unprotected. There was widespread concern that the problem was out of control. There was speculation that the authorities were aware of the true scope of the problem but were hiding information to keep beef sales buoyant. This was based on the fairly commonly held view that the main driving forces in Spanish society are economic and political interests that put profit above all else.

> *'I believe that they are hiding something from us.'*
>
> *'There are lots of vested interests.'*
>
> *'They're manipulating us.'*

Only a few people in our sample thought information was being covered up because the authorities wanted to protect the population and prevent widespread alarm.

Interestingly, the available quantitative data on meat consumption at the time showed that in spite of the major drop overall, on certain days sales of beef rose strongly. We developed two hypotheses to explain this.

First, consumers are psycho-physiologically dependent on beef, which they find highly motivating and appetising. The body needs it and the mind needs it. Consumers cannot automatically shake off such a deeply rooted habit: they feel nostalgia and long for a good steak. Therefore, on occasions, they relativized the problem and ate beef.

Giving up beef for a long period of time is psychologically difficult. It is easy to give in to temptation. Respondents justified their occasional consumption of beef because they believed the chances of catching the disease were minimal.

Our other hypothesis was linked to media coverage. When there was less news about the problem consumers felt that the situation had returned to normal, and resumed beef eating.

At a latent level, we saw the problem in terms of a conflict between nature and culture. The negative side of culture, that which is artificial and chemical, developed a feed that harms the positive side of nature: cows, and humans too. The underlying fear was the denaturing of the Earth.

The bloody and extreme images shown on television were associated with a regressive world that consumers thought advanced European countries had moved beyond. They took society back to a past of insecurity and vulnerability, to a hostile and aggressive world of epidemics and plagues.

To understand the fear felt by the population, it has to be emphasized that 'mad cow disease' attacks values that are very important to society: animals and nature, dietary habits, health and individual responsibility. Those who buy meat, usually women, do not wish to be responsible for 'poisoning' their families with infected beef.

Most respondents had reduced their consumption of beef, but they were at different places on a continuum which ran from total rejection, through avoiding it as much as possible, to consuming it without any concerns. We identified three basic segments:

- Type 1: individuals who were aware of the problem. They did not eat beef in or out of the home. They carefully scrutinized pack labels to make sure there was no beef in processed products they bought. In extreme cases these individuals were scrupulous and obsessive.

- Type 2: moderate or intermediate individuals. They no longer ate beef in restaurants. However, they did eat it at home, because they trusted their butchers and asked them where their meat came from. For processed products they looked for trustworthy brands, as the brand was more important to them than the ingredients. When there was less news about the problem they increased their consumption of beef. Conversely, when media coverage of the problem increased they once again went on the alert.

- Type 3: those unworried by or unaware of the problem. They had hardly altered their beef purchasing and consumption habits. They considered the chance of contamination to be almost zero, or even claimed that because the authorities were exercising a lot of control over the beef industry, there was no safer time to eat beef. They used the psychological mechanism of denying the problem.

Interpretation

An eclectic and multidisciplinary team of qualitative researchers (psychologists and sociologists, with different theoretical orientations) met for an analytical meeting. They looked for models to help them understand and explain the consumer behaviour.

Seven theoretical models from different sources and disciplines proved to be highly effective tools in this process. These models were not mutually exclusive but complementary, and it was not possible to rank them in terms of their suitability. Each one offered us clues about different facets of this social problem.

The anthropological model

Anthropologists have made a highly interesting contribution to our understanding of the relationship between 'nature' and 'culture'. Structuralist Claude Levi-Strauss* was an outstanding figure in this field.

Analysed in depth, our respondents echoed the thesis that nature has two dimensions: a positive part (sometimes seen as divine) and a negative side (sometimes seen as diabolical). On the plus side, nature offers us plants, fruit, the meat of animals, milk, wonderful landscapes, beaches and the countryside, and so on. The negative side includes natural catastrophes such as earthquakes, floods, volcanoes and tsunamis.

Many elements in nature have both positive and negative values. For example, the sun is a primordial source of life, but too much sunlight can cause skin cancer.

In the same way, culture has its good and bad sides. On its positive side are all the advances that enable us to live in a secure and enjoyable society, with better-quality and longer lives than in the past. Medicine, vaccination, all of the products and services that make our lives more comfortable belong to this group.

But there are still social problems such as crime and terrorism. Again, some aspects of culture are simultaneously positive and negative: for instance car usage can enhance our lives, but at the cost of pollution, traffic jams and accidents.

The following figure summarizes this anthropological context in which the 'mad cow disease' crisis occurred.

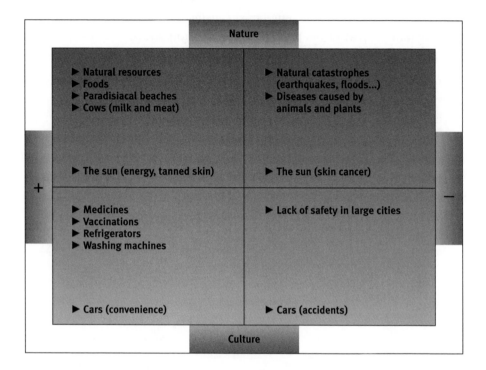

The problem is positioned in the lower right-hand sector, of diabolic culture. Cows are naturally peaceful animals, symbols of life, health and nature, but the 'food industry' has denatured them, creating something monstrous and frightening.

The cognitive model

Cognitive psychology was a major improvement over earlier reductionist behaviourism. Thanks to input from cybernetics, information theory, computing, data processing and general systems theory, it has developed far beyond the simple stimulus–response model, and views consumers as highly complex systems that interact with an environment which is itself very complex. To make it possible to analyse and gain a better understanding of consumer behaviour, it is broken down into different modules, each one of which fulfils a different function. The system is very sophisticated, because all these modules are interrelated in multiple ways.

This discipline tries to understand the connections between cognitive thought, the emotions, language and action, plus aspects such as perception, attention and memory. Applying a cognitive model to the BSE issue, the stimulus is a negative one, worry that eating contaminated beef may infect humans with CJD. This negative stimulus activates the emotions, causing alarm, fear, terror and panic. The more rational part of the brain then comes into play, seeking to understand the issues and control the emotional response.

However there is a large amount of information about the problem, and much of it is confusing and contradictory. There are no clear criteria or guidelines, and this can lead to a new emotional reaction: anger and frustration. The rational mind tells customers they should stop eating beef until the situation is clarified, but habits and motivations are rooted in the mind, and this gives rise to conflict. When levels of negative media coverage, and thus worry, fall slightly, consumers go back to eating beef.

The next figure shows the working of the cognitive model:

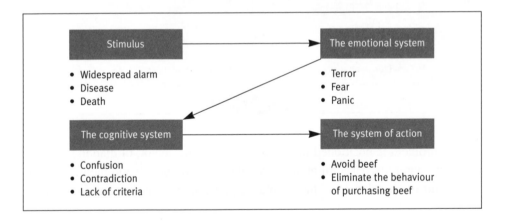

The psychosocial model

The theory of cognitive dissonance was developed by Leon Festinger*. He studied the consequences for an individual of deciding on one of several alternatives. Once the decision has been made the subject tends to behave in a way that is consistent with it, and to reject the other possibilities. The purpose of this is to reduce dissonance.

Festinger's theory is essentially a framework for analysis after decisions have been taken. Applying this to Spanish consumers' reactions to the BSE crisis, we found a high level of dissonance between vectors of:

- positive forces: consumers enjoyed and wanted to eat beef, and were not prepared to stop
- negative forces: eating contaminated beef could cause disease and death.

We concluded from the focus group data that consumers reduced their psychological dissonance in two ways:

- accepting that there was a problem, and trying to repress their desire for beef.
- negating the problem, arguing that it was under control and beef was safe to eat.

The following figure shows the working of the psychosocial model:

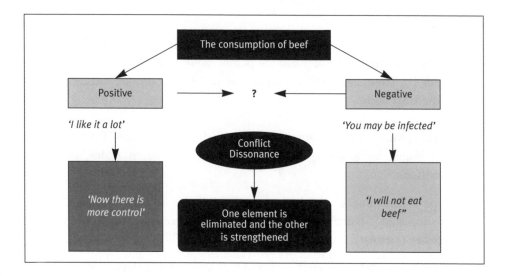

The psychodynamic model

Psychoanalytic theory argues that our behaviour is determined to a great extent by unconscious factors. The relationship we establish with our environment is an extension and prolongation of our first and most important relationship, with our mother. Our unconscious minds operate at the level of symbols and archetypes. (Jung* was one of those who studied this phenomenon most closely.)

The cow is a symbol of motherhood, it represents nature and goodness, and like the mother it is an universal symbol for food in the form of milk.

The natural tendency of babies is to put everything into their mouths, giving them what Freud* called oral pleasure. When children grow and develop, the mother teaches them what they can safely place in their mouths and what they cannot. Regulatory bodies and brands also play a maternal role for consumers, helping them decide what is suitable for consumption.

So when a problem such as BSE arises, consumers feel fear and panic because there is no sociological mother to offer them clear information and guidelines on how to behave. In the focus groups our respondents wanted the government or scientists to offer clear guidelines. When the authorities were unable to function like a mother who brings peace of mind, anxiety emerged.

The transactional model

Transactional analysis is a theory about personality and how it influences interpersonal relations. We outlined the parent, adult and child behavioural roles on chapter 18. These can be mapped onto the different reactions consumers showed to the BSE issue:

- Type 1, the concerned individuals who had eradicated beef from their diet and home, were acting in the register of the parent (rules, duty and sacrifice).

- Type 2 individuals, who had modified their behaviour but within limits, trusting some sources of beef but not others, were functioning in the adult register (maturity, common sense and responsibility).

- Type 3, those who denied there was a problem and had chosen not to modify their beef-eating, were functioning in the register of the child (impulse and desire).

The brand archetypes model

See chapter 17 for an outline of the brand archetypes model, and the ten basic archetypes and their shadows.

The BSE crisis led to a major change in the archetypal representation of cows and beef. Cows, milk and beef are normally represented by the archetype of the Mother, who symbolizes life, care, protection, growth, health, support, unconditional love, sustenance, nutrition, devotion and generosity. The appearance of this strange disease in cows transformed beef to its shadow archetype, the Stepmother, who symbolizes just the opposite: selfishness, coldness, negligence, lack of interest, unscrupulousness and emptiness.

The semiotic model

One of the main concepts of semiotic analysis, the 'semiotic square', also had relevance to this issue. Semiotics is interested in how the value of 'veridicality' (truth-speaking) is created from within an expressive system. This not only involves correct expression, it also and importantly involves creating the *effect of the sense of truth* from within a communication, because of its internal consistency.

As we have seen, consumers were very confused because they had received contradictory messages about 'mad cow disease' and the possible effects on human beings. From the semiotic viewpoint, the chief problem centred on the credibility of the messages from the different agents. This was a problem of 'verification': of discovering who, if anybody, was telling the truth.

Veridicality is assessed by the projection onto the semiotic square of the concepts of 'being' and 'seeming', and their negatives, 'not being' and 'not seeming'. The truth game is created by moving from 'seeming' to 'being', thereby deducing the truth values present in discourse. If we establish the code of veridical positions we obtain the following modes:

- Being + Seeming = True.

- Seeming + Not being = Lie.

- Not seeming + Being = Secret.

- Not seeming + Not being = False.

Graphically this is shown in the next figure.

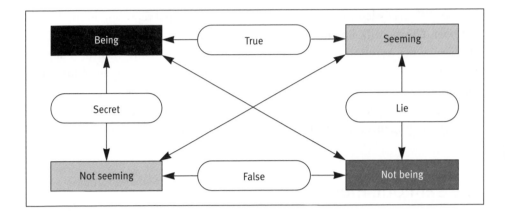

From the point of view of the consumers in our study, the different social agents were trying to occupy the territory of 'truth' (Being + Seeming) in relation to the BSE problem. But they were not usually credible, and tended to be seen as occupying the territory of a 'lie' (Seeming + Not being).

Final reflection

Qualitative research analysis is more productive and effective when it takes place in a group, due to the advantages of team work, a multidisciplinary environment, the heterodox approach and an eclectic viewpoint.

In the case of 'mad cow disease' we have tried to show that the different theoretical approaches are complementary. In each case it is prudent to use the model that is of most use in helping us understand and explain the market situation. This is because it will also be the most effective when making changes to attain the desired objectives. When we are able to interpret data well, we have the keys we need to develop a good marketing strategy.

Summary and conclusions

- At the start of 2001, Millward Brown Spain carried out a qualitative study in Spain on the 'mad cow disease' (BSE) crisis. The main objectives were to determine the effects the crisis had had on beef purchase and consumption habits.

- Focus groups revealed that consumers experienced BSE as a serious problem which gave rise to major concern at a psychological as well as a social level. Although much information was available, it was contradictory and not always credible.

- The respondents had adopted three different responses to this situation, which we categorized as Types 1, 2 and 3, ranging from a punctilious avoidance of beef in all forms, to a decision to ignore the problem and continue as before.

- To interpret the information we used seven different theoretical models from different sources and disciplines: the anthropological, cognitive, psychosocial, psychodynamic, transactional analysis, archetype and semiotic models. All of them provided useful insights into the situation.

26
Making and selling soup in France

GUILLAUME CADET

Introduction

In 2007, Millward Brown France was asked by a major manufacturer of ready-made soup to explore whether people who made their own soup could be persuaded to switch to ready-made, to grow the market. They drew an analogy with yogurts, where now almost everybody uses the manufactured product. Soup is a mainstay of French cuisine, and the marketing team felt strongly that the jump to ready-made should be easy for French housewives. But in fact penetration of ready-made soup in France was relatively low, and the market was not growing as quickly as our client would have liked.

Objectives of the research

At the outset, we questioned the client's strategy (a marketing campaign targeted at French soup-making housewives) and persuaded them to conduct some qualitative research. They needed to understand the relationship those who make their own soup have with it. What rational and psychological benefits do they feel they get in return for their effort?

Methodology

Our research approach involved 24 in-home depth interviews with women of different ages in different parts of France who make their own soup at least twice a week in winter. These covered the relationship they have with soup, and the way they prepare, serve and eat it.

We also held eight conflicting paired in-depth interviews, each bringing together a heavy ready-made soup user and a heavy home-made soup user. Respondents were asked to defend their views on what they believed was the right type of soup to serve their families. We were also keen to uncover any flaws in their arguments.

The following table shows the distribution of our sample.

Technique	Individual interviews		Conflicting pairs	
Age	Mothers (aged 30–50)	Older women (aged 55+)	Mothers (aged 30–50)	Older women (aged 55+)
Paris	4	4	2	1
Rural area	4	4	1	1
Small city	4	4	2	1

Main findings

Consumers do not consider ready-made soup as a replacement option for home-made

Our research showed that home-made soup was irreplaceable. There was no way that French women who make their own soup would consider switching to ready-made. It was not that they had negative perceptions of ready-made soup – we worked hard to get them to criticize it when our ready-made soup users argued that it was faster, easier and objectively as good as home-made soup. In fact, they agreed with them. But they did not want to switch.

This is part of one debate from a conflicting paired depth interview (H is the home soup maker, R the ready-made user).

R: *'I can't understand why you spend so much time making soup. Perhaps you're not working, so you've got time for that kind of stuff.'*

H: *'Actually, I work full time. And I've got three kids. So you'll appreciate that time is an issue for me. But anyway, I spend something like one hour cooking per day.'*

R: *'You're a kind of anti-industrial food purist, aren't you?'*

H: *'No actually, we usually eat frozen prepared meals. I've got a microwave. I have nothing against modern food.'*

R: *'OK, I see. So you think that the ready-made soups are not good. Is it a question of taste? A question of nutritional values?'*

H: *'I don't think they are not good. I ate a chilled soup at a friend's. It was very good. I thought it was home-made and I must say I was surprised to hear that it was ready-made.'*

R: *'Did you know that with commercially produced soups the vitamins are better preserved than when you buy vegetables and cook them at home?'*

H: *'I didn't know that, but fair enough, I can believe it.'*

R: *'What would make you change your habits and eat more ready-made soup?'*

H: *'That's a good question. If I think about it, it's obvious that ready-made has many advantages. But I can't imagine life without buying, chopping and cooking vegetables.'*

And here's another exchange:

R: *'You must think I'm a lazy housewife who doesn't give her family the best food.'*

H: *'No, to be perfectly honest with you I think you're a lucky housewife.'*

The reality is that making their own soup is something they do without thinking about it. It is an integral part of their culture. They do it as an unconscious duty: to carry on a tradition, keep a link with their family roots. They know their soup isn't the best in the world, but it is theirs and in a way it is part of them. Substituting ready-made soup for home-made makes no sense to them at all!

> *'I've been using the same recipe for years. It came from my mother. Frankly they're all a bit fed up with that soup at home, and I am too. But this is how it goes, they can't tell me they're fed up, and I can't admit it to myself either.'*

Three types of commercially resistant consumer

Based on their attitude and their psychology of (politely) ignoring the ready-made option, we identified three different types of home-made soup makers (here categorized as women, which they usually are).

The dogmatic

This woman lives in the city centre in a large, bourgeois type of flat. She has children and her values are fairly conservative. Pleasure is not at the top of her list of food concerns. However, 'good' food is extremely important to her, and it is important that she is seen to be a good wife and a good mother.

By making home-made soup she is able to fulfil this duty. It gives her an excuse for being more relaxed about the food she serves at other meals. In France, soup is seen as the symbol of food perfection. These consumers like the idea of home-made soup more than they do their actual soups.

The voluntary

This woman is more mainstream in social class and lifestyle. She tends to live in the suburbs and is a responsible mother who tries hard to combine work and family life. Cooking offers her the best opportunity to express her generosity. Making soup is the best way to manage the guilt she feels, and to meet the massive social expectation of providing five vegetables per day. It also gives her a chance to experiment with new recipes. After all, making soup does not require a lot of time or talent. It is just a question of willpower.

The instinctive

The instinctive home-made soup maker lives in the provinces and resembles the archetype of the 'traditional' French way of life. For her, each of the stages involved in making soup is a pleasure, from growing her own vegetables to perpetuating the tradition of the family together enjoying the smell, warmth and taste. Soup recipes are passed down from generation to generation and play an unstated role in preserving French rural culture.

Apart from these very deep-seated reasons for making soup, there is also a very pragmatic motivation: for gardeners the vegetables are already there, available free, and taste so much better than those sold in the supermarket.

Five motivational axes

In our analysis we uncovered five psychosociological dimensions of women's relationship with soup:

- Nutritional:
    - vegetables' wholesomeness
    - the five a day recommendation
    - complete food
    - food control.

- Sensory:
    - good smell in the house
    - fresh, natural colour
    - warmth
    - texture
    - generosity.

- Psychological:
    - emotional heritage
    - filial/maternal feeling
    - passed down from generation to generation/shared
    - provide the best food
    - being a good mother.

- Pragmatic:
    - easy to make
    - not so expensive
    - suitable for everyone in the family
    - people have their own vegetables
    - complete meal.

- Social:
  - soup is trendy
  - back to authentic things
  - creativity
  - sharing
  - maintaining tradition.

The whole picture

The three typologies we identified have very different motivations for making soup, summarized in the following table. However, their soup-making behaviour is the same: home-made soup remains a pillar of their food repertoire, and they ignore the ready-made alternative.

	Primary	Secondary
The Dogmatic	Psychological	Nutritional, social
The Voluntary	Social	Nutritional, pragmatic
The Instinctive	Sensorial	Pragmatic, psychological

The next figure shows the five motivational axes, and the dynamic between home-made and ready-made soup:

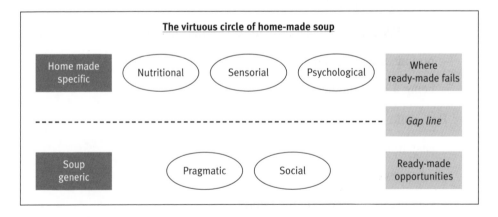

What we found in the course of our research came as a shock to our client. However, we recommended that the client should continue the quest to grow the ready-made soup market. Our research had given us some pointers on how this might be done:

- no longer comparing home-made to ready-made soup in communications, and promoting it as a solution for other occasions (at work, as a snack and so on)

- also developing products to help consumers improve their home-made soup, such as ready-to-use unusual vegetables.

Summary and conclusions

- We undertook a study in France in 2007 on perceptions of home-made and ready-made soups. Its ethnographic approach combined in-home depth interviews and conflicting paired interviews.

- It was apparent that French home-made soup makers do not see ready-made soup as an acceptable substitute, for a variety of reasons more psychological than practical.

- We were able to advise our client to promote ready-made soup as a product for different occasions than home-made soup, and to find ways of supporting the home-made soup sector.

27

100 Mexican families

ANDRÉS LÓPEZ

Introduction

In 2002, when Millward Brown opened a qualitative department in its Mexico City office, it undertook a study of Mexican families and consumption. Although some changes may have taken place since, we believe the core findings are still valid. We also wanted to explore how family structures influence the consumption process not just in Mexico, but in other countries too.

Objectives

The objectives were:

- to understand the changes that were taking place in Mexican families and their lifestyles

- to explore the purchasing process and families' relationship with different types of product (food and drink, household cleaning products and home appliances, health care, financial services, personal care and hygiene, leisure and technology).

Methodology

We carried out an ethnographic study, using 100 in-home family interviews each lasting approximately three hours. All family members were present during most interviews. The interviews were very open, and although we used a rough guide, the only instruction to the interviewer was to understand the family and its relationship with different product categories.

We segmented family types into:

- individuals who live alone (7 interviews)
- couples without children (ten)
- couples with small children (13)
- couples with adolescent children (14)
- couples living with dependents aged 18–25 (15)
- adults living alone with their children (five interviews, all with women).
- couples whose children have left home (five)
- senior couples (five)
- families of immigrants (five)
- families with a member in the United States (four)
- homosexual couples (three)
- multi-generation families (ten)
- multi-family households (four).

The sample was not designed to be statistically representative. Rather, we wanted a minimum sample of each type of family, so that we could make comparisons.

Similarly, the study took place in a cross-section of towns of different sizes: a metropolis, Mexico City (25 interviews), two large cities, Guadalajara (15) and Monterrey (15), and six medium-sized towns: Tijuana (ten), Mérida (ten), Mazatlán (five), Puebla (six), Morelia (nine) and Oaxaca (five). This included towns from the north and south, the coast and the interior, and representing different cultures and mindsets. Monterrey and Tijuana, for example, are strongly influenced by the United States; Puebla is considered to have a traditional mindset; and Oaxaca has a different but also deeply rooted traditional culture.

Socioeconomically, there were:

- 30 interviews with upper-middle and upper-class families (social class B/C +)
- 40 interviews with middle and lower-middle-class families (social class D +/typical C)
- 30 interviews with lower-class families (social class D).

Double standards

Almost all the families, younger and older, defended traditional values. One young couple said:

> *'We want to educate our children in the same way that we were educated, with the same values ... religion is an important part of our marriage.'*
> (Monterrey)

However, this does not necessarily reflect reality. Things in Mexico, as everywhere, are changing with increasing speed. But while in some countries modernity is considered desirable, Mexican families do not describe themselves as modern. Why?

One possibility is that respondents were trying to impress or please the researcher. Double standards are very much part of Mexican society. For instance, often the father spoke most at the start of the interview, solemnly presenting his family history which was full of traditional values and in which he naturally played a prominent role. But after about half an hour, once the atmosphere was more relaxed, the other family members told a quite different story.

The importance of the family in Mexican identity

Other factors are also at play. In defending the family Mexicans are defending something they feel is under threat because of changes in society.

In Mexico the family plays an essential role in subjective life, and is strongly emotionally charged. Most people spend weekends with their extended family, including teenage children who might have preferred different activities. The family is also a sign of national identity. In the interviews family life in Mexico was often compared favourably with families living in the United States, seen as 'non-families', mere groupings of individuals with no emotional ties.

Power and relationships

A change is evident in the balance of power in the family. The father is no longer the king of the home, and perhaps never was. Women are gaining more power. Interestingly, with lower-income families, where women must work for financial reasons, and have little job choice, so they often work in the informal sector (for example selling articles from a catalogue), couples rarely mentioned the woman's job. When they did, it was in a way that undervalued its importance. Working outside the home is a way for women to gain independence. This desire to hide or even deny reality therefore has much to do with defending the status quo.

One interview with a young couple started before the husband had returned from work. The woman described how she wanted to get a job and become economically independent. But she said no more of this once her husband arrived home: instead she talked about wanting children and how they should be educated.

Individualisation, hedonism and tolerance

Three factors contributed to changes in family dynamics: increasing individualism, the growing trend towards hedonism and a (relative) absence of values, and a greater tolerance of, or indifference to, certain life choices.

For women, being a mother no longer subordinated other aspects of their lives. Zygmunt Bauman* describes how in conditions of 'liquid modernity', committing yourself to a role for life ceases to be rational. People must feel sufficiently free and unencumbered by lifelong obligatory roles to be able to adapt to continuous change. Solid ties that last forever cease to be functional. However, their lack is counterbalanced by the creation of other more temporary ties, such as virtual communities.

In the quest to meet long-term objectives, hedonism replaces the values of renunciation and sacrifice, with emphasis on the search for new experiences. It is clearly one of the factors that most undermines the institution of the family.

The idea in itself of having values is now in crisis. Values have been replaced by a type of absolute relativism, which makes other options in life easier to accept.

Changes in the Mexican family

All this means that the nuclear family has ceased to be the only, or only legitimate, type of family. Perhaps it is less that other types of family are emerging, more that they have always existed, but are now being considered as legitimate.

Other important developments include changes in the nature of the bond that binds a couple. Personal plans and individualism are starting to take priority. Emotions become more important than obligations. The same movement towards individualism also explains why roles, especially women's roles, are becoming more flexible. It is not that women are ceasing to accept their traditional role (emotional, expressive, personifying family relationships and bringing up children) but rather that they are playing it in a different way. Women have switched from communicating traditional values to aiding communications within families; from sacrificing themselves for the sake of the family to combining duty with pleasure; from being the children's ally against the father (often absent and almost always distant) to allying themselves with him over issues such as the education of children.

We also need to interpret men's roles in a new way. They continue to fulfil a role as provider and source of authority, but are moving more into the role of negotiator. They are more prepared to have a relationship with their wife based on equality. They are more open and tolerant with their children, and display more emotion with them. They are closer to them and more willing to take on child-rearing duties. They are also a little more prepared to help with housework, although the kitchen remains the woman's domain.

Attitudes to these changes are highly ambivalent: they are both accepted and rejected, desired and feared. But there is less ambivalence about children's education, where parents now tend to respect the choices their children make.

As in other countries, the boundaries parents set have become so loose that children no longer define their identity by challenging them. Instead they define themselves by peer-group differences (urban tribes, different types of music and brands and so on).

Resolving ambivalence to change

This ambivalence is resolved in different ways, depending on age and socio-economic level.

- Lower and lower-middle-class women see working outside the home as more a necessity than a vocation. They would often prefer not to have to, and hope their job will not last for long.

- Middle-class women, whose husbands earn enough to meet all expenses, do not want to work outside the home (and often instead become perfect home managers).

- In the upper-middle classes women often show a genuine desire to work outside the home, but only until the birth of their first child.

- Attitudes to change also vary with age. Unsurprisingly, perhaps, the youngest respondents were found to be the most open to change.

Lower-class families have more traditional attitudes and are more defensive about them. In part, this is because among this group the family provides a social and support network in difficult times, very necessary in a country that has never had a 'welfare state'. In the middle and upper classes people have a reasonable level of education, more choices and less need for such a support network. They are more willing to accept the underlying values of change. But the most conservative values are found in the highest classes, based on a mix of religion and ideology.

Hedonism is more common among the upper middle and upper classes. They have the means to enjoy themselves, like to do so, and wish to do so ostentatiously. People in the lower socioeconomic groups struggle to make ends meet; values such as honesty, hard work and discipline predominate. The middle classes work hard to improve their social and economic standing, and their values are associated with effort *('a bit more, and I could buy a car or send my children to a private school')*.

The variation in individualism too is easy to explain. The upper classes can afford plans: the better your current situation, the more you can allow yourself the luxury of thinking about the future.

We imagine that in the near future, middle and upper-class Mexican families will be similar to those in other (European or North American) societies, while life for the lower classes will change at a different rate.

The family and consumption

Although it might seem obvious, the role the family plays in the consumption of products and services tends to be ignored by marketers and researchers. We are used to thinking of consumption as something individual (which it is), and design our strategies and research on this premise. But ethnographic studies, many of which involve in-home interviews in the presence of several family members, are helping to change our views.

Consumption and emotional structure

We suggest that emotional structures exist within families just as they do for individuals. They might be described as emotional lines of power, which differ depending on the family composition. For example, it was apparent in the interviews that overloading single mothers with responsibilities that made them feel they had to work outside the home gave rise to strong feelings of guilt. This tended to make them be very practical, but also spoil their children: for example they might use ready-made meals, but buy lots of electronic toys.

Another example: in families where the father had emigrated to the United States, teenagers sometimes ran away from home. Mothers tried to dissuade them by looking for ways to share leisure time free of charge with their children. Consumption in these families too tended to be governed by guilt. This leads to austerity, to saving money on cleaning products for the home and products for personal care, as well as on food (these families avoided impulse buys).

The home was particularly important for the homosexual couples. In such a traditional society, it is a place for freedom and the expression of difference. This was shown in the purchase of home-related products.

Consumption and family structure

The different life stages of families (before children, with young children, with adolescent and older children living at home, after children have left home) are each associated with characteristic emotions, each of which helps to determine how the family relates to the marketplace. This is not an exhaustive description, but a flavour of how this mechanism works.

Families without children are in the process of creating their own space, breaking away from their family of origin and (usually) enjoyably building a home and a relationship:

- Nutrition centres on pleasure: meal times are unregulated, and people choose food they enjoy.

- Leisure is of vital importance (these couples eat out and take holidays relatively often).

- For some couples the home has a strong emotional charge, but others (especially when the woman has a job) distance themselves from it.

- Shopping is something to be shared and enjoyed, with some product choice changes from habits acquired in the family of origin.

The arrival of small children is a key moment in the formation and consolidation of the family unit. The couple must each decide how they will play their role.

- Nutrition has to be controlled and this replaces pleasure as the most important factor in food choice. The arrival of children often leads to healthier eating habits for the whole family.

- Leisure activities centre on the child, as it did when our couples lived as children with their family of origin.

- For women, care for their appearance is transferred onto their child.

- Shopping is now a necessity, and what had been a time for enjoyment with their partner becomes a time when mothers fulfil their maternal role.

In families with teenagers and older children, individual personalities emerge strongly. The family shows signs of dissolving or separating. The children bring fresh air into the home: new ideas, habits and trends:

- Several different criteria for eating coexist, so negotiation is necessary. Practicality becomes the most important factor, and because at this lifestage meals are often eaten at different times, family togetherness is threatened.

- Shopping completely loses its emotional charge. From being a 'family outing' it becomes a simple necessity.

- The places where parents and their children enjoy their leisure time are no longer the same, and shared places are sought to keep the family together.

- Young people are open to advertising and fashion, and this influences their parents.

- The home becomes like a service infrastructure in which everything has to work seamlessly and efficiently.

When the children leave home the emotional structure involves building life together again as a couple, rediscovering spaces for leisure and enjoyment. These couples become concerned about the future, and they tend to save and express concern for their health.

- These couples rediscover enjoyment together. They eat out more often, and some aspects of their lives take on new meaning (for example, vacations are no longer spent with their children).

- Shopping becomes more ascetic (the tendency is to save).

- What people save on everyday items is often invested in impulse buys that can be enjoyed with their partner.

- Much less effort is expended on equipping and cleaning the home. The extra free time may lead them to feel empty, in which case they try to fill it in different ways.

Last, for senior citizens a strong feeling of nostalgia dominates (the past and memory, above all in men, come to substitute for the future). They struggle against decline, of both their bodies and their household:

- They keep in touch with their children and grandchildren as a way of filling the emptiness. If they are not working (which many in the lower classes are), they seek leisure activities to fill the void.

- Men start to play a more active role in shopping.

- Few new products are purchased, and the home is not redecorated. It is now a place for memories, where the extended family meets.

- Meals are determined by medical parameters. They no longer have emotional value, which is reserved for meals prepared for children and grandchildren.

Summary and conclusions

- In 2002 Millward Brown Mexico undertook a major qualitative study about the changes taking place in Mexican families, how they are experienced, and the relationship families have with different types of products.

- Although most Mexican families describe themselves as traditional there have been major changes in recent years, including a wider variety of acknowledged family types and changing gender roles.

- Family structure, the way it is expressed emotionally, age and social class all have a significant influence on consumption patterns.

28
What's in a book title? (case study)

PEPE MARTÍNEZ

Introduction: objective and methodology

This case study of creative research focuses on a topic very close at hand: the title of this book.

Once we had written the book the only thing left was to find a title. We held a productive and enjoyable brainstorming session with the aim of generating possible alternatives. In the immersion phase the moderator explained the objective, and the criteria for the title were discussed. The creative phase involved asking those taking part to use their imagination to generate as many titles as possible. The suggestions were written on a flip-chart. In the final stage a group of people looked at a long list of the titles and selected all those they considered to be the most suitable in terms of the objectives.

This basic approach can also be used for creating the name for a new product or brand, developing a new product concept, new communication concepts, preparing future scenarios for the development of a brand and so on.

The immersion phase

Here members of the group were shown the index of the book, and were told that we were looking for a title that would attract our clients, and make them want to read the book from cover to cover. It was agreed the title had to be striking, attractive, magnetic, 'sexy' and seductive, as well as expressing clearly what the book was about.

The idea-generation phase

The technique we used was free association. Those taking part were encouraged to name out loud all the possible titles they could think of. The meeting lasted approximately one and a half hours, and the following names emerged:

- The essence of qualitative research
- The formula of qualitative research
- Interpret-action
- The art of qualitative research
- The laboratory of qualitative research
- Anatomy of qualitative research
- 'Insight-ders'
- Qual insights
- Qualitatology
- Qualitology
- Why do they call it quali when they mean …?
- Do you believe in qualitative research?
- Qualitative research in the XXI century
- Qual or no qual?
- 3rd generation qualitative research
- The new qualitative generation
- A new vision of qualitative
- The qualitative telescope
- The qualitative microscope
- Qualitative research: knowing how to listen
- The lens of the mind
- Nobody listens to me
- Is there anybody there?
- Life after qualitative research

- Planet Qualitative
- Deciphering qualitative research
- The genome of qualitative research
- The x-ray of qualitative research
- The qualitative net
- Novelties in qualitative research
- Discover qualitative research
- A journey through qualitative research
- The consumer's voice
- 100,000 leagues in qualitative travel
- 100,000 tongues in qualitative travel
- 2008: The Odyssey of qualitative research
- Qualitative e-motion
- Qualitative emotions
- The discovery of qualitative research: an inconvenient truth
- Get excited about qualitative research
- The qualitative connection
- Qualitative connection
- Connect with qualitative research
- I love qualitative research
- Qualitative heart
- The soul of qualitative research
- The qualitative personality
- I want to be qualitative when I grow up
- Qualitative research: sense and sensibility
- Feeling qualitative
- Quali, my friend
- Be Quali, my friend
- Qualitative research: the compass
- Qualitative indoor

- Qualitative inspiration
- Qualitative immersion
- Qualitative dip
- Diving in qualitative
- Qualitative nautilus
- Navigating in qualitative research
- Navigating the qualitative sea
- The engine room: qualitative research
- The gears of qualitative research
- The turbines of qualitative research
- The essence and science of qualitative research
- Qualitative research: essence and science
- Believing qualitative
- Be-living qualitative
- Don't worry, be quali!
- What does qualitative research smell of?
- The qualitative gene
- The qualitative revolution
- The re-evolution of qualitative research
- The qualitative recipe
- Designer qualitative
- Into the kitchen: the ethnographic approach
- Qualitative 2.0
- Qualitative research: more than data
- A window open onto consumers
- The qualitative window
- Discovering the consumer mind
- The qualitative route
- The mind reader
- The qualitative compass

- Consumers are moved, too
- Qualitative feeling
- Qualitative: a reason to believe
- The quest for qual
- Qualitative shouts
- Do you understand consumers?
- The voice of qualitative research
- Homo Qualitative
- The secrets of qualitative research
- Unlocking the secrets of qualitative research
- The magic of qualitative research
- The keys of qualitative research
- Homo Verbum
- The practice of qualitative research

Back to reality

We then had to come back to reality and select the names we felt stood out as most attractive and best suited to the objective. We selected ten possible titles.

The quantitative phase

After the creative meeting we undertook a quantitative research phase. One hundred people were shown the alternative titles, and were given the following instructions:

> 'You will now be shown ten alternative titles for the book about qualitative research. We suggest that first you read all of the potential titles quickly, as if you were looking at a shelf in a bookshop. Then rate each one of them from 1 ('I do not like it, it does not seem suitable') to 7 ('I like it a lot, it seems highly suitable').'

Based on their responses, we calculated the average score for each title and ranked them from highest to lowest. The results of this quantitative study gave us the winner:

> *Qualitology*
> *Unlocking the secrets of qualitative research.*

Summary and conclusions

- To find a good title for this book we held a creative meeting with three main phases: immersion in the problem, idea generation using brainstorming, and the return to reality.

- It generated over 100 alternatives. In a quantitative phase we scored 10 of them, the main ones, each one for appeal and suitability, and this led to *Qualitology: Unlocking the secrets of qualitative research.*

Notes on authorities

Althusser, Louis Pierre (1918–1990): Algerian philosopher who lived in France and developed Marxist structuralism.

Aristotle (384 BC–322 BC): Greek philosopher, a student of Plato.

Aschaffenburg, Gustav (1866–1944): German psychiatrist.

Barthes, Roland (1915–1980): French writer and semiologist.

Bauman, Zygmunt (1925–): Polish sociologist.

Berne, Eric (1910–1970): Psychiatrist who developed transactional analysis.

Bleuler, Eugene (1857–1940): Swiss psychiatrist.

Boethius, Anicius Manlius Severinus (480–524/525): Roman philosopher.

Comte, Auguste (1798–1857): Positivist, the creator of sociology.

Cousin, Victor (1792–1867): French philosopher.

Derrida, Jacques (1930–2004): Algerian-born French philosopher.

Descartes, René (1596–1650): French philosopher, mathematician and scientist.

Durkheim, Emile (1858–1917): Founder of modern sociology.

Erikson, Erik (1902–1994): German–born US psychologist notable for his contributions to developmental psychology.

Federn, Paul (1871–1950): Austrian-American psychologist and psychoanalyst.

Festinger, Leon (1919–1989): North American social psychologist who studied with Kurt Lewin and developed the theory of cognitive dissonance.

Foucault, Michel (1926–1984): French philosopher, sociologist, historian and psychologist.

Freud, Sigmund (1856–1939): Austrian doctor, neurologist and free thinker. The creator of psychoanalysis.

Gadamer, Hans–Georg (1900–2002): German philosopher who studied hermeneutics, author of *Truth and Method.*

Galton, Francis (1822–1911): British explorer, scientist, psychologist and biologist, who worked in disciplines including technology, geography, statistics and meteorology.

Garfinkel, Harold (1917): Developer of phenomenological sociology and ethnomethodology.

Hegel, Georg Wilhelm Friedrich (1770–1831): Famous German philosopher.

Jung, Carl Gustav (1875–1961): Swiss psychiatrist, psychologist and essayist. Founder of the school of analytical psychology (with a psychoanalytical viewpoint)

Kant, Immanuel (1724–1804): A famous German philosopher.

Kraepelin, Emil (1856–1926): German psychiatrist.

Lacan, Jacques (1901–1981): French doctor, psychiatrist and psychoanalyst.

Lévi-Strauss, Claude (1908–): French anthropologist who developed a structuralist approach.

Mead, George H. (1863–1931): Pragmatic philosopher, sociologist and psychologist who developed symbolic interactionism.

Montaigne, Michel Eyquem de (1533–1592): French writer, politician, essayist and politician of the Renaissance.

Ortega y Gasset, José (1833–1955): Spanish philosopher who developed *raciovitalismo*, a theory that bases knowledge in the radical reality of life.

Piaget, Jean William Fritz (1896–1980): Swiss experimental psychologist, philosopher and biologist.

Plato (427/428 BC–347 BC): Famous Greek philosopher.

Ricoeur, Paul (1913–2005): French philosopher and anthropologist who tried to combine phenomenological description with hermeneutic interpretation.

Rogers, Carl Ransom (1902–1987): North American psychologist who founded the humanist approach.

Rousseau, Jean Jacques (1712–1778): Franco-Swiss philosopher.

Saussure, Ferdinand de (1857–1913): Swiss, founder of modern linguistics.

Socrates (470 BC–399 BC): Famous Greek philosopher.

St Thomas Aquinas (1225–1274): Medieval philosopher and theologian.

Vygotsky, Lev Semyónovich (1896–1934): Byelorussian psychologist, who worked on developmental psychology and whose work was a forerunner of Soviet neuropsychology.

Watson, John Broadus (1878–1958): North American psychologist and the founder of behaviourism.

Weber, Maximilian (Max) (1864–1920): German philosopher, economist, jurist, historian, political theorist and sociologist.

Wundt, Wilhelm (1832–1920): The creator of the first psychology laboratory.

Bibliography

AEDEMO (2000): *La investigación en Marketing* (Investigations in marketing), Vols I and II, Celeste Ediciones.

AGUILAR, María José (1991): *Cómo animar un Grupo* (How to enliven a group), Editorial El Ateneo.

ALONSO, Luis Enrique (1998): *La mirada cualitativa en sociología,* Editorial Fundamentos (Colección Ciencia).

ANSART, Pierre (1990): *Las Sociologías Contemporáneas* (Contemporary sociology), Amorrortu Editores.

ANTISERI, Dario and REALE, Giovanni (1995): *Historia del pensamiento filosófico y científico* (History of philosophical and scientific thought), 3 vols, Editorial Herder.

ANTONS, Klaus (1975): *Praxis der Gruppendynamik,* Göttingen/Toronto/Zurich: Dr C. J. Hogrefe.

ANZIEU, Didier and MARTIN, Jacques-Ives (1997): *La dynamique des groupes restreints* (Dynamics of group breakout sessions), Presses Universitaires.

BÁEZ Y PÉREZ DE TUDELA, Juan (2007): *Investigación Cualitativa* (Qualitative research), Editorial ESIC.

BARNARD, Alan (2000): *History and Theory in Anthropology,* Cambridge University Press.

BAUMAN, Zigmunt (2001): *La sociedad individualizada,* Cátedra.

BECK, Ulrich (1998): *La sociedad del Riesgo,* Paidós.

BENGOA RUIZ DE AZÚA, Javier (1997): *De Heidegger a Habermás (Hermeneútica y fundamentación última en la filosofía contemporánea)* (From Heidegger to Habermás: hermeneutics and the foundation of contemporary philosophy), Editorial Herder.

BENNE, Kenneth D. (0000): *T-group Theory and Laboratory Method,* Wiley.

BERKO, J. and BERNSTEIN, N. (1999): *Psicolingüística* (Psycholinguistics), McGraw-Hill.

BERNE, Eric (1973): *Games People Play: The Psychology of Human Relationships,* Penguin.

BERNE, Eric (1975): *What Do You Say After You Say Hello?* Corgi.

BOURDIEU, Pierre (1986): *Distinction. A Social Critique of the Judgment of Taste,* London.

BOURDIEU, Pierre (1998): *Contrafuego,* Paidós.

BRADFORD, Leland P.; GIBB, Jack R. and BENNE, Kenneth D. (1964): *T-Group Theory and Laboratory Method Innovation in Re-education,* Wiley.

BRÜGGEN, E. and WILLEMS, P. (in press): 'A critical comparison of offline focus groups, online focus groups, and e-Delphi', *International Journal of Market Research.*

BRUSKO, Marlene (1987): *Living with Your Teenager,* McGraw-Hill.

BUCAY, Jorge (2002): *El camino de la felicidad* (The road to happiness), Random House Mondadori.

CODERCH, Joan (1995): *La interpretación en psicoanálisis (fundamentos y teoría de la técnica)* (Interpretation in psychoanalysis: foundations of theory and practice), Editorial Herder.

DELVAL, Juan (1975): *El animismo y el pensamiento infantil (Psicologia y etologia),* Siglo Veintiuno.

DENZIN, Norman K. and LINCOLN, Ivonna (1998a): *Collecting and Interpreting Qualitative Materials,* Sage.

DENZIN, Norman K. and LINCOLN, Ivonna (1998b): *The Landscape of Qualitative Research: Theories and Issues* (Handbook of Qualitative Research), Sage.

DENZIN, Norman K. and LINCOLN, Ivonna (1998c): *Strategies of Qualitative Inquiry,* Sage.

ETCHEGOYEN, R. Horacio (1993): *Los fundamentos de la técnica psicoanalítica* (Fundamentals of psychoanalytical theory), Amorrortu Editores.

FEDERACIÓN ESPAÑOLA DE MARKETING (1999): *Diccionario Profesional de Marketing* (Professional dictionary of marketing), CISS Especial Directivos.

FERNÁNDEZ NOGALES, Ángel (2004): *Investigación y técnicas de mercado,* Editorial ESIC.

FESTINGER, Leon and KATZ, Daniel (1972): *Los métodos de investigación en las ciencias sociales* (Methods of investigation in the social sciences), Editorial Paidós.

FLICK, U. (2004): *Introducción a la investigación cualitativa* (Introduction to qualitative research), Ediciones Morata.

FLOCH, Jean-Marie (1993): *Semiótica, marketing y comunicación* (Semiotics, marketing and communications), Paidós Comunicación.

FLORCZYK, Andrzej (1990): *Kto nie lubi Lecha* (Who doesn't like Lech Walesa), Warsaw.

FROMM, Erich and MACCOBY, Michael (1970): *Social Character in a Mexican Village,* Prentice-Hall.

GADAMER, Hans-Georg (1994): *Truth and Method,* Continuum.

GADAMER, Hans-Georg (1998): *Arte y verdad de la palabra*, Paidós Studio.

GIBB, Jack R. (1959): *Dynamics of Participative Groups*, Colorado University.

GIDDENS, Anthony (2006): *Sociology*, 5th edn, Polity Press.

GIL RODRÍGUEZ, Francisco and ALCOVER DE LA HERA, Carlos María (1999): *Introducción a la Psicología de los Grupos* (Introduction to the psychology of groups), Ediciones Pirámide.

GINER, Salvador; LAMO DE ESPINOSA, Emilio and TORRES, Cristóbal (1998): *Diccionario de sociología* (Dictionary of Sociology), Alianza Editorial.

GONZÁLEZ LOBO, Mª Ángeles (2000): *Investigación Comercial (22 casos prácticos y un apéndice teórico)* (Market research: 22 case studies and a theoretical appendix), Editorial ESIC.

GRONDIN, Jean (2000): *Hans-Georg Gadamer. Una biografía* (Hans-Georg Gadamer: a biography), Editorial Herder.

HARRIS, Marvin (1985): *Culture, People, Nature: An Introduction to General Anthropology*, Harper & Row.

HARRIS, Thomas A. (2004): *I'm OK – You're OK*, Harper.

ÍÑIGUEZ RUEDA, Lupicinio (2003): *Análisis del discurso (Manual para las ciencias sociales)* (Analysis of discourse: a manual for social sciences), Editorial UOC.

JAÚREGUI, José Antonio (1998): *Cerebro y emociones (el ordenador emocional)*, Maeva.

JOHNSON-LAIRD, P. N. (1983): *Mental Models*, Cambridge University Press.

JUNG, Carl Gustav (1968): *Man and His Symbols*, Dell.

KING, Gary; KEOHANE, Robert O. and VERBA, Sidney (2000): *Designing Social Inquiry: Scientific Inference in Qualitative Research*, Princeton, NJ: Princeton University Press.

KRUEGER, Richard A. (1998): *Focus Groups. A Practical Guide for Applied Research*, Sage.

LAPLANCHE, J. and PONTALIS, J. B. (1983): *Diccionario de Psicoanálisis* (Dictionary of psychoanalysis) Editorial Labor.

LATIESA, Margarita (1991): *El pluralismo metodológico en la investigación social*, Universidad de Granada. Biblioteca de Ciencias Políticas y Sociología.

LÉVI-STRAUSS, Claude (1967): *Structural Anthropology*, Doubleday.

LINDSTROM, Martin with SEYBOLD, Patricia B.: *BRAND child*, Millward Brown.

LLOPIS GOIG, Ramón (2004): *Grupos de discussion* (Discussion groups), Editorial ESIC.

LYUBOMIRSKY, Sonja (2008): *The How of Happiness*, Penguin.

MARINOFF, Lou (2007): *The Middle Way: Finding Happiness in a World of Extremes*, Sterling.

MARTÍN POYO, Ignacio (1978): *Teoría y práctica de la creatividad* (Theory and practice of creativity), Instituto Nacional de Publicidad.

MARTÍNEZ SILVELA, Jorge (1998 *Breve historia de la filosofía* (A short history of philosophy), Ediciones Globo.

MILES, Matthew B. and HUBERMAN, A. Michael (1994): *Qualitative Data Analysis*, Sage.

MIRALLES, Francesc (2007): *Conversaciones sobre la felicidad,* Alienta Editorial.

MONEDERO, Carmelo (1986): *Psicología evolutiva del ciclo vital.* Editorial Biblioteca Nueva.

MORGAN, David (1990): *Focus Groups as Qualitative Research*, Sage.

MORRIS, Desmond (2006): *The Nature of Happiness*, Little Books.

ORTIZ-OSÉS, A. and LANCEROS, P. (1998): *Diccionario de Hermenéutica* (Dictionary of hermeneutics), Universidad de Deusto.

PIAGET, Jean (1955): *The Child's Construction of Reality.* London: Routledge and Kegan Paul.

PINILLOS, José Luis (1998): *La mente humana* (The human mind), Círculo Universidad.

PINKER, Steven (2000): *Words and Rules: The Ingredients of Language*, Phoenix.

PUNSET, Eduardo (2005): *El viaje a la felicidad (Las nuevas claves científicas),* Ediciones Destino.

RATEY, John J. (2002): *A User's Guide to the Brain: Perception, Attention, and the Four Theaters of the Brain*, Vintage.

RECAS BAYÓN, Javier (2006): *Hacia una hermenéutica crítica (Gadamer, Habermas, Apel, Vattimo, Rorty, Derrida y Ricoeur)*, Editorial Biblioteca Nueva.

RODRÍGUEZ DELGADO, José M. (1994): *Mi cerebro y yo,* Ediciones Temas de Hoy.

ROGERS, Carl R. (1961/2004): *On Becoming a Person*, Constable.

ROGERS, Carl R. (2003): *Client Centred Therapy: Its Current Practice, Implications and Theory*, Constable.

ROJAS ORDINA, Octavio Isaac; ANTÚNEZ, José, CASAS, Roger, GELADO, José Antonio, and DEL MORAL, José Antonio (2008): *Web 2.0. Manual (no oficial) de uso* (The unofficial Web 2.0 users' manual), Editorial ESIC.

ROVIRA, Alex and MIRALLES, Francesc (2007): *El laberinto de la felicidad,* Santillana Ediciones Generales.

RUBIA, Francisco J. (2000): *El cerebro nos engaña,* Ediciones Temas de Hoy.

RUIZ OLABUÉNAGA, José Ignacio (2003): *Metodología de la investigación cualitativa* (Methodology of qualitative research), Universidad de Deusto, Bilbao.

SÁNCHEZ MECA, Diego (1996): *Diccionario de Filosofía* (Dictionary of philosophy). Alderabán Ediciones.

SANDÍN ESTEBAN, M. Paz (2003): *Investigación Cualitativa en Educación* (Fundamentos y tradiciones) (Qualitative research in education, fundamentals and methods), Editorial McGraw-Hill.

SARABIA, Bernabé and ZARCO, Juan (1997): *Metodología cualitativa en España* (Qualitative research in Spain), CIS.

SELIGMAN, Martin E. P. (2003): *Authentic Happiness: Using the New Positive Psychology to Realise Your Potential for Lasting Fulfilment,* Nicholas Brealey.

SHAW, Marvin E. (1976): *Group Dynamics*, McGraw-Hill.

SOLER PUJALS, Pere (1993): *La investigación motivacional en Marketing y Publicidad* (Motivational research in marketing and publicity), Ediciones Deusto.

SULEK, Antoni (1990): *O rzetelnosci i nierzetelnosci badan sondazowych w Polsce. Proba analizy empirycznej. In: W terenie, w archiwum i w laboratorium* (On reliability of survey methodology in Poland: an attempt at empirical analysis, in the field, archive and laboratory), Warsaw.

TIERNO, Bernabé (2008): *Los pilares de la felicidad* (The pillars of happiness), Ediciones Temas de Hoy.

TIERNO, Bernabé (2007): *Vital optimism,* Editorial Temas de Hoy.

TUSÓN VALLS, Amparo (1997): *Análisis de la conversación* (The analysis of conversation), Ariel Practicum.

VALLÉS, Miguel S. (1999): *Técnicas cualitativas de investigación social (Reflexión metodológica y práctica profesional)* (Qualitative methods in social research: methodology and practice), Editorial Síntesis.

VERGÉS, Juan Salvador (2008): *La felicidad de Alicia,* Editorial Planeta.

VILLAMARZO, Pedro F. (0000): *Hermeneútica psicoanalítica,* Universa Terra Ediciones.

WALDENFELS, Bernhard (1997): *De Husserl a Derrida* (Introducción a la fenomenología) (From Husserl to Derrida: introduction to phenomenology), Editorial Paidós.

WORCESTER, Robert and DOWNHAM, John (eds) (1986): *Consumer Market Research Handbook,* Cambridge.

ZELLER, Richard: *Qualitative Approaches to the Study of Human Sexuality.*